The Seattle General Strike

THE
SEATTLE
GENERAL
STRIKE

By ROBERT L. FRIEDHEIM

University of Washington Press   Seattle

Acknowledgments

IN WRITING this book, I have accumulated a number of practical and intellectual debts which should be acknowledged. Grants from the American Council of Learned Societies and the Purdue Research Foundation helped finance preparation and publication of the manuscript. The unpublished materials that I used were located with the generous and able assistance of Richard C. Berner, curator of manuscripts, University of Washington Library, who also helped in many other ways; Jane F. Smith, chief of the social and economic branch, National Archives; and Louise Heinze, librarian of the Tamiment Institute Library, New York. Both James A. Duncan and the late Harry E. B. Ault were very generous with their time and patiently answered my numerous oral and written questions. They also read an early draft of the manuscript and made valuable comments. Hugh Bone, chairman of the University of Washington Department of Political Science, was helpful in the early stages. I am also grateful to Dorothy Johansen of Reed College and Lance Davis of Purdue University for reading the manuscript, and especially to Robert E. Burke of the University of Washington, who aided and encouraged me so frequently that his acts of kindness are beyond specification. My greatest debt is to my wife, Robin. In addition to the usual uxorial inspiration, she contributed her professional editorial skills. To her this volume is dedicated. If, after all the aid I have received, errors have survived in the text, I alone am responsible.

West Lafayette, Indiana   R.L.F.

May, 1964

Contents

The Seattle General Strike

I

Prelude

At ten o'clock on the morning of February 6, 1919, the city of Seattle was ominously quiet. Some sixty thousand organized workingmen had failed to report to work. Buses and trolleys remained in their barns. No smoke poured from the chimneys of factories, workshops, or foundries in the ordinarily bustling industrial portions of the city and its waterfront. On that Thursday morning even the public schools of the Northwest's Queen City were closed. The downtown streets were virtually deserted; only a few people moved quietly past closed stores and shops. In fear of hardships and violence, Seattle consumers had long since emptied the store shelves of food and fuel—and rifles and pistols. Wealthier families had left the city for a haven in Portland hotels. The first major general strike in American history had begun.

The whole country anxiously awaited news of the events unfolding in Seattle. Reports carried by the wire services, and magazine articles that followed, branded the general strike a revolution. These reports helped to frighten the American public into believing that revolution stalked the land, and thus in part helped convince them of the necessity for the infamous Palmer raids of 1919 and 1920.

The Seattle general strike also produced a colorful new American hero—the city's mayor, Ole Hanson, who, according to his own immodest account of the events in February, 1919, suppressed a revolution. The personal publicity he garnered because of the strike gave Hanson delusions of grandeur; he proclaimed himself a candidate for the Republican nomination for the presidency of the United States.

Although the Seattle general strike helped to mold the history of the early twenties, no full account of the strike has been written. As a result, more than forty years after its occurrence, analyses of the strike are based as much upon myth as on fact. The strike has been variously designated: as a Bolshevik type of revolution planned and carried out by Soviet agents; as a one-man revolution engineered by a local radical, Leon Green; as an uprising of the Industrial Workers of the World attempted under cover of a strike by American Federation of Labor unions; as an insurrection led by James A. Duncan, secretary of the Seattle Central Labor Council, defying Samuel Gompers and the other conservative leaders of the AFL international craft unions; and, as Seattle labor itself alleged, merely a demonstration of Seattle labor's sympathy with their striking fellow workers in the shipyards.[1] While all of these views contribute something toward understanding the causes and meaning of the strike, none contains more than partial and distorted truth.

The causes of the general strike were numerous and complex. For purposes of analysis, they can be discussed in three categories: general instability during this era throughout major portions of the world, felt both locally and nationally; the organization, ideology, and mood of the Seattle AFL movement; and the immediate cause, the Seattle shipyard strike directed against yard owners and the Emergency Fleet Corporation, a wartime subsidiary of the United States government.

I

In February, 1919, the fighting of World War I had ceased less than three months before. The losing powers were militarily defeated and socially and politically unstable. Most of the victors had extended themselves to the limit in blood and treasure to achieve their victory, and many of their peoples were disillusioned and tired. Revolution and revolt occurred in the lands of both victor and vanquished. In this unstable postwar world, governments had to face the problem of reconverting their manpower, resources, industries, and farms to meet the needs of a goods-starved world. Even more difficult than material conversion was the task of reorienting men's minds. Both soldiers and civilians were said to have been brutalized by their participation in the war, and many social critics wondered whether traditional social and political patterns could ever be restored.

With the exception of acts of sabotage and overseas battle casualties, the United States was exempt from the direct effects of all of the violent energy expended on the slaughter of men. Yet Americans too were concerned with the psychological problems of the postwar world. The war, it is often said, brought on the end of American innocence. Before the war, to those who look back, the United States seemed to be unique and unspoiled. Wrapped in its mantle of moral righteousness, sure in its isolation from the foolish quarrels of Europe, confident in the ability to perfect man, the United States seemed justified in its smugness and Victorian complacency. As a result of the war, so the popular myth runs, this Eden was destroyed; America was no longer innocent; social and political upheaval replaced the known traditional standards. This is, of course, a highly romanticized view of the American past. Even before the war industrialization had begun to transform American society, and social rebels had been "cheerfully laying dynamite" to sweep away Victorian values.[2]

Nevertheless, the war was the great event marking the transition between the nineteenth and twentieth centuries. The United States characteristically entered the war with exaggerated expectations of its ability to reform the world. As Richard Hofstadter has pointed out, "the war was justified before the American public—perhaps had to be justified—in the Progressive rhetoric and on Progressive terms. . . ."[3] Disillusionment was inevitable.

Americans did not have long to wait to discover that the world might not be safe for what they envisioned as democracy. For any reader of American newspapers, 1919 was an extraordinary and upsetting year. Stories datelined from all quarters of the globe told astonishing tales of violence, war, revolution, and civil upheaval. There were putsches fomented by the right and revolutions instigated by the left. This was the era of the Kapp putsch in Berlin to overthrow the recently created Weimar Republic from the right and the Spartakist uprising to overthrow it from the left. Hungary too was undergoing a Red revolution led by Béla Kun. Argentina lay prostrate, with all activities halted by a general strike. The president of Portugal was murdered. The Lloyd George government was returned to power in the United Kingdom in the "Khaki Election" on the promise of harsh peace terms for Germany. The American press reported rumors that the United States would declare war on Mexico, a step made necessary, it said, by the infringement of vital American interests in our revolution-scarred neighbor.

The reports of these events were tinged with hysteria. Perspective was lost and journalistic objectivity thrown to the winds. Newspapermen presented facts and rumors in the same inflammatory prose. The leaders of the Spartakists—Rosa Luxembourg and Karl Liebknecht—were reported killed several times before they actually were murdered. Americans were deliberately being frightened by headlines of turmoil abroad. One newspaper ran a startling front-page-center spread, titled in bold letters, "Anarchy Plot to Hit Us?" The accompanying article carried the prediction of the Argentine dictator that his country's general strike was part of an anarchist movement which would spread to the United States and the rest of the world unless it were stamped out at once.

The effort to restore peace was another dramatic event of 1919. The gathering of the victorious leaders—Woodrow Wilson, David Lloyd George, Georges Clemenceau, and Vittorio Orlando—at Versailles was hopefully observed by the people of the world for any sign of agreement on a lasting peace. The newspapers obliged their publics by covering the conference in great detail. They sent special correspondents, well-known experts, and their foreign-affairs editors abroad to send back first-hand reports. Unhappily, they had to report disquieting rumors and incidents—rumors of difficulties over the League clauses, and the walkout of the infuriated Italians after they were balked by Wilson on the Dalmatian Coast issue. There were even rumors from Washington that certain senators approved neither the composition of the American delegation nor the results achieved.

Columnists were predicting a fight in the Senate over the ratification of the treaty even before it was signed.

These events, however, were overshadowed by another occurrence of transcendent importance—the Bolshevik Revolution. The March, 1917, revolution overthrowing the Russian czar was widely acclaimed in the United States, if only because it removed an obviously undemocratic member from the Entente.[4] Not so the Bolshevik Revolution of November, 1917. The November revolution, the civil war, and Allied intervention that followed, split opinion in democratic states into two antagonistic camps— the left, defending the revolution as the beginning of paradise on earth, and the right, attacking it as hell on earth. The conflicting attitudes on what should be done about Russia affected domestic political struggles within other lands.

The importance of these world-shaping events was not matched by developments in the United States. There were, however, disquieting signs that the mood of unrest had crossed the Atlantic. A rash of Negro lynchings broke out in the South. Mobs there no longer seemed content to wait for the ordinary process of Justice. The Eighteenth or Prohibition Amendment, to be associated with widespread lawlessness, was adopted in haste two months after the Armistice. In the first fifteen days of January, 1919, twenty state legislatures voted for the passage of the amendment which was to make the manufacture or sale of intoxicating liquors for beverage purposes illegal. On January 16 the Nebraska legislature became the thirty-sixth state to vote positively, thus fulfilling the constitutionally required three-quarters majority. Thirteen days later the Congress ratified the amendment.[5] Imbibers had only one year from that date in which they could drink legally. The state of Washington, like a number of others that had banned drinking, presented a warning of how easily people could foil Prohibition. By early 1919 a smoothly operating bootlegging system was supplying alcohol to all who wanted and could afford it.

Even nature seemed to conspire against stability: an influenza epidemic which had littered the land with dead was still killing numerous victims. With monotonous regularity obituary columns in the daily newspapers recorded the passing of "flu" victims, young and old, in February, 1919. Public officials issued ominous warnings of the danger of infection. The medical directors of school systems often reminded parents that they ought not allow their children to attend "promiscuous gatherings" during the Christmas holiday.

Wartime hatreds against dissenters, aliens, slackers, "Huns," saboteurs, and all varieties of radicals had not abated. Too often whipped up by official propaganda, large segments of the American public and press found the declaration of war an excuse for an emotional orgy expressing their hates, fears, and frustrations. Even when the fighting was over, the newspapers sedulously kept the "Hang the Kaiser" movement alive; he and his military commander, von Hindenburg, deserved that fate, they said, because they were "cowards," as our winning the war had proved. Editors also delighted in running stories of pranksters who registered "Bill Hohenzollern" to vote in elections in a free America. More serious was the press's savage approval of Germany's postwar economic and social instability. When German emissaries appealed to the United States for food, their pleas were greeted with outraged editorial cries.

The press and public cannot receive all the blame for the savagery with which dissent was treated in the wartime United States. The United States government imprisoned thousands of persons who disapproved of American entry into the war; and this did not stop when the war ended. Rather, the campaign to rid the United States of "undesirables" by imprisoning or deporting them was just then beginning to operate at maximum efficiency. The Industrial Workers of the World, which made no secret of opposition to America's participation in the "Capitalists' War," was particularly hard hit by government repression. Jails throughout the West held many "class-war victims," as the IWW called them.[6] In December of 1918 forty-six members of the IWW (popularly known as Wobblies) were indicted in Sacramento, California, for the bombing of Governor William D. Stephens' residence. Rather than resting his case on proving the specific acts alleged, the district attorney used the trial as a vehicle to prove the outright illegality of the IWW organization.[7] The trial quickly became a *cause célèbre* and sentiment for conviction seemed overwhelming in the press and respectable society.

Because the radical threat was viewed with alarm, there was widespread support for a bill to outlaw the IWW submitted in the California legislature at the time of the Sacramento trial. In fact, criminal syndicalist laws were looked upon as a popular nostrum for ridding the country of unpatriotic radicals; and they were before many state legislatures in 1919. The state of Washington adopted one in January, 1919, over the veto of Governor Ernest Lister and the protests of labor-backed King County representatives.[8] The Seattle general strike one month later was to spur other legislatures into adopting similar legislation.[9]

II

Seattle felt all of the symptoms of the contemporary instability. But the problem of radicalism seemed more real in the Northwest—Seattle was a center of numerical strength for the IWW. Local residents—both officials and private citizens—thus had numerous opportunities to catch a disease known locally as the "Wobbly-horrors." Wobblies were unable to hold any open meetings in the city until July, 1919. Prior to that, Wobbly-supported affairs had to be advertised under the banner of either another or a dummy organization.[10] The police would periodically raid the IWW hall (as they did in May, 1918, February, 1919, and June, 1919), close the hall, and arrest a few Wobblies.[11] When the IWW reopened the hall, the police would bring down a Board of Health doctor to condemn the place as unsanitary and order it closed again.[12] The police even had a guard at the Equity printing plant to prevent it from publishing IWW materials. The Wobblies did not particularly mind; the guard was good propaganda.[13] They did mind, however, when another plant they had previously used was wrecked by a mob. In January, 1918, two civilians and twenty sailors caused $15,000 damage to the plant that printed the IWW's *Industrial Worker*. Death threats were also made to anyone who would print Wobbly literature in the future. When the leader of the mob, G. Merle Gordon, was apprehended, eleven Elks rushed to post his $1,000 bond. In April he was "released on his plea of 'mental irresponsibility' caused by the seditious articles published by this press." [14]

Seattle witnessed several other incidents of official repression of dissenters which aroused various segments of the local labor population. The Wobblies were enraged by the prosecution of Louise Olivereau for violation of the Espionage Act. Emotional and high-strung, she was a voluntary stenographer for an IWW local in Seattle and a self-proclaimed anarchist and pacifist. The indictment accused her of sending letters to draftees "urging those who are about to engage in the project of war, seriously consider what it is." [15] There was no question of her personal guilt. But what infuriated the IWW was the prosecution's allegations that she had sent her anticonscription propaganda on the organization's orders and paid for it with gold supplied the Wobblies by the Imperial German government. The IWW hotly denied that it had sponsored her efforts and pointed out that she was an employee of the IWW organization but not a member. Wobblies were indignant that anyone would think that they would trust an emotional, irresponsible girl in such an important undertaking.[16] The jury needed only one-half hour's deliberation to find her guilty. She was sentenced to ten years in a federal penitentiary.[17] She did not, however, serve her full term. Two years and seven months later she was released from the federal women's prison at Canyon City, Colorado, and returned to the thick of radical activities in Seattle.[18]

Another federal prosecution aroused the ire of Seattle's AFL unions. Two well-known and well-liked members of the AFL movement were put on trial for conspiring against the execution of the conscription law. Hulet Wells, a former president of the Seattle Central Labor Council, and Sam Sadler (both members of the Socialist party) had distributed a circular entitled *No Conscription, No Involuntary Servitude, No Slavery* when Congress was debating the draft bill. Although they desisted after its passage, they were nevertheless brought to trial. The result was a hung jury. The two were retried, convicted, and given a two-year prison sentence on a new indictment alleging that they had conspired "to prevent the execution of the joint resolution of Congress declaring war." [19]

Among labor and liberals their conviction was viewed as manifestly unfair. Before they left for prison in the spring of 1919, they were feted at a banquet at which the speakers were George Vandeveer, their attorney, and the acting mayor of Seattle, W. D. Lane. A few months later labor was stunned to hear a report that Wells was being tortured in the McNeil Island prison. Wells, claiming to be in poor health, refused to make railroad ties; as punishment he was forced to stand for eight hours a day with his hands chained over his head. He also supposedly was put on bread and water and was denied visits from his wife. The labor movement erupted with a storm of protest. The Central Labor Council immediately organized a delegation to visit him which included a prominent doctor not previously associated with the labor movement. When they reported that the charges of ill-treatment were true and that Wells's health was poor, the anger of Seattle labor and sympathizers rose to fever pitch. Protests were made directly to President Wilson, protest strikes were proposed, and giant street rallies were held.[20]

The repression of dissent fostered the habit of spying and made it acceptable to the public at large. While not a new method of controlling American labor,[21] labor spying—official and unofficial—increased vastly during the war. One Wobbly in a soapbox speech is reported to have said: "The I.W.W. is going to use new tactics in strikes. Now all you secret service men and detectives get out your paper and pencil and put this down. . . ." And they did! [22] Labor and radical movements in Seattle were honeycombed with "patriotic" infiltrators, some of whom rose to positions of leadership.[23] The spies were sponsored by a variety of groups—local management,[24] the United States government,[25] and semiofficial patriotic organizations. The most active, and most powerful, was an organization called the Minutemen. A branch of the American Protective League, the Minutemen had twenty-five hundred investigators in the field as infiltrators and *agents provocateurs*.[26] Although theoretically operating under the direction of the United States Department of Justice—federal officials served on each state committee—the

Minutemen had few controls imposed on their actions. Their irresponsibility was particularly unfortunate in light of the important tasks delegated to them. The Minutemen were empowered to assist in the "suppression of anarchy, sedition and sabotage." [27] They also controlled investigations "upon general army matters, all applications for passports, Red Cross, Y.M.C.A. and Knights of Columbus. . . ." [28] While ferreting out "un-American" activities, Minutemen agents were assured "that in case of any trouble . . . [they had] the United States and the Department of Justice . . . behind [their] back[s]." [29]

The Seattle middle class, which supported the attempts to suppress radicalism, was to some extent justifiably suspicious of the ideological position of Seattle labor. Strange new organizations were being formed in the community, as well as in Butte, Montana, and Portland, Oregon—Soldiers', Sailors' and Workingmen's councils.[30] Sponsored by the AFL-affiliated Seattle Metal Trades Council, the new organization suspiciously resembled the Bolshevik Soviet. The metal-trades spokesman did not deny that the Soviet was the original model for the council; and some of its other sponsors hoped it would serve the same revolutionary function as its archetype.[31] This was viewed as an ominous development by middle-class Seattleites, as was the news that in establishing the council the local AFL and IWW worked together for the first time.[32] Fear that returned servicemen would be organized into revolutionary cadres was even expressed on the floor of the United States Senate; California's Senator Hiram Johnson charged that the plight of destitute veterans was so desperate in Seattle that the IWW was able to buy their loyalty with a meal and a bed. This accusation was publicly denied by Seattle's mayor, Ole Hanson.[33]

Perhaps the mayor correctly assessed the radicals' ability to organize the veterans because he knew how thoroughly the Soldiers', Sailors' and Workingmen's Council had been infiltrated by the Minutemen.[34] Eventually their control was such that the council's and the Minutemen's offices were in the same building and were served by the same stenographer! [35] Moreover, the council went into trusteeship because of financial irregularities, which the radicals said were caused by spies' efforts to destroy the organization.[36] The radicals, mostly Wobblies, abandoned the council when they realized that "Stoolies" were firmly entrenched. Instead, they formed a new organization, the Soldiers', Sailors' and Workingmen's Union. The existence of dual organizations whose object was the organization of the same group of men led to a furious battle on the floor of the Central Labor Council for organized labor's recognition and endorsement.[37] To complicate the situation further, a third organization—the Private Soldiers' and Sailors' Legion—was formed and it also asked for recognition from the Central. It claimed to lie ideologically between the newly formed American Legion and the Soldiers' and Sailors' Union. Its chief appeal to labor was the fact that it did not admit officers.[38] But these organizations too were rapidly infiltrated by labor spies.[39] All three—council, union, and legion—led short but tumultuous lives; they were dying by the summer of 1919.

None of the attempts by labor and the left to organize the veterans of the recent war had sufficient impetus to threaten the power structure of Northwest society. Their organizational efforts did, however, have symbolic importance which was completely neglected by the major Seattle newspapers. They should have been taken as indicative that Northwest labor intended to protect its wartime economic gains and protest against wartime political repression. Labor was concerned with the organization of veterans as one element in its attempt to head off possible adverse developments in the postwar readjustment. In all the furor over the allegedly revolutionary character of the Soldiers', Sailors' and Workingmen's Council, few readers of Seattle newspapers saw that the metal-trades spokesmen emphasized self-protection rather than revolution. In offering aid and assistance to returning veterans—finding them jobs, easing their initiation into unions, sheltering and feeding them, and in general helping them re-enter the civilian work force—the AFL unions of Seattle hoped to prevent management from using ex-servicemen as strikebreakers and disrupters of closed-shop industries.[40] Labor feared that disruption of labor's gains was the motivation for management's efforts to aid the veterans. With its economic power, management was in a competitively advantageous position for solving the most pressing problem of the veteran—employment. The *Daily Bulle-*

tin, later called the *Journal of Commerce,* organ of the Seattle business community, offered to print a free "employment wanted" advertisement for one week for any serviceman who requested it.[41] Its effort was duplicated by the Seattle *Times* and the Seattle *Post-Intelligencer,* two of the major conservative city newspapers.[42] The effort of labor and management to organize veterans presaged a full-scale confrontation of Northwest labor and management.

The signs of imminent labor-management conflict were already evident two to three months after the war's end. A powerful open-shop movement had come to the attention not only of the Seattle AFL unions but the newspapers as well.[43] The successful wartime effort to repress dissident groups had encouraged Northwest citizens interested in maintaining privilege. They were not averse to the continuation of harsh repression of those who demanded change, as indicated by an advertisement in the Tacoma *Leader* and Seattle *Post-Intelligencer*:

> We must smash every un-American and anti-American organization in the land. We must put to death the leaders of this gigantic conspiracy of murder, pillage, and revolution. We must imprison for life all its aiders and abettors of native birth. We must deport all "aliens," Socialists, Non-partisan Leaguers, "closed-shop unionists," Syndicalists, "agitators," "malcontents"—all these "must be outlawed by public opinion and hunted down and hounded until driven beyond the horizon of civic decency." [44]

Seattle labor knew it must accept the challenge. While numerically the AFL movement in Seattle had benefited by wartime prosperity, it chafed under the wartime restrictions on its freedom of action. Much of what it produced, especially in the shipyards, was for the United States government. As a result the ordinary labor-management confrontation on questions of wages, hours, and working conditions was halted in favor of government regulation. The Seattle AFL was also made restive by the insistence upon "loyalty" during wartime. The measures used— antisyndicalist laws, arrests, spying—were viewed by Seattle AFL labor as attempts not merely to rid the country of foreign-inspired enemies but to break the labor movement by moving first against labor extremists, then against all organized labor. Thus the Seattle Central Labor Council bitterly protested the arrest of workingmen on open charges.[45] This was also the reason that the Seattle AFL sought to protect its rival, the IWW, from hysterical attacks. As Seattle AFL spokesmen saw it, once the IWW was destroyed, the AFL would be accorded the same treatment in turn.[46]

The Central Labor Council would not accept such treatment without a fight. The Seattle AFL, at least in relation to the position on politics and economics generally associated with the AFL as a whole, was a radical organization. It was also a powerful and strongly organized city union movement which commanded the loyalty of its members and produced the economic results they sought. Because of the organization's efforts, Seattle workers toiled for high wages under favorable closed-shop conditions. The gains that the movement had made during the war were, in the opinion of leaders and rank and file alike, worth trying to protect. In December, 1918, the Seattle AFL agitated for national and state legislative programs to insure the permanence of labor's gains.[47] The Central Labor Council went one step further in hope of protecting the postwar position of labor; it requested that the peace terms decided upon at Versailles be subjected to a popular referendum for validation.[48] The Seattle AFL leaders realized that brave words alone would not stop a concerted attempt by reactionaries to manipulate government power, destroy the labor movement, and possibly harm or imprison its outspoken members. But until an overt open-shop maneuver—not merely a newspaper manifesto—became evident, labor leaders were struggling against a phantom opponent.

Preventing a successful antiunion effort depended to a great degree upon the reputation organized labor enjoyed with Seattle's middle class. If not thoroughly frightened, the middle class would never support or condone vigilante tactics. Those interested in destroying organized labor had to convince the middle class that its status was threatened, in which case labor's position would become untenable. In the struggle for middle-class sympathy, labor was at a disadvantage. The IWW was known by all to be strong in Seattle, and the local AFL was widely reputed to be radical, with some justification. Thus, all Northwest labor was vulnerable to the diatribes of the reactionaries. What endangered the Seattle AFL's public image most was its enthusiastic and unqualified support of the Bolshevik Revolution. The growing domestic crisis between Seattle labor and the reactionary segment of local management was often spurred on by differences on the question of Russia.

The business press hammered home an image of the evils the Bolsheviks had perpetrated. The *Daily Bulletin* fulminated against labor and liberals for not believing the worst of the Bolsheviks. Middle-class liberals particularly were the target for its jibes. It was their weak attitude, the *Bulletin* claimed, which was responsible for allowing the alarming world-wide increase in radical agitation. The *Bulletin* was particularly incensed that liberals did not give proper credence to the "infamous decree issued by the Bolsheviks at Saratow which called for the socialization of women, the vilest document ever penned." [49] This tale of alleged moral perversion was picked up by another Seattle business paper, the *Business Chronicle,* and became a main theme in the propaganda of the coalition of local open-shop, anti-Bolshevik, nativist, and hundred-per-center forces. It was repeated in speeches before businessmen's groups in towns and smaller cities around the state; reprints of the articles were sent to farm families.[50] This is only one example of the extreme alarmist tactics used by the growing coalition of right-wing forces. It aimed to create blind terror, and not to reject left-wing ideas rationally. If the latter had been the purpose, by 1919 there was sufficient accurate information on the nature of the Soviet regime to reject it on more reasoned grounds.[51]

The labor defenders of the Bolshevik Revolution were, however, the equal of their opponents in depth of feeling and lack of objectivity. They viewed the issue in black-and-white terms— support the Bolshevik government or acquiesce in the restoration of czarist autocracy.[52] Almost daily, the labor-owned newspaper, the Seattle *Union Record,* ran articles castigating the United States' participation in the Siberian expedition. Its headlines asked "Why Did We Enter Russia?" and demanded "Recall Army." [53]

The factions within the Seattle labor movement were united

in viewing the destruction of the Bolshevik regime as a calamity to all laboring men.[54] Support from labor conservatives was even forthcoming because of the naïve belief shared by Seattle unionists that all working-class movements were essentially the same and that a victory for one was a victory for all. Enthusiasm was certainly not lacking, but accurate information and knowledge of the realities of the Soviet system were. In her autobiography Anna Louise Strong, then a reporter for the *Union Record,* excellently captures the feeling of the Seattle labor movement about the proletarian adventure in Russia:

> Still cheerfully unaware of the theoretical basis of Russia's revolution, and ready to cheer any workers who had taken power, we remained in the period before the American Communist Party was organized, perhaps the only newspaper in America that was consistently pro-Soviet. But our cheers were based on feeling rather than knowledge.[55]

Seattle labor did, however, attempt to learn more about the situation in Russia. Its thirst for knowledge led to a parade of speakers appearing before the members of the Central Labor Council during its regular meetings. Any friend of labor recently returned from Russia with fresh information was invited to lecture; among them were Raymond Robins, Louise Bryant (Mrs. John Reed), Wilfrid Humphries, and Albert Rhys Williams.[56] In an effort to discover the true situation in Russia, the Central passed a resolution asking the United States government to guarantee delivery of a telegram to Lenin inquiring about the feasibility of sending an American labor delegation on a fact-finding trip to Soviet-held territory. In the expectation that Lenin's reply would be positive, the Central Labor Council established a Bureau of Russian Information to begin planning for the trip.[57]

Talk, reading, and private discussion were not sufficient outlets for the enthusiasm of the Seattle labor supporters of the Russian revolutionaries. They tried to give more tangible support by stopping the flow of arms through the port of Seattle bound for Vladivostok. Weapons had been shipped to Siberia via Seattle since June, 1917, after the establishment of the Kerensky government.[58] After the Bolshevik Revolution, the arms were consigned to Admiral Kolchak, self-styled "Supreme Ruler of Russia" and leader of the white forces in Siberia. Longshoremen in Seattle appealed to workers in munitions factories to stop producing war materials for the anti-Bolshevik forces. The Seattle branch of the International Longshoremen's Association promised that if the arms workers took the initiative, Northwest longshoremen would cooperate by refusing to load arms shipments already at the docks. After the general strike, the Seattle dockers were more willing to proceed without outside support. On September 23 they refused to load fifty railroad cars of arms and munitions purchased by Kolchak from the Remington Arms Company onto the steamer *Delight,* chartered from the United States government. When the "scabs" began to load the vessel, the situation became fraught with violence. The first gang of forty scabs was met at the gate of Pier 5 after work hours by four hundred ILA men; not many of them arrived home unscathed. Nevertheless, sufficient scabs were found to continue the loading process. The longshoremen then turned to the courts, hoping to get an injunction to stop the loading by nonunion men.[59]

Labor supporters of Russia's experiment had still another method for demonstrating their support—large-scale open-air rallies. One was held on January 12, 1919, and a riot took place as a direct result. Two to three thousand people were present when the meeting, held on a vacant lot at the corner of Fourth Avenue and Virginia Street in downtown Seattle, was called to order. Spectators heard S. W. Brookes of the Socialist party, who presided, Walker C. Smith, an IWW spokesman, and Vincent Brown of the IWW and the Hope Lodge of Machinists rail against American intervention in Russia. According to newspaper accounts, they "urged a general strike to tie up all industries and shipping engaged in the manufacture of supplies for the maintenance of the American army and its allies in Siberia." [60] After the speeches, which received the warm approbation of the militants present, they sang Wobbly songs, a collection was taken, and a parade formed. By this time the militants were being watched by three thousand additional spectators drawn to the scene by the noise. At this point city and military police moved into action. They broke up the formation with their clubs and arrested thirteen men for disorderly conduct. The "experts" on radicalism, the Minutemen, helped the police determine who among the participants was the most radical and, therefore, the most disorderly.[61]

Naturally, the *Union Record* was incensed by the action of the police. Its headline on January 13 claimed, "Men Clubbed By Police Until Blood Flows." Its indignation was stated in the strongest possible terms in an editorial entitled "Citizens Outraged." Although the major downtown dailies varied in their opinions of the purpose of the meeting and the resultant police action, they all viewed the events without passion. A *Post-Intelligencer* editorial called it a "Useless Riot," a waste of the demonstrators' energy because, first, all Americans wanted United States troops out of Russia and second, most Seattleites were not even aware that the protest meeting was to take place. "The city wasn't at all shocked—certainly not terrified." [62] Nor was the Seattle *Star* shocked, although it felt that the meeting degenerated into a riot because of overzealous police action. As long as no sedition or treason was advocated, the *Star* opined, it was best to allow the powerless radicals to vent their grievances in speech: "Just what harm there is to allow the spouters to spout in a vacant lot, where traffic is not disturbed, the *Star* cannot see." [63]

The business press, however, thought the riot a more serious matter. It predicted the worst. According to the *Daily Bulletin*, the situation had deteriorated to the point that "What is needed today is a carrying of the war to the IWW. Let us give him all the hell he is looking for instead of waiting for him to prepare his own particular kind for this city as he most certainly is doing." [64]

The "hell" soon occurred. A second riot took place at a meeting organized to protest the police tactics at the first. On the evening of January 16, again on the vacant lot at Fourth and Virginia, five hundred militants assembled for an open-air meeting. The meeting attracted five thousand other persons, who listened as A. J. Wieland castigated the action of the police; Fred Nelson, a vice president of the Metal Trades Council, spoke about free speech; and F. C. Clifford told his listeners "that the workers ought to take over, own and run the machines of industry." [65] When the militants, singing rousing and irreverent

Wobbly songs, led the large, curious crowd into the street for a march on the city jail, a contingent of mounted police charged, dispersing the mob without difficulty. No one fought back and no arrests were made. Mayor Ole Hanson was present during the entire meeting,[66] doing his civic duty and sniffing the political wind to see which way it would blow.

III

Watchful waiting was an attitude characteristic of Ole Hanson. He was a man with an acute sense of political timing. His political career is a case study of how far a man can go in American politics by first discerning the direction of public opinion and then giving the public what it wants. Every move Hanson made in politics was the result of careful consideration. If the hesitations required while a firm line of opinion formed, or the rapid changes in his own political affiliations and opinions made him appear foolish, fickle, and even "crazy" to the various politically committed groups he wooed, won, and dropped, he was anything but the "clown" or "buffoon" that large segments of the Seattle population thought him to be. Rather, he was a shrewd, calculating opportunist who consistently prepared himself for auspicious openings which would further his fortunes.

Hanson was well aware of the social circumstances which helped to mold men's political behavior. He had a good mind and was a first-rate observer. For example, he realized that the loathsome conditions in the lumber camps of the Northwest were the major reason for the IWW's hold over the minds of the loggers. He told the Boston City Club:

> The I.W.W. swarmed in the lumber camps, and made trouble. Why should this be? Because of the injustice with which they had been treated in the past. The shacks in which they were housed were unsanitary, and the men were marooned in a wilderness without any amusement whatsoever, even a chance to read. When they were paid off and visited Seattle, nobody greeted them but the I.W.W. agents, and the only places where they got any welcome were the saloons, where they dumped their dunnage and even deposited their pay checks.[67]

On the basis of this insightful comment, one might expect that he would advocate measures which would improve the logger's lot and thereby undercut the effectiveness of the message of the revolutionary syndicalists. Not Ole Hanson! There was nothing in it for him. That is, there was no powerful group to support such a proposal; the lumber companies were opposed, and the Seattle middle class, which was physically segregated from "Skid Road," was indifferent. Postwar public opinion in the Northwest seemed to demand repression as the cure for the Wobbly problem. Hanson, never a man to fight a trend, boasted that he "cured" Seattle's IWW situation by closing down the Wobbly halls.[68]

One of Hanson's most important political assets was his ability to convince any audience of his sincerity. This was not necessarily a mere subterfuge to disguise his self-seeking. The reason he sounded sincere was, no doubt, that he had first convinced himself of the justice as well as the seeming profit of any scheme he proposed. A highly emotional man, he allowed himself to be carried away by the flight of his own rhetoric. "A political associate of Hanson's said years later 'He just seemed to be wound up too tight. I never heard anything like old Ole until Hitler came along. He'd get so worked up he'd be almost screaming. He sure sounded sincere.' " [69]

Born in Racine County, Wisconsin, in January, 1874, Hanson did not arrive in Seattle until late 1902. Soon after he settled his family, he opened a grocery store on Beacon Hill. He quickly disposed of it "after learning that the grocer is the king of philanthropists. . . ." [70] He then entered the insurance business. Rapid growth in Seattle's population, however, made him realize that the business for an ambitious young man was real estate. At the time of the strike, Hanson was the president and sole owner of the Sequamish Land Company.[71]

As he testified personally, Hanson's political attitudes were molded by an overwhelming admiration for Theodore Roosevelt. He began political life, like Roosevelt, as a Republican reformer. Hanson was elected to the lower house of the Washington state legislature and proved to be an outspoken and effective lawmaker. But when Roosevelt bolted the Republican party in 1912, Hanson too was drawn into revolt against the party regulars. "Teddy's" death in 1919 affected Hanson profoundly, causing another switch of political position: he dropped an important group of political supporters—labor—because it had insulted Roosevelt's memory.[72]

Hanson's one break with his mentor was on the issue of the United States' participation in the Great War. Believing that his country ought to remain aloof from Europe's quarrels, he had supported Woodrow Wilson in 1916. His pacifism, however, had little depth. With the entry of the United States into the conflict he became a 100 per-cent patriot. He even ran for mayor, so he said, as a patriotic duty in March, 1918. Once elected, he demonstrated his ardor for getting on with the war by occasionally working after hours as a "bolter-up" in the Seattle shipyards, where vessels were being constructed for the United States government.[73]

The support of organized labor contributed to Hanson's victory in the mayoralty race. He claimed to be inordinately proud of his honorary membership card in Boilermakers' Local 104, given to him after his symbolic labors in the shipyards. Business, on the other hand, distrusted Ole. He was characterized by the *Business Chronicle* as "Oily Ole (mayor by mistake)" and worse, a "socialistic demagogue."[74] But Ole knew that today's political enemy might be tomorrow's political ally. The events of February, 1919, would offer an opportunity for him to win business' allegiance.

II

The AFL in Seattle

Aʟᴛʜᴏᴜɢʜ instability was characteristic of the immediate post-war years in the entire world and in Seattle, it was certainly no newcomer to the scene in that city. Seattle had had a short history, dominated by the quick growth of a latter-day frontier. Two events at the turn of the century, which made Seattle "Queen City" of the Northwest, also brought instability in their wake—the completion of James J. Hill's Northern Pacific Railroad in 1893 with its terminus at Seattle,[1] and the discovery of gold in Alaska four years later. As the terminus of the new railway, Seattle could hope to dominate the entire Northwest. And because of its location, the fine harbor, and the railway, local citizens also had inflated expectations that Seattle could be America's gateway to Asia. The Alaskan gold rush provided Seattle with wealth and people. As Murray Morgan put it, Seattle became a city which annexed a territory.[2] It was through Seattle's port that Alaskan gold was shipped; it was to Seattle that gold-seekers came to outfit themselves, seek transport to Alaska, rest on their return, and be entertained. Business boomed. Within twenty years Seattle was transformed from a small outpost at the end of the northern frontier to a great metropolis. In 1890 Seattle had 42,000 inhabitants, by 1900, 80,671—an increase of 88.5 per cent. By 1910, 237,194 people crowded the city—a new increase of 194 per cent.[3]

This growth was gratifying to those who envisioned a great future for their city. But it was not based on industry—and even a city with an attached territory could not depend upon the flow of gold for permanent prosperity. According to many of its boosters, Seattle was too dependent upon gold production and such extractive industries as lumbering. What industry there was serviced and finished the products of the Northwest natural resources. This situation could be remedied by attracting many new industries, as Frederick Jackson Turner suggested in 1914 at the University of Washington, when he proclaimed the end of the "old frontiers of wilderness" and the need for "new frontiers" of science and industry.[4]

Until World War I (and perhaps a good deal later),[5] Seattle had a typical colonial economy, dependent upon extractive industries and eastern capital. World War I seemed to offer the opportunity for the development of a genuine industrial economy controlled by local capital. Wartime demands did foster a great increase in industrial production in Seattle. In 1914, 1,014 industrial establishments produced $64,475,000 worth of manufactured products; by 1919, 1,229 establishments produced $274,431,000 worth.

Naturally, the labor force rose with the upward curve of the industrial graph. In 1919 more than forty thousand workers employed in true industrial pursuits were being paid over $63,000,000 in wages—an increase of more than 190 per cent— well more than double the national wage increase for that year.[6]

The men swarming into Seattle were quickly organized by the existing labor unions. The American Federation of Labor, which Samuel Gompers established in the Northwest in 1887,[7] grasped this opportunity to increase its power in the community, for Seattle was a labor town with a tradition of vigorous labor activity.

In 1915, before the war boom, fifteen thousand men were union members; by 1917 there were forty thousand; by late 1918, sixty thousand—an increase of over 300 per cent in three years.[8] The vigor of the unions' organizing activities is indicated by the larger number of unionists than industrial workers. Labor leaders were proud that Seattle seemed likely to become a closed-shop town. In addition to the industrial workers in the shipyards and metal trades, there were the craftsmen of the building trades, the teamsters, tailors, barbers, and some retail and drugstore clerks working under union-shop conditions.[9] Labor claimed that 50 per cent of the eligible labor force in Seattle was unionized in 1919.[10]

The Seattle union movement differed quite sharply from the general line of policy of the AFL as established by Samuel Gompers and the General Executive Board. Its ideas were distinctly its own, and local leaders were interested in putting those ideas into practice. They built an organization with tight discipline and pride in itself; the primary loyalty of local unionists was to their local and regional organizations. The parent body looked upon the Seattle AFL as a radical organization. Let us examine the situation of Seattle labor as it faced the immediate postwar problem of retaining its great wartime gains.

I

The Seattle unions were, at least formally, part of the AFL. They most resembled the parent organization in formal structure, for the local unions were based upon the craft principle— that is, small groups of men with associations based on their skills rather than the industry in which they worked. Craft unions tend to be highly decentralized and autonomous and usually elect their own officers—generally president, vice president, secretary, treasurer, and business agent. With increasing specialization, the number of locals proliferates, and each group jealously guards the boundaries that separate it from similar trades, often leading to the ubiquitous jurisdictional disputes associated with the AFL.

In 1919 there were 110 AFL local craft unions in Seattle.[11] Theoretically, in any matters going beyond their constitutional powers, local unions are responsible to their own craft national and international unions, which are largely independent of one another. The AFL, as the name states, is a federation, depending for its success on the cooperation of its autonomous components. The president of the AFL and its highest organ, the General Executive Board, have the function of promoting such cooperation.

Other organizations, however, cut across the hierarchical pattern; regional and local coordinating bodies exist to promote the cooperation of separate unions within a geographic area, or a particular industry within an area, such as metal trades. There are three such types of coordinating bodies: state federations, city centrals, and trade councils. These groups serve to overcome the tendency toward craft exclusiveness within the AFL. Obviously labor problems arise which primarily concern a particular region or industry. If possible, these problems are to be settled locally by the regional or trade council. These groups, however, cannot compel locals to take action not approved of by their national or international.

Locals have the most frequent contact with the trade council. To coordinate the many special skills within an industry, each local sends a delegate to the trade council, which ordinarily has its own headquarters and officers. In Seattle, the most important of these councils were the metal trades, with a heavy concentration of shipyard locals, the building trades, and the teamsters.

The capstone of AFL local labor organization was the Central Labor Council, which was organized in Seattle on May 1, 1905. It had its own officers and building—the Labor Temple at Sixth and University in downtown Seattle. During its regular Wednesday-evening business meetings, all the affairs of Seattle laboring men were discussed. Craft locals, even those with membership in trade councils, were often also affiliated with the Central Labor Council. Each local sent to the Council a slate of three rank-and-file delegates. There was no AFL requirement that a local affiliate with a city central, but Seattle men boasted that their central had the highest participation of locals in the country.[12]

While trade councils were not responsible to the Central Labor Council, they were often closely connected with it. In Seattle there was a high degree of cooperation in which both organizations expressed mutual concern—each sent delegates to the other's meetings.[13]

Seattle labor was not formally organized in a distinctive manner. But the use to which the organization was put *was* distinctive. Rather than feeling primarily responsible to their craft nationals and internationals, Seattle locals gave their loyalty primarily to their local coordinating bodies—the trade councils and the Central Labor Council. No matter what union a Seattle worker belonged to, he was most conscious of being a member of a *Seattle* labor organization. This intense localism was unique. The AFL did not seek the same goals the Seattle workers sought; it did not envision the same place for workingmen in American society that the Seattle workers envisioned. The Seattle labor movement caused the AFL leaders endless trouble. It stood for everything Samuel Gompers rejected—labor in politics, industrial unionism, and nationalization of key industries.[14] The Seattle labor movement was so distinctive that even the IWW characterized it as a movement "affiliated—more in form than in spirit—with the American Federation of Labor." [15]

The Seattle AFL manifested its distaste for the parent body by sending its best-known local leader, James A. Duncan, to the AFL conventions in 1919 and 1920 to cast the sole vote in opposition to the re-election of Samuel Gompers. Preventing his election from being unanimous was a source of great satisfaction to Seattle labor, a symbol of defiance that could be indulged in without great cost. But although relations between Seattle and AFL headquarters were often strained, they were never broken. Some vocal elements in the local union movement advocated breaking with the AFL, but Seattle's responsible labor leaders, for all their differences with AFL leadership, refused to be isolated from the mainstream of American labor. Thus, defiance was often breathed in speeches before the Seattle Central Labor Council, but only rarely carried out.[16]

AFL leadership was viewed with distaste mainly because it was identified with the East. To Seattle workers, "the East" meant Wall Street. Workers and their unions believed that local employers were mere puppets operating at the command of hidden eastern power. Seattle workingmen were determined to fight this surreptitious control in order to obtain their rights in the American economic system. Even relatively conservative Seattle workingmen were affected by this feeling.[17] Eastern labor, and therefore the AFL leadership, was viewed as insufficiently militant.

In summarizing his experiences at the 1919 AFL Convention,

James A. Duncan is said to have made the following remarks to the Central Labor Council:

> I found in my travels across the country that in the East the people are more conservative. Of course we have radicals in every part of the country, but the rank and file of the workingmen are more conservative. The One Big Union idea is not very well developed in the East. It exists there but is not very strong. It seems to me that if there is any reform in the labor movement they will come from the West. The people in the East cannot even realize that Booze is injurious to the working class. I think that when the working people sober up in the East, they will advance very rapidly, but their only hope is prohibition. A sober mind is the only mind that can reason and their brains are pretty well pickled. This talk of One Big Union in Washington is not very practical here in this state alone. If anything like that is adopted, it must be nationwide. We will have to do a lot of educating in the East. To establish O.B.U. in this state at this time would be committing suicide, as far as organized labor is concerned. Canada had a better chance of success, but failed, and we could not do any better in the State of Washington.[18]

Charles Doyle, business agent for the Central and delegate to the convention, who was later called an "old-guard reactionary," [19] also indicated some of the distinctions he noted between eastern and western laborers:

> You would be surprised at the intelligence of some of the eastern delegates to the A. F. of L. Convention. Actually our Newsboys union members are much better posted on economics than some of the eastern delegates to the A. F. of L. Convention. They think more of their dinner parties and socials than they think of business. They have to take care of [sic]. The western delegates have to show them that the west means business and they do it. We had a report to make at one of the conventions, and I was on the committee with a delegate from New York, a great big husky, much bigger than I was. When we got together he said that it was all right for me to write the report and that he would sign anything that I would write. I told him that I would do no such thing. That he would stay right there and write the report with me, in spite of the fact that he said he had to keep an engagement to a dinner party. Some of the delegates thought that there would be a scrap, but he did not fight, and we got out the report. Later, some of the delegates asked me if all the delegates were fighters like I was. I told them that I was nothing compared with Jimmy Duncan. That he was a fighting fool. After that Seattle delegates were always respected.[20]

While Seattle labor had an intense local loyalty, it did not feel completely isolated within the AFL. Seattle felt bonds of kinship with other West Coast labor movements. The term "western" implied the entire West Coast—north to Canada, south to San Francisco, and inland to Butte. Night after night in Seattle, union meeting reports were made on the progress and problems of brother unionists on the coast. Visitors from Vancouver, B. C., were encouraged to describe the conditions of the Canadian "One Big Union" movement.[21] Guests from San Francisco, Oakland, Portland, and Butte were asked to address local labor audiences.[22] Local unions gave visitors permission to raise funds for their embattled unions. For example, Seattle Boilermakers' Local 104 donated $56,000 to the San Francisco Metal Trades Council.[23]

The Seattle AFL movement was more radical than most other American city-wide movements. While other cities had radical fringes, in Seattle there was wide consensus on radical solutions to the question of labor's place in society. This agreement was voiced by Harry Ault, editor of the Seattle *Union Record:*

> I believe that 95% of us agree that the workers should control the industries. Nearly all of us agree on that but very strenuously disagree on the method. Some of us think we can get control through the Cooperative movement, some of us think through political action, and others think through industrial action. . . .[24]

While this statement is not in itself a sufficient summary of Seattle labor's point of view, it does give certain psychological clues to the feelings and actions of Seattle workingmen. First, the idea of class consciousness was implicitly accepted. Seattle labor looked at itself as a class apart, denied its birthright. The prevalent feeling was that workingmen had a natural feeling toward each other as class brothers. The corollary to class consciousness was class conflict—if some were brothers, others were natural enemies. While in actuality Seattle labor did not treat all employers as irrevocable enemies, and in fact prized some nonlabor liberals and farmers as friends and allies, still the jargon of class conflict was in constant use.

Whether they understood the terms they used is a moot point. For example, Ault presented the concept of labor ownership of industry as a point of wide agreement among Seattle labor. But how would the workers control industry? Through the socialist state, syndicates, guilds, or some other scheme? Seattle labor was simply not concerned with this, one of the major problems of leftist thought. It implicitly accepted the labor theory of value but felt no particular need for a careful definition of the terms. Doctrinally, Seattle labor was extremely unsophisticated. Knowledge of the Marxist classics was rare among Seattle laboring men. Few had read them and even fewer understood them. Anna Louise Strong, of whom more will be said later, tells an illuminating story on this point. In the wake of the Bolshevik Revolution, Seattle unionists expressed their curiosity about the ideas of the great revolutionary leader Lenin. Until then, Lenin's writings were unknown to local union men. Miss Strong received from the Rand School of Social Science in New York a pamphlet by Lenin which also contained a detailed analysis and notes by Alexander Trachtenberg. In her view, Seattle union men were simply incapable of understanding the pamphlet as she received it. Labor's own publishing company had to republish the pamphlet[25] with notes and analysis omitted in favor of Miss Strong's shortened foreword and simplified paragraph summaries.[26]

The Seattle labor movement was hospitable to any leftist idea, with no thought for selectivity or refinement; all leftist ideas were tolerated. Many of the ideas bandied about were contradictory, but Seattle workingmen were unconcerned. Ideas per se were not of value, but rather served as contributors to a fighting, spirited organization. Seattle union men were eclectics—a seemingly good idea was a good idea, no matter what its derivation, as long as it led to action.

Their pragmatism in programs for action can also be seen in Ault's comments. Anything that might work was worth trying. Industrial action with political or purely economic goals, cooperatives, or political action—these schemes at one time or another were all considered and used. If one did not work, there was no doctrinal barrier to dropping it and transferring enthusiasm to another course of action.

With a goal as vague as "labor ownership," and with means as flexible as theirs, Seattle workers were easily sidetracked. Since the relationship of a particular means to the vague end had never been carefully analyzed, the end itself could and did change. For example, if workers' ownership could be obtained only by the use of violence, and not peacefully as many Seattle unionists blandly assumed, the end was dismissed as not worth the cost. For this reason, while the initial goal might have called for revolution, the final achievement was only specific economic gains and a general rebelliousness. But this limitation was not recognized at the time; Seattle labor did not realize that its pragmatic focusing only on the next step worked toward a scuttling of larger goals.

Seattle labor was also faddish about doctrine. Any new development in labor movements throughout the world was emulated locally. One Seattle radical, in a mood of self-examination, spoke on the subject, "Why Look to Europe":

> It seems to me that we are great imitators, and we imitate every movement that is originated in Europe, but we get no results from imitating these movements because in every country different conditions exist. In France they have the syndicalist movement; we have it here in the U.S. Then when the Russians overthrew the Czar, we were all for Kerensky. When the Bolsheviki overthrew Kerensky, we all became Bolshevists. When they organized the Workmen's, Soldiers, and Sailors Council there, we organized one here. . . . Then in England they have the shop steward system. We also have it here. We talk about it in the Labor Temple, and that is as far as it goes. We grasp at every movement that is originated in Europe. . . .[27]

Like all fads, the new ideas captured the imaginations of the Seattle workers; they were discussed and became the basis for enthusiastically sponsored schemes or organizations which were regarded by their proponents as panaceas. But they were short-lived and did not interfere with Seattle laboring men's concern for their more immediate problems.

No fad could deter their concern for American labor's main problem—the craft principle on which the AFL was organized. Seattle was an early center of agitation for some form of industrial unionism. That the craft principle was obsolete in an age of mass-production industry was a belief shared by all but the most conservative of Seattle union men. The workers of Seattle felt that no matter what might be the ultimate goal—revolution, nonviolent but sweeping changes in American society, or merely a full dinner pail—industrial unionism would be more appropriate than the prevailing organization.

As the result of their own experiences—particularly in the metal shipyards—Seattle workers wanted a new form of organization. They had the usual difficulties with craft unions—each was too small to face a powerful employer, and their autonomy made it hard for them to act in concert.[28] And there were the usual jurisdictional disputes—employers would often play off one complementary trade in an industry against another. Craftism seemed to lead to the fractionization of the working class by "the interests" or "big biz." [29] This was anathema to the class-conscious majority of Seattle labor.

Seattle was strong for labor unity. Industrial unionism would represent all workers in an entire industry regardless of their individual skills. Thus all labor in a single industry would operate as a unit when bargaining with the management. Proponents of this system hoped for two major gains: representation of less skilled and unskilled labor in the industry; and elimination of the frequent problem of one specialty of an industry on strike, yet unsupported by other specialties still under contract with the management. The industrial union seemed simplicity itself— all workers in, all workers bargain together, all workers strike together.

If enthusiasm were the only requirement, Seattle labor would have organized industrially in 1919. However, Seattle labor was still affiliated with the AFL, which staunchly maintained craft unionism. Although a few industrial unions—notably, the United Mine Workers and the Brewery Workers—were members of the AFL, after the 1901 Scranton convention the AFL took an increasingly stringent line on the organization of an industry.[30] Since workers looking to the Seattle Central Labor Council for leadership represented a variety of crafts, their national and international officers made it obvious that they would greatly disfavor any attempt to organize local industrial unions.

According to responsible labor leaders, Seattle's problem was how to organize along industrial lines and still maintain its connections with the AFL. These labor leaders had a difficult task in restraining the industrial-union enthusiasts, some of whom did not care what price had to be paid, others of whom advocated an open break with the AFL. Radicals of all persuasions agitated in meetings of locals, trade councils, and the Central Labor Council for the formation of industry-wide unions. On occasion the enthusiasts gained sufficient support to overwhelm the recognized leaders' pleas for patience. The radicals even succeeded in having the Central Labor Council endorse the industrial-union concept.[31] Further, they pushed through a request for an industrial-union referendum during the 1919 convention of the State Federation of Labor. The executive board of the AFL immediately threatened to suspend the state charter if the referendum were carried out.[32] The radical cause split asunder when state and local labor officials explained to the Seattle rank and file that a successful referendum would mean secession from the AFL.[33] Many radicals backed down when they realized that workers holding cards from Washington State industrial unions could not work outside the state. It was to be expected that the AFL would fight the revolt of Washington labor and that local employers would probably side with them.[34]

Thus, the outright adoption of an industrial-union plan seemed highly unlikely to Seattle workers. But they did not give up hope of acquiring the benefits of the system; they looked, rather, for alternatives to give them the substance if not the name. One such scheme was the federated-union plan under which all craft unions in an industry would remain in existence, but arrangements would be made for all contracts with the employers to expire at the same time. The craft unions would then be federated. To see that everyone cooperated, however, the sponsors of the federated-union plan also proposed the creation of a city-wide central federated labor organ. Although it generated some enthusiasm among local laboring men, the scheme smacked too much of dual unionism and was strenuously fought and defeated in the Central Labor Council.[35]

Enthusiasm for industrial unionism did not preclude use of other means for improving labor's lot. As noted earlier in the remarks of Harry Ault, Seattle labor was too pragmatic to rely upon one method or to look upon various reform schemes as mutually exclusive. The Seattle labor movement had invested heavily and enthusiastically in businesses owned either cooperatively or by the unions themselves. There was little dissension within labor as to the value of these investments. Radicals could view them as a useful adjunct to more stringent schemes for social change; moderates could view them as valuable in themselves. Labor was interested in an enormous variety of enterprises. For example, Boilermakers' Local 104 had $12,000 invested in a cooperative food store, $15,055 in the labor-owned daily newspaper, *Union Record,* and $3,100 in a labor-owned laundry.[36] All reported good business.[37]

The Seattle labor movement was also engaged in somewhat riskier enterprises—a union-owned theater under the auspices of the Union Theater Company was set up. A proposal for establishing a labor-owned bank had wide support. The Seattle longshoremen planned to establish their own stevedoring firm, a venture which would surely succeed, they believed, if they could hire Robert Bridges, former head of the Seattle Port Commission, to run the firm.[38] The Central Labor Council even established a Workers' College, with the assistance of Dr. Henry de Man, a Belgian labor leader and educator. Although initially most of its teaching personnel were linked with the University of Washington, the Workers' College reportedly wished to emancipate itself from the University's influence because the teaching of its borrowed professors was "offensive to the workers." [39]

Another exotic flower of labor's imagination was the proposal to establish labor-owned motion-picture companies—the Union Label Film Company and the Federation Film Company. They hoped to produce pictures for the edification of the working class and the "education" of the general public. Arthur Nelson of the Federation Film Company read before a union meeting a synopsis of a typical script that he hoped to produce. The film was to deal with a strike. In silent sequences, it would tell the terrible tale of labor's suffering. Through all travails the striking laborers maintain their solidarity, making possible a happy ending—the employer going broke and the business reopening under the cooperative plan.[40]

Even the grandiose did not frighten the laboring men of Seattle. Harry Ault, editor of the Seattle *Union Record*, reporting to the Central Labor Council on his trip to Chicago to attend the National Cooperative Congress, spoke about prospective plans for establishment of a labor-owned press service. The initial cash outlay would be $100,000. To continue operation, the service would have to supply news to more than the one existent labor-owned daily, the Seattle *Union Record*. Thus twenty more labor-owned papers would be established around the country. But even this was not an end to the problem. Newsprint was in short supply. Before more labor papers could be established, organized labor would have to form a company to manufacture paper. Ault was enthusiastic, though, and assumed that labor would encounter no great difficulty in raising the necessary $1,750,000. He did, however, warn his labor audience "not to invest in anything, for we will want your money to promote your own establishments." [41]

The leaders of Seattle labor also wanted to command the political loyalty of their union members. The eclecticism of the Seattle movement allowed, in addition to all other methods of bringing about social change, the use of political action. Labor plunged into politics with its usual verve and enthusiasm. Although Seattle city elections were by law "nonpartisan," labor-sponsored candidates, as everyone in Seattle knew, were regularly elected to city and local offices. Usually two or three men on the City Council were not only labor-sponsored, but themselves members in good standing of organized labor. Labor-sponsored candidates also ran for mayor, the Seattle School Board, and the Seattle Port Commission. But labor had greater political ambitions than merely capturing some local offices. It was interested in and ran candidates for statewide, and even national, positions. Contrary to the policy of the AFL, Seattle labor tried to form its own party—not a Labor party but rather a coalition of Seattle labor with other disaffected groups. With the state Grange and the Railroadmen's Welfare League, the State Federation of Labor formed a Triple Alliance, which they hoped would sweep the statewide and congressional elections of 1920. (This too had its foreign model—the 1914 Triple Alliance of the British trade-union movement, which, as one Seattle worker put it, was "show-ing us the way." [42]) Although Seattle labor groups continually referred to their amalgam as the Triple Alliance, it ran candi-dates on the Farm-Labor party ticket. Seattle labor thought of itself as the heart of the Triple Alliance and disputed control of it with the state Grange.[43]

During 1919 Seattle labor was deep in preparations for the 1920 campaign. Hopes were high. Labor claimed to have raised $250,000 for campaign funds. Since the organizers of the Seattle branch of the Triple Alliance hoped to keep it a rank-and-file controlled organization, they expected overwhelming support from Seattle union men.[44] Doing nothing by half measures, labor plunged into a strenuous effort to get all workingmen registered, indoctrinated to the vital role their individual votes might play, and organized into a well-knit party right down to the precinct level.[45]

The enthusiasm for reform made Seattle labor somewhat puri-tan. The more vocal leaders saw the purpose of the movement to be the improvement not merely of the economic condition of laboring men but also of their moral character. Although the movement as a whole was not pro-Prohibition, it was not, as were many labor movements at that time, vehemently anti-Pro-hibition. As we have seen, James A. Duncan was an ardent Dry; nor was he the only one. One reason for conflict between Seattle labor and the AFL was a rumor that Samuel Gompers supported sending a trainload of people to Washington, D.C., to protest Prohibition. The "Booze Special" was said to have been organ-ized by an eastern brewery syndicate.[46] The association of drink-ing and loose moral habits with the East and eastern labor served to heighten Seattle's suspicion of Samuel Gompers and his AFL. To local labor Dries, "booze" was injurious not merely to the workingman but also to his organization. Thus, a resolution could be submitted to the Seattle Metal Trades Council

. . . condemning the plan of President Wilson to have the Prohibi-tion law repealed. It stated that prohibition is the greatest blessing to labor that ever happened. That doing away with whiskey caused the Russian workers to wake up and overthrow their oppressors; therefore

Labor should demand of their Congressmen and Senators that the Prohibition law stand as it is.[47]

II

With the multiplicity of ideas in the air, it would be too much to expect that Seattle labor would have been of one mind on philosophical and tactical questions. The remarkable degree of unity was brought about by a conscious effort to respect differences of opinion and position while still maintaining the ability to work together. In fact, if any characteristic of Seattle labor of the time stands out, it was this ability to "agree to disagree" without loss of cooperation.

Seattle labor recognized three general groupings within the movement—the "conservatives," the "radicals," and the "progressives." These were not distinct entities, but rather tendencies, as the men of Seattle clearly understood. The boundaries were not sharp or well-defined; among men categorized by these labels there was some range of opinion, particularly among "conservatives" and "radicals." Only the "progressives" were a coherent faction. As we examine each group separately, it should also be remembered that standards of some forty years later are not applicable to these 1919 labels.

As a group, although politically to the right of the other wings of Seattle labor, the local conservatives were considerably more liberal than the ordinary run of AFL conservatives. But the term "conservative" was applied to many men with disparate points of view. Some were "pie-card artists," as the Wobblies put it, that is, concerned with bread-and-butter issues and content to leave the property system alone. These men were at most mildly reformist. As viewed by the other contingents of Seattle labor, the price of the full dinner pail was lack of reforming zeal. This brand of conservatism was often espoused by the men and leaders of Seattle unions with strong craft traditions, such as the carpenters, plumbers, painters, and cooks. This point of view was also strong in unions such as retail clerks, which recruited their members from the lower middle class. The leaders of the conservatives were drawn from the latter unions. Among the most prominent were Louis Nash of the retail clerks, Ed Levi of the cooks, and H. F. Jones of the Building Trades Council.

But the Wobbly judgment was extreme. Certainly not all conservatives were pie-card artists. Many who classified themselves as conservatives absorbed some of the prevalent leftist ideas. Nevertheless, even these less doctrinaire conservatives were suspicious of the whole leftward drift of the Seattle labor movement. Their greatest objection was not toward the ends so vaguely stated by their more fire-breathing colleagues, but toward the means advocated. Men classified themselves as conservatives primarily because of temperament. They saw themselves as common-sense thinkers. They were goal-oriented, and they wanted to realize their goal in the foreseeable future, with the steps for attaining it clearly patterned out. The conservatives prided themselves on their organizational sense and lavished great care on such matters as proper timing in the economic struggle. They considered their method to be the application of common sense to improving the laboring man's lot. In the intemperate personalities of the radicals, the conservatives saw the very opposite of common sense. The conservatives felt that the radicals' effort to bring the far future into the present meant a hasty abandonment of step-by-step planning, organizational efforts, and proper timing.

F. A. Rust, a prominent conservative, summed up the differences between conservative and radical in Seattle labor as follows:

> I am called a conservative by many that don't know me, but I want to tell you I am just as radical as any of you, only I use common sense in trying to get certain things. If I wanted to go to Spokane I would take a train to get there at the present time. That would be the most practical way of doing it. A wobbly might want to go by airplane or jumping over there. They want to use methods that are not practical at this time. I want just as much as the wobblies do and understand economics as much as they do, but I am not foolish enough to think that we can do anything like that now, and just because I believe only in going as far as I can get results, I am classed as a conservative.[49]

Another prominent conservative, J. P. Martin, president of Boilermakers' Local 104, displays the concern for organization and the relative liberalism of many Seattle labor conservatives:

. . . we are all more or less radical. It's all right to be a sensible radical but not to be crazy like some of the I.W.W. that we have in our Local. I believe that the One Big Union principal [*sic*] is good but we are not prepared for it and all of us that have been in the game for years know it. There is no use disorganizing and letting organizations that we have got go to the winds and have nothing definite in its place.[50]

Conservatives were deeply entrenched in official positions in many craft locals and well represented among presidents, secretaries, and business agents of Seattle unions. This was true in some important unions reputed to have a large radical following among the rank and file, such as Boilermakers' Local 104 and the Hope Lodge of Machinists. The radicals in J. P. Martin's union persistently attempted to oust him; but for all their numerical strength, they could not force him out of office. He even ran a successful purge of radicals.[51]

The conservatives' entrenchment in positions of power and influence gave them significant voice in Seattle labor affairs. Because they made fewer demands and proposed less than spectacular practical schemes, they were not as often heard from on the floor of the Central Labor Council and the trade councils.

The radicals *were* heard from—continually and loudly. To understand Seattle labor one must realize that the appellation "radical" was loosely applied. Anyone was considered a radical who vociferously demanded rapid and far-reaching changes in the position of labor in society. Enemies of radicalism—such as labor conservatives, labor spies, and respectable members of the community—used the term as a pejorative and made little attempt to distinguish between the shades of opinion on the left. Although opinion formed along a spectrum, the radicals can be essentially categorized into two groups: the "free-wheeling" radicals with no outside organizational ties, and the IWW "borers." The two were frequently allied on specifics, but there were important differences between them. Mainly, most free-wheeling radicals considered the costs of revolutionary changes and backed down from their positions; the IWW borers did not.

The borers were members of the Industrial Workers of the World who simultaneously held AFL cards and participated in the action of AFL unions. Although boring was not approved as official IWW policy,[52] men holding Red cards joined Seattle unions for any of three reasons: first and most important was the fact that the AFL unions had job control in what was essentially a closed-shop town. A man without a valid AFL card could not get work. As a Wobbly named Freinberg put it:

> I belong to the A. F. of L., the machinists' organization, and some of the A. F. of L. members might say that I had no right to do this. Well, I want to say that I have just as much right to do this as the A. F. of L. members have to dine and associate with the Employers and I want to say this—that I belong to the I.W.W. for a principle and to the A. F. of L. for a job.[53]

Second, and more traditional, was the idea of infiltrating the AFL in the hope of converting it to revolutionary syndicalism.[54] This reason for boring made the orthodox Wobblies most suspicious of the tactic—converting the AFL would eliminate the IWW's reason for independent existence. Nevertheless, the IWW was unable to discipline its members, and individual Wobblies infiltrated, hoping dramatically and quickly to increase the size of the syndicalist movement. Third, Wobblies bored in order to create havoc in the rival organization. They accomplished this purpose, often unintentionally, because of their chronic lack of discipline.

Borers were particularly significant in the various metal-trades unions working in the shipyards. They claimed at one time (although Wobbly figures must be viewed *cum grano salis*) that of the fifteen thousand members of Boilermakers' Local 104, nine hundred held Red cards.[55] Borers were also strong in the Hope Lodge of Machinists and fairly significant in the electrical workers' unions and various construction unions whose craft specialties were relatively unskilled. Shipyard work accounted for so much of the borers' strength because, as a result of the war boom, it was the great source of new and temporary jobs in Seattle. The labor shortage was sufficiently acute for the yards to put on virtually every available man, however unskilled or ideologically extreme.

The Wobblies made much of their numbers in the shipyards and at various times hoped either to organize them in their own name or, failing that, to convert the AFL unions that already had job control. They wildly exaggerated their power, basing their hopes on totally unreliable membership statistics. Admittedly, accurate statistics were difficult to gather. Because of the migratory nature of the typical Wobbly and the high rate of turnover in the yards, a single Wobbly might well be carried on the books of two or three different IWW locals in two or three industries. Furthermore, they operated in the shipyards on the job-delegate system, that is, a floating delegate would collect the member's monthly dues. But since delegates were ambulatory, a member might pay one delegate one month and another the next—thus doubling the size of the membership in IWW records. The main reason for unreliability of Wobbly membership claims in the shipyards, however, is simple exaggeration by the IWW. It is less that Wobblies deliberately lied than that, completely indifferent to the mundane facts of reality, they wanted to *will* the revolution, with nonexistent numbers if necessary.[56]

Even in those AFL unions where Wobblies had significant numbers, they were less influential than might be supposed, because they had bored only to get a job. They paid their dues, and beyond that gave little attention to AFL affairs. Far fewer Wobblies bored for the second and third reasons, but these directed borers were very noticeable because of their outspokenness and exaggerated demands. They were present at every meeting; they would perpetually take the floor to make an impassioned speech; they hatched countless schemes to drive the AFL unions further to the left. While their propaganda helped familiarize a generation of Seattle laboring men with radical ideas, the borers themselves were never able to capture any local they entered. On occasion, one would be elected as a rank-and-file delegate to the Metal Trades Council or Central Labor Council, but that was the extent of their power.

The borers were surprisingly easy to identify. Like the Mr. Freinberg mentioned above, they could not keep their affiliations secret. Because of their pride in being members of the IWW, they trumpeted their dual status in speeches to all who would listen. The most conspicuous borer in the AFL movement was Vincent Brown, one of the Hope Lodge of Machinists' delegates to the Central Labor Council, whose speeches on the Council floor made it plain that he was a Wobbly. But he resigned and left for his home in England in 1920, exasperated with his inability to convert or overturn the Seattle AFL movement.[57] William Coffey, a member of the Building Laborers' Union and the IWW, also gloried in his dual affiliation.

The borers were also distinguishable on other grounds. They had little concern for the viability of the Seattle labor organization per se. Radicals whose affiliation was primarily with the AFL organization would desist in their efforts if convinced that they would hurt the labor movement as a whole. Wobbly borers would push any radical scheme no matter how costly in terms of labor unity or the reputation of the Seattle labor movement.

A third way of identifying IWW borers within the Seattle AFL movement was their attitude toward politics. As we have seen, the mercurial enthusiasm and eclecticism of Seattle labor often inclined it toward pursuit of goals through the accepted political system. The borers would have none of the idea of putting laboring men or labor's friends in public office. Whenever such a scheme was proposed, the borers would shout with anguish, as they did when Seattle labor became involved with the so-called Triple Alliance.[58] As a syndicalist organization, the IWW was antipolitical, assuming that the politics allowed by the capitalists was a subterfuge to trap unwary workingmen and make them slaves to "the system." Although this philosophic position was vague and unsubtle, so strong was its emotional pull that the borers could not hide their feelings on the matter.

Because of their closer association with the Seattle AFL movement, the "free-wheeling" radicals were the more influential of the two radical groups. Men such as Frank Turco of the Blacksmiths' Union, and vice president of the Metal Trades Council, Phil Pearl of the Barbers' Union, and Percy May of the International Longshoremen's Association, had large followings among the stable labor population of Seattle. They were in the forefront of every attempt to propose radical solutions for the problems of Seattle labor.

Although they were not known by the term "free-wheeling" radicals, this sobriquet is appropriate. These men were well to the left, but they were not doctrinaire and had no set creed. Also, to some extent they were responsible for the eclecticism of Seattle labor, for any kind of scheme, as long as it seemed radical and promised action in the immediate future, received their support. Loud and boisterous, suspicious of softness, accusing those who disagreed with them of "selling out," persistently speaking on the floor of the Central Labor Council—they were a bane to the organization. But their opinions, even when rejected, were always given respectful attention. Percy May, in a mood of self-examination, reveals why the free-wheelers acted as a constant annoyance to the organization: "Since I have been in the labor movement in Seattle, I was always with the radicals, but at times they get on one's nerves. The trouble with many radicals is that unless they are the ones that are doing certain things they do not trust anyone else. . . ." [59] For all their rabble-rousing, the free-wheelers had a message that Seattle workingmen wanted to hear.

The free-wheeling radicals can be distinguished from the IWW borers by reversing the criteria used to identify the borers. First, their primary loyalty was to the Seattle AFL. For example, although ardent supporters of the idea of industrial unionism, they backed down when outright advocacy of it brought on the wrath of Samuel Gompers. Turco and Pearl originally supported the industrial-union referendum adopted at the State Federation Convention. They had second thoughts when the AFL Executive Council threatened to suspend the State Federation's charter if the vote were carried out;[60] and subsequently they voted with the conservatives and progressives to call off the referendum.[61] Nor was this the only time they backed down. After vociferously championing that curious substitute for outright industrial unionism, the federated-union plan, they both voted against it, fearing to harm the existing organization by creating a dual-union problem.[62]

Again, unlike the Wobbly borers, the free-wheelers supported political action and were especially enthusiastic about labor- and cooperative-ownership plans. For example, the proposed labor-owned stevedoring company, mentioned above, was sponsored by Percy May. Although not as enthusiastic about political action as the progressives, they acquiesced to its use with no qualms, unlike the Wobblies.[63]

The final distinguishing characteristic of the free-wheelers was their refusal to act as an organized faction. They were a collection of individuals who frequently came down on different sides of a controversial issue. In contrast, the IWW borers would seldom differ fundamentally from each other or from their Wobbly brethren on the outside: their purpose was always to destroy the AFL and to promote the vague but emotional IWW ideology of direct action and revolution.

Frank Turco, an important participant in the general strike, can serve as a typical example of the free-wheeling radical. An Italian immigrant, Turco was loud of voice, ardent and hot-tempered, free with his fists—a ferocious battler who was constantly on the attack with no holds barred. No one in the labor movement was neutral toward Turco; one was his friend or his enemy. As an enemy, he was apt to be accused of selling out or invited out into an alley. Inevitably, on occasion Turco was wrong in his accusations and was himself justly censured, as when the head of the State United Mine Workers "denounced Turco and called him a liar and a disturber of organized labor." [64] Turco had a strong sense of working-class solidarity. He was a fervent rank-and-filer who feared the creation of permanent officials because of what Robert Michels would call the "iron law of oligarchy." [65] Then as later, Turco tried to play the role of one-man protector of the ordinary union man. He was a spectacular, if difficult, figure in Seattle labor. No matter what the point of view of current labor leaders, Turco made their efforts to operate with maximum solidarity a trial. Often accused of being a Wobbly,[66] he always denied this charge.[67] But he never denied that his feeling for working-class solidarity led him to support any action in which the entire laboring class could operate together. Far from being a member of the IWW, he saw no reason for the organization's existence, and in fact encouraged all Wobblies to join the AFL. Then, he claimed, their good rank-and-file voices could be heard within AFL halls on the issues of industrial unionism and working-class solidarity.[68] His relations with Wobblies were excellent; his boast that his name was as well known in the IWW as the AFL[69] was another annoyance to Seattle AFL leadership.

After his important part in the general strike, Turco became less dangerous to the Seattle labor movement. He was, however, as flamboyant as ever. When the shipyards shut down and he could no longer gain employment as a blacksmith, he became a newsboy at Third and Pike in downtown Seattle. In 1964, at eighty-five years of age, he was still on the job and still involved in local labor as a member of Seattle Newsboys' Local 621. His hoarse voice and enormous mane of gleaming white hair were the trademarks by which many thousands of Seattleites could recognize Turco. His only absences from his stand were for annual pilgrimages to the AFL convention, where he would treat the delegates to the speech they had come to expect—thunderingly denouncing labor racketeers, lauding John L. Lewis, and lamenting the declining moral values of labor leadership.[70]

Although the borers and free-wheeling radicals constituted the bulk of the radical members of the postwar Seattle labor movement, there was a scattering of other radicals who do not fit either category precisely. Not particularly powerful, they are still worthy of mention. In a later era, due to temperament, national origin, or ideological beliefs, they would be Communists, but since the Communist party of the United States and its rival splinter, the Communist Labor party, were not organized until the summer *after* the general strike (August-September, 1919), we may call them "incipient Communists." Their numbers were small because the requirements were special: a knowledge of Leninist theory and the discipline required to follow an ideologically rigid path to revolution. Most of the Northwest laboring men who were drawn to revolutionary ideas were more attracted by the less demanding and more emotionally satisfying Wobbly call to action.

One leader of Seattle labor who played an important role in the strike was undoubtedly an incipient Communist—Leon Green. A mystery man, he drifted into town during the war. No one knew where he came from, although he was said to be of Russian origin. He worked for a short time as a reporter on the labor paper, the *Union Record,* became a member of its Board of Directors, was a delegate to the Central Labor Council, and managed to secure the position of business agent of Electrical Workers' Local 77.[71] Here he played an ominous role in the strike, lending color to contemporary and later accusations that the general strike was the first step of the Bolshevik Revolution in America. But there is no evidence that "incipient Communists" had any importance in the Seattle labor movement. Certainly they were not in positions of influence and leadership; Green is the exception.

The third group, the progressives, were the cement binding Seattle labor together. Without them, conflict between conservatives and radicals would have been inevitable and bitter. For, although many who were called conservatives considered themselves liberal, they would have none of the hare-brained schemes the radicals were proposing. On the other hand, the radicals heaped bitter scorn on conservatives, accusing them of being "pie-card artists" or of selling out the working class through their willingness to abide by contracts. A movement as volatile as Seattle labor is always susceptible to internecine conflict. Nevertheless, Seattle labor's unusual tolerance between conflicting groups was the work of the progressives. But they did far more. They were responsible for "mold[ing] the trade unions into an organization as single in its unity of action as the IWW." [72]

The power of the progressives was based on their ability to lead the labor movement in a direction acceptable to conservatives and radicals. Lacking the power to control the entire movement themselves, the groups to the left and right had to content themselves with the progressives' leadership. As a result, the progressive policy was middle-of-the-road, reflecting elements of both sides. In the words of one progressive leader, they were attempting to "slow up the radicals and speed up the American Federation of Labor. . . ." [73] They tried to maintain a balance between what Daniel Bell calls unionism as a social movement, and as an economic force (market unionism). [74] As a social movement the progressives tried to build an organization that would be a vehicle of social change. At the same time, their effort to create the closed shop in Seattle and their willingness to bargain with management for workable agreements were characteristics of market unionism —that is, they attempted to eliminate wages as a factor in Northwest economic competition (for example, in the shipyards they tried to standardize wages at the high level paid by the largest yard, Skinner and Eddy).

Strong, militant leadership was characteristic of the men whom their fellow unionists called progressives. While many progressives occupied formal positions of leadership in their unions or councils, they themselves looked for leadership to James A. Duncan, whose power was far greater than might be implied by his title of secretary of the Central Labor Council. The influence of Harry Ault, editor of the *Union Record*, was only slightly less than Duncan's. Ably supporting these men were J. C. Mundy, president of the Central Labor Council; James A. Taylor, president of the Metal Trades Council; Bert Swain, its secretary; John Ballinger of the Plumbers; Andy Mulligan of Boilermakers' Local 104; Ben F. Naumann of the Hoisting Engineers; John Von Carnop of Hope Lodge of Machinists, and John McKorkle of the Building Trades Council.

These were the men who gave the Seattle organization its pragmatic character. They were discontented with craft unionism like the radicals, but they feared the cost of adopting an avowedly industrial-union plan in the face of opposition from Gompers and the international presidents. They wanted both industrial unionism and membership in what they considered the mainstream of organized American labor. As long as they gave up the outward form of industrial unionism and attempted to gain only its substance, they saw no reason why they could not have both. Thus these leaders sought alternatives to outright industrial unionism, to which the AFL could not object as strenuously.

Theirs was a radicalism of the practical. The progressives sought only slightly more than what they expected their enemies would concede; they operated by the methods that would engender the least opposition. In addition, they strongly believed in the value of a solid organization. While they wished to change labor's place in society, the progressives realized, in contrast to both borers and free-wheeling radicals, that demands do not automatically bring results. They were critical of the radicals for assuming that "education" of the workers would light the spark that would bring about great social changes. The progressives realized that each advance of labor required effort and protracted bargaining backed up by a labor organization with unity and discipline. As a result, much of their effort went into creating such an organization.

Another decidedly important reason for their emphasis on organization was the strong competition offered by the IWW in the Northwest. In order to compete with the IWW, the progressive leaders must have an organization sufficiently militant to discredit any IWW claim that it was merely a protective association for a small, skilled labor elite. Additionally, the progressives realized that the Seattle AFL would have to offer workers something the IWW did not—a powerful and effective organization based upon disciplined, united effort.[75]

These various influences on their course of action—the desire for change, reliance upon organizational solidarity, dependence upon hard work, creating an organization that could compete with the IWW, and the avoidance of precipitant action—were summed up in the following remarks attributed to James A. Duncan:

> There is absolutely no danger of any other organization taking place of the A. F. of L. It's too valuable a machine to do away with and then try and build up another one. The labor movement will not stand for anything like that. But the A. F. of L. itself will change right along. The I.W.W. may exist as a secondary organization. They are really pacesetters. After an idea gets old with the I.W.W. then the A. F. of L. begin thinking about it. But the I.W.W. as it is today will never take the place of the A. F. of L. as an organization, but those radical ideas are being rapidly absorbed by the A. F. of L. and what some of us consider radical today will be conservative tomorrow. As we get ready we absorb those ideas but see no reason why one has to join the I.W.W. to carry out those ideas. Good ideas we can absorb. Some of those bad ones that get them into trouble they can keep. The trouble with some people is that they want to change the intelligence of the workers in a few days, when it takes years to do it in.[76]

"Jimmy" Duncan lent his name to the unique form of organization that characterized Seattle AFL unionism. "Duncanism" was the substitute for industrial unionism. It consisted of three elements: (1) strong central control of all unions in the area by the Central Labor Council; (2) close cooperation of allied trades in an industry through the trade councils, cooperation of trade councils, and their informal allegiance to the Central Labor Council; and (3) the attempt to get all agreements between management and the various craft locals within a single industry to expire simultaneously so that labor could bargain as a unit.[77] Duncanism, therefore, led to the accumulation of vast power in the hands of the Central Labor Council—power which reduced the hold of the international unions over their Seattle locals. Until 1920 Duncanism operated informally in order to avoid giving the AFL Executive Council grounds for punitive action against the Seattle Central. But in that year an attempt was made to formalize this centralization of power. The Seattle Central Labor Council tried to modify its constitution to permit itself final authority over wage contracts negotiated by member craft locals. This brought a rapid rebuke by Samuel Gompers, who demanded that the Seattle Central rescind the altered constitution.[78]

The man who ran the Central Labor Council was Jimmy Duncan, a tough, canny, hard-headed Calvinist, sure in his faith that he represented right and truth. This certainty in the justice of his cause allowed him to assume responsibility and an often back-breaking burden of work. Greatly respected by Seattle union men, he held the office of secretary of the Central Labor Council through the tenure of three presidents. He was Seattle labor's favorite delegate to the AFL conventions and was a labor sponsored candidate for the mayoralty of Seattle and the United States Senate. At the time of the strike he was president of the Hope Lodge of Machinists and president of the Machinists' District Council.[79]

A Scottish immigrant, forty years old at the time of the strike, James Alexander Duncan was born on December 28, 1879, in King Horn, Fife. When he was a child his family moved to Southampton, where his father worked as a shipwright. At seventeen he began his apprenticeship as a machinist in the Napier Engine Works, Southampton. Later he spent several years as a marine engineer on an American-flag steamship on the New York–Southampton run. In 1904, when he was twenty-four, he went around the Horn to Seattle and decided to settle there. He sent home for his fiancé, and they were married on her arrival in 1905. Duncan was a member of the Westminster Presbyterian Church in Seattle and taught Sunday School there. He was also a member of the Young People's Christian Endeavor Association and for three years was the superintendent of its Good Citizenship Department.[80]

Duncan's character was heavily influenced by this background. A rigid Calvinist morality molded his view of life. He had an absolute horror of alcohol and immoral conduct, and he insisted that those in contact with him live up to his own personal standards of behavior. When running for mayor in 1920, he is reported to have said of his opponent,

> Caldwell said in one of his speeches that you cannot make a Sunday school out of a seaport. Well, I want to say that as far as booze and vice goes I will make a Sunday school out of Seattle. I will make them all obey the law, whether he lives on Capitol Hill or in the Rainier Valley, it will be all the same to me, they will all toe the mark.[81]

If Jimmy had been elected, Seattle might have become the new Geneva!

Although not a Socialist at the time of the strike, Duncan had been a member of the Socialist party.[82] But he knew little about Marxist theory and cared less. The vast generalizations of Marxist analysis were foreign to his mind and training. The end to be reached did not have to be carefully defined. Rather, effort and thought had to be expended on the details of the step-by-step process of moving men in any direction. Duncan's thinking was a "bump by bump" effort, as he put it, "casting around for a real solution of our problems . . . and figuring where we would get to after we did this and after we did that. . . ." [83]

Duncan's power in Seattle labor did not result from his ability in long-range planning or sophisticated economic analysis, but rather from his force of character, will power, and willingness to work. For all his toughness and rigid moral views, he was not dictatorial. He would not have dominated Seattle labor without the support of other men with similar views who were themselves well-known and well-placed in the labor movement. With these men, Duncan was *primus inter pares*. He could lead them and the rest of Seattle labor because he knew just how far they could be pushed without rebelling.

III

No analysis of Seattle labor in the early postwar years would be complete without a word on the important role played by the Seattle *Union Record.* It is unique in the annals of American labor as the only daily labor-owned newspaper. The *Union Record* was the official organ of the Seattle Central Labor Council, which owned 51 per cent of its stock; the remaining shares were in the hands of Seattle locals and trade councils. The Central appointed the *Record's* twenty-one-man board of directors and its editor.[84]

The *Union Record* was a complete daily newspaper with all the features usually associated with a major journal—wire-service coverage of major national and international stories, women's section, coverage of the arts. After World War I, circulation boomed, reaching at one point a total paid daily circulation of 112,000.[85] With a large, faithful readership, the *Union Record* was a powerful voice in the community. As its circulation increased, it caused some consternation among businessmen and the other local newspapers for its uncompromising if somewhat over-enthusiastic support of causes close to the hearts of Seattle laboring men. Roy John Kinnear, president of the Seattle Chamber of Commerce and Commercial Club, said of it,

> In Seattle, a newspaper owned and operated by the Central Labor Council has almost continuously been open in its advocacy of Bolshevist Propaganda, full of the defense of Russian Soviet Government. It has even gone so far as to denounce the United States Government in a manner that is rebellious and unlawful.
>
> This representative of Union Labor in Seattle has advocated and supported movements of a seditious nature. Continuously it justifies and defends violence, intimidation, and force. It openly ridicules the authorities who enforce our laws and forever strives to engender a feeling of disrespect and contempt for Government.[86]

Through the *Union Record,* Seattle workingmen could communicate with one another; the paper was extremely important in creating the characteristic unity of local labor. It also helped give workingmen a sense of place in the community, serving notice on Seattle of labor's aspirations.

Its editor, Harry E. B. Ault, aligned the editorial policy of the paper with the views of the progressives. As the man in a position to communicate with all Seattle labor, Ault's voice was important, even if he was less often in the limelight than James A. Duncan. But it was clear that he must agree before any major policy was proposed by that middle group.

Thirty-five years old at the time of the strike, Harry Ault was the editor of the *Union Record* from its inception in 1917 until its demise in 1928. When he was fourteen his family had migrated from Kentucky to the Northwest to join the Equity Co-operative Colony, near Bellingham, Washington. After early training as a printer, Ault served for a time as publicity secretary for Eugene V. Debs. He also served before Duncan as secretary of the Seattle Central Labor Council.[87]

Keeping the *Record* in operation and consistently behind the progressives was no easy task. Not only did he have to perform the usual editorial chores, but those of the publisher as well. The *Record* was essentially a one-man operation. Developing a labor newspaper as he wished to do—free from "capitalist propaganda," the emotional outbursts of super-patriotism so rife in the period, and the suspected "biased reporting" of the wire services[88]—forced Ault to rely heavily upon the work of amateur reporters and a news staff drawn from the local labor movement. His personnel were long on verve, short on balance and professional journalistic technique.

One of the staff whose enthusiasm for labor and leftist causes led her to play an important part in the general strike was Anna Louise Strong, feature editor, poetry contributor, and sometime editorial writer. Her background was not what one would expect for a working member of organized labor. Her family could be traced back to settlers arriving in New England in 1630. Her father was one of the most prominent clergymen in Seattle, known for his theological liberalism; her brother was a rising young light in the YMCA movement. After a year at Bryn Mawr, she graduated from Oberlin College. She was one of the earlier woman PhD's, taking her degree at the University of Chicago. Her early career reflected the family background—her dissertation was entitled "A Study of Prayer from the Standpoint of Social Psychol-

ogy," her first job, associate editor of *Advance,* a Protestant funda-
mentalist weekly newspaper. Later she was active in child-welfare
work, setting up exhibits organized by the United States Child
Welfare Bureau.

In 1915, when her father was called to a Seattle congregation,
Anna Louise accompanied him. She immediately threw herself
into organizations devoted to civic improvement. She organized
"Know Your City" trips to acquaint Seattleites with the beauties
and facilities of the Queen City. Because of her humanitarian
work with civic and child-welfare organizations and the fact that
she was one of the best educated women in town, she was elected
to the Seattle school board with the solid backing of women's,
civic, and good-government organizations.

Her introduction to socialism came in Kansas City in 1911
when, as supervisor of a child-welfare exhibit, she had to lay off
a craftsman. In sympathy, she tried to break the news gently.
From this worker she first heard of the Socialist party and of the
fact that some men believed that by deliberate action the in-
equalities of society could be eliminated. She immediately tried
to join the party. But Miss Strong was always a person of mercurial temperament, and her interest died rapidly.

Just before America's entry into World War I that interest
revived. She immersed herself in campaigns to keep the United
States out of the war. This fight was her first chance to meet
some real proletarians. The more she worked with groups opposing war the more she came to admire left-wing ideas. For a
while she worked on a four-page radical Seattle paper, the *Daily
Call.* Her flirtation with the left, however, made the middle-class
groups that had supported her for the school board suspicious.
Their fears seemed to be confirmed by her testimony on behalf of
Hulet Wells at his first trial. A recall movement was begun, but
lay dormant until Miss Strong again showed her sympathy with
those who opposed America's entry into the war. The recall petitions were reactivated when she sat on the defendant's bench to
comfort Louise Olivereau during her trial for violating the
Espionage Act.[89]

Deserted by her middle-class supporters, Anna Louise Strong
moved leftward permanently. Her attachment to socialism, pri-

marily a product of her humanitarian instincts, became increasingly ardent, although woefully weak in terms of knowledge of formal doctrine. According to James A. Duncan, at the time of the strike, he was much more radical than Miss Strong, who was still essentially a middle-class sympathizer with a naïve conception of the problems of operating a working-class organization.[90] She was to learn more about such practical problems and the length to which a true supporter of the proletarian cause must go.

III

The Shipyard Strike

AMID exciting accounts of the riots over American participation in the Siberian expedition, a quiet little news story appeared in Seattle newspapers which escaped the notice of most readers. Its effect would be that of a delayed-action bomb. The Pacific Coast Metal Trades District Council, the report revealed, had decided to discontinue dealing with the Shipbuilding Labor Adjustment Board and instead to negotiate directly with the shipyard employers.[1] This decision was in part the result of already unsettled conditions prevailing in Seattle and was a harbinger of important events and still greater unrest to come.

In the last months of 1918, the Seattle shipyards hummed with activity. Most of these yards, like many others in all United States coastal and lake regions, had been hastily constructed with the encouragement of the United States government. The outbreak of war in Europe in 1914 found the United States virtually without a merchant fleet, most American exports reaching their destinations in foreign bottoms. At the beginning of the war, the British Navy prevented Germany from engaging in international commerce, and Great Britain and her allies kept their own ships in port in fear of German raiders. As a result, American exports dropped precipitously, causing a financial panic. Later, as it became possible to trade with the Entente, the relative shortage of shipping drove freight rates to exorbitant heights, and the threat of German submarines made marine insurance prohibitive.[2]

These were compelling reasons for the United States to attempt to create a merchant marine which would break American dependence on foreign-flag shipping. As the war progressed, campaigns for "preparedness" and the United States' eventual entry into the war were additional motives for such an effort.

To attain this goal, government supervision and massive financial assistance were necessary. Shipbuilding, once a great American industry during the age of the wooden ship, had declined.[3] With the replacement of the wooden by the steel-hulled vessel, American yards could no longer compete with foreign shipyards: first because of the higher price of American steel, later because of the greater cost of American labor.[4] To provide the supervision necessary for the revival of American shipbuilding, Congress on September 7, 1916, passed legislation creating the United States Shipping Board. The Board was endowed with the power to regulate merchant shipping under the American flag and to promote creation of shipyards and the construction of ships. The Board itself retained its regulatory function and overall supervision of shipyard construction and shipbuilding. Active promotion of construction, however, was delegated to a subsidiary of the Shipping Board, the Emergency Fleet Corporation.[5]

From the start, the organization and operation of the Shipping Board and the Emergency Fleet Corporation were slow and inefficient. The Board was not organized until January 30, 1917, and the Corporation only on April 16, 1917, after the United States had entered the war.[6] In their early histories both were crippled by the inability of their appointed officials to agree on policy. Resignations were frequent. It was only after Edward N. Hurley became president of the Shipping Board and the Emergency Fleet Corporation and Charles Piez became general manager and vice president of the Corporation that the internal struggles were resolved.[7]

It was under Piez's direction that enormous shipyards were constructed, hundreds of ships fabricated. By 1919 the Emergency Fleet Corporation had accepted delivery of 647 vessels aggregating 3,603,434 dead-weight tons.[8] Piez planned ultimately to add 13,000,000 dead-weight tons of new vessels to the United States merchant fleet.[9] Charles Piez was a dominating personality. Born in Germany in 1866 of naturalized American parents, he was an engineer by profession. A graduate of the Columbia University

School of Mines, he was successful both as a practicing engineer and a businessman. Since he sat on a number of boards of directors, he was familiar with the requirements of the direction of large enterprises.

The Emergency Fleet Corporation, of which he was the operative head, had a dual function—to create shipyards and ships, and to supervise the use of the ships the Corporation built. The United States government, under the 1916 act creating the Board and Corporation, was neither to own nor to operate the shipyards. Although the government would own the ships, they were, in the main, to be operated by private interests.[10] Thus one of the two main functions of the Emergency Fleet Corporation was to use government funds—originally $50,000,000, then increased to $750,000,000, and finally to $2,884,000,000—not merely to purchase ships but to provide the capital required by private interests to create the shipyards.

The lucrativeness of the ship contracts and the virtually unlimited funds available for the construction of shipyards encouraged businessmen all over the country to go into the shipbuilding business. Northwest entrepreneurs quickly saw the advantages of this arrangement. Before 1914 only one firm—the Seattle Dry Dock and Construction Company—was manufacturing steel-hulled vessels in Seattle. From 1914 to 1917 two more steel-ship yards were built.[11] By the end of 1918, five firms in Seattle were constructing steel-hulled vessels. In addition, since the Emergency Fleet Corporation also encouraged the construction of wooden-hulled vessels, and because the primary materials were available locally, shipyards capable of building wooden ships proliferated even more rapidly. Twelve were producing ships in Seattle by 1918.[12]

Federal funds made Seattle a boomtown again. More than thirty-five thousand men were employed in the metal and wooden shipyards and allied trades. Backed by EFC funds, twenty-three new shipways capable of holding large vessels—some up to 17,500 tons—were erected. The new giant of the Seattle shipyards, Skinner and Eddy, put up ten of them.[13]

Seattleites viewed their wartime shipbuilding record with great pride. During 1918 Seattle yards contributed ninety-six ships of

651,000 dead-weight tons to the war effort, sixty-one of which (535,200 dead-weight tons) were steel freighters.[14] The Northwest district of the Emergency Fleet Corporation was the most productive district in the country in terms of tonnage.[15] During the course of the war, Seattle alone produced 26.5 per cent of all ships constructed for the Emergency Fleet Corporation.[16] The shipyards' record-setting performance of fabricating metal freighters in seventy-eight working days, indicative to Seattle's citizens not only of patriotism, but also of the high quality of the equipment, leadership, and workmanship of the shipyard organizations, seemed to augur a bright industrial future in the coming days of reconversion.[17]

But the price of a wartime boom, which Seattleites hoped would supply the sinews of future industrial prosperity, began to be questioned by some of the city's older residents. Seattle could not supply from its domestic labor force sufficient workers to operate the shipyards at peak capacity. A large proportion of the thirty-five thousand men in the shipyards and allied trades had to be recruited from all over the West. Newspaper advertisements were placed in western dailies urging skilled men to come to Seattle to work in the yards. The United States Department of Labor sent out "scouts" to recruit. The employment departments of the shipyards sent Seattle unionists to visit locals in other cities to recruit men for Seattle.[18]

Many older residents of Seattle believed that the influx of labor could change the character of their city. The problem of accommodating these men had already caused tension between newcomers and more settled residents. Housing was short. The competition for limited facilities, accelerated by wartime restrictions, caused a rapid rise in rents. The newcomers charged that too many local landlords and merchants demanded higher prices from them than from older residents (and in some cases sub-rosa payments), thus making the official cost-of-living index inapplicable to them.

More important in its implications for changing Seattle than the temporary tensions of the migration itself was the resultant increase in the power position of organized labor. The shipyards had become the largest employers in Seattle.[19] The shipyard unions grew enormously; for example, Boilermakers' Local 104, with fifteen thousand members, boasted that it was the largest local of any union in the world.[20] The Metal Trades Council, with which the shipyard unions were affiliated, was the largest component of the Seattle Central Labor Council. Organized labor entrenched itself deeply in the shipyards. Although an agency of the federal government had forbidden discrimination between union and nonunion employees by the shipyard employers,[21] the employers did not use this to attempt to maintain an open shop. Nonunion employees saw the advantages of joining a union soon after they were hired; although in theory restricted by the afore-mentioned ruling, the United States Employment Service "advised" the men it recruited to take out a union card.[22] Thus, though not officially closed shops,[23] the yards were almost 100 per cent unionized,[24] as nearly everyone in Seattle knew.[25]

Many people in Seattle feared that the unions were taking advantage of their power. Although the production record of the shipyards was excellent, local editorial writers and correspondents complained that it could have been even better if the unions had been more cooperative. The newspapers often printed accusations of a deliberate inflation of the shipyard work force. The metal-trades unions were blamed for forcing management to hire many more men than necessary. "Slackerism" (later to be called "featherbedding"), it was charged, was rife; two men were hired to do the work one man could adequately perform. Fictitious helper and supervisor jobs were said to have been created as sinecures for union leaders and their friends.

The power of the Seattle unions was all the more frightening to the pre-war Seattleites because of the political opinions of the new workers. The mayor of Butte, W. H. Maloney, on a visit to the Skinner and Eddy plant, found a large number of ex-miners —known for their radicalism—at work on the shipways.[26] In addition, some of the shipyard workers were Wobblies and ex-Wobblies. Local critics said that the Wobblies were particularly attracted to the shipyards because defense workers were exempted from the draft. Being opposed to fighting wars for "capitalism," they went to work in the shipyards, these critics said, either to avoid conscription or to sabotage the war effort or both.[27] This view may have been extreme, but in general the men and leaders of the shipyard unions were "impatient of tradition." [28]

The volatile situation in the Seattle shipyards greatly concerned the Emergency Fleet Corporation. Charles Piez charged that the Seattle shipyard owners in their efforts to recruit workers were upsetting the entire program of the EFC in the West. He was particularly incensed by the recruiting tactics of Skinner and Eddy, the largest yard, whose success forced the other Seattle shipyards to emulate them. To bring in workers from other cities, the Seattle shipyards "lured" them away with offers of higher wages than those prevailing, either in nonshipyard work in Seattle or in the shipyard industry as a whole.[29] Men working in shipyards as far down the coast as Portland and San Francisco responded to the bait. The ship production schedules in those cities became disarranged, making Charles Piez and the down-coast shipyard owners look at Seattle's recruiting tactics with somewhat jaundiced eyes.

For its part, Seattle labor and its leaders were not thoroughly satisfied with the way the far-off bureaucrat Piez dealt with what they considered to be pressing problems. Labor feared that the Emergency Fleet Corporation was attempting to interfere with its ability to deal with its employers, who had been remarkably generous in the shipyards. Skinner and Eddy paid the men not only far more than the national average, but also more than other local yards. For labor, Skinner and Eddy's wages became minimum bench marks. The Emergency Fleet Corporation saw the situation differently:

> The contracts and the policies of this company were instrumental in causing a great deal of the unrest that later developed. As this company was in a position to execute its contract profitably under any wage situation that was likely to arise, its employees received the impression that it was willing at its own expense materially to increase their compensation and that it was their generous advocate. . . . The mental attitude thus created was reflected in all attempts at adjustment throughout the whole period of the war.[30]

Seattle labor argued that it deserved higher wages for comparable work than shipyard workers in other areas of the country. Seattle laboring men were naturally locally oriented; they thought in terms of *their* problems and not in terms of the problems of the shipbuilding industry as a whole. In any attempt at dealing with them, they would immediately indicate that in their view the wages of the men in the Seattle shipyards should be established only by relating them to the current wages being paid in Seattle for nonshipyard work. To them, establishing Seattle shipyard wages in relation to wages in shipyards in other areas of the country ignored the fact that, owing to the distance of the Northwest from other industrial sections of the nation, both wages and prices in Seattle had for many years been higher than the national average. Seattle labor clung to this argument even after a careful investigation of the cost of living on the West Coast revealed that it was no more expensive to live in Seattle than in other western port cities. Their argument was economically valid against a national shipyard wage scale, but not a regional one.

Pride in the efficacy of their local labor organization, however, was the primary reason that Seattle labor—men and leaders— viewed with suspicion Charles Piez's efforts to treat their problems as only one component of a larger problem. High wages in Seattle, they believed, were achieved by the union movement's vigorous efforts at organization. The labor unions feared that the creation of a regional or national standard would not mean elevating all shipyard workers to Seattle's high standards but rather destroying Seattle's advantage to labor by applying the lowest common denominator. They needed only to point to the shipyards of Portland as an indication of what would happen if other than local standards were applied. Wages in that city were considerably below the pay scales for similar work in Seattle.[31] Furthermore, Portland employers were able to run the shipbuilding industry on the open-shop plan. Seattle labor was particularly apprehensive that a regional standard would be used as a first step in taking away advantages its labor movement had won by its own efforts, thus helping to destroy the organization itself.

The suspicion of Piez grew quite intense. To Seattle labor, Piez was committed to the destruction of their movement. His conduct as director general of the EFC, said the *Record*, was motivated by his desire to protect personal investments in another of the new shipyards built with EFC funds—the Hog Island yards on the mud flats south of Philadelphia.[32] The *Record* darkly hinted that Piez had engineered a deal between local shipyard owners and a group of eastern capitalists to destroy the Seattle labor organization. The local capitalists were to be paid in eastern shipyard stock in case their antilabor efforts resulted in the destruction of the entire shipbuilding industry of Seattle.[33]

Although the labor situation in the Seattle shipyards proved to be the most troublesome to the Emergency Fleet Corporation, it was not the only indication of labor discontent the Corporation faced. As ultimate employer of all American shipyard workers, the Corporation was in a compromised position in dealing with labor because it had to protect the interests of the United States government. To rectify this, there was established on August 20, 1917, the Shipbuilding Labor Adjustment Board—better known as the Macy Board after its chairman V. Everit Macy. Set up by agreement of the Navy Department,[34] the Emergency Fleet Corporation, and (after consultation with Samuel Gompers) various craft international union presidents, the three-man Board was to remove from labor and shipyard management the problem of bargaining over all disputes involving questions of wages, hours, and working conditions for the duration of the war. Macy, a New York bank director, was appointed by President Wilson. E. F. Carry, president of the Haskell and Barker Car Company, was added to the Board as the Emergency Fleet Corporation appointee. The third member, A. J. Berres, secretary of the Metal Trades Department of the AFL, was appointed by Gompers.

Because its powers were undefined and under dispute, the Board got off to a bad start. The delays required for shaking down the organization of the Board directly interfered with its initial attempt to settle a wage dispute on the West Coast. As a result, western labor's expectations that its problems would be handled fairly and expeditiously were upset, and the Board began its work in bad repute with that group. Unfortunately, it continued to fumble and render unclear decisions on wages in the western shipyards. Its handling of the wage question in Seattle was a very unfunny comedy of errors to local labor. This must be kept in mind when Seattle labor's subsequent actions over the final Macy Board decision are evaluated.

In July, 1917, the Metal Trades Council of Seattle, negotiating for all of the shipyard unions, presented shipyard managements with a set of demands for a new blanket agreement. It provided for wages of $6.00 per eight-hour day for skilled craftsmen and increases in pay for semiskilled and unskilled labor. Skinner and Eddy, because its contracts were more recent and reflected rising ship prices, agreed to comply with union demands after January 1, 1918. The other shipyards, however, had contracts which they announced would not allow them any profit if they agreed to the union demands. The Metal Trades Council prepared to call a strike in all metal-trades establishments in Seattle. Edward Hurley sent a telegram to the Seattle Metal Trades Council on September 2, 1917, to head off the strike. In it he proposed that the Council send, at government expense, three delegates to Washington, D.C., to present the union case before the Macy Board. He further promised to make any Macy Board decision retroactive to August 1, 1917.

The Seattle delegates arrived in Washington in the middle of an institutional crisis in the Shipbuilding Labor Adjustment Board. When it was originally constituted, the members assumed that the decisions of the Board would be final and binding. But on September 7, Hurley demanded an EFC veto of Macy Board decisions on the grounds that the EFC could not be responsible for the cost of ships without that power. As a result of Hurley's demand, Carry resigned from the Macy Board, leaving it without authority to hear the complaints of the Seattle delegates. In fury and disgust the three Seattle unionists left Washington for home on September 23. Ironically, hours after they left, the Board's power to make binding decisions was restored.[35]

By the time Carry rejoined the Board and it began again to consider the problem of West Coast shipyards, most of them had been struck. The Board sent the Seattle Metal Trades Council a telegram indicating that it would repair immediately to Seattle to hold hearings on the spot. The departure of members of the

Board, however, was delayed when Carry became ill and was forced to resign a second time. It was October 3 by the time Louis A. Coolidge was appointed as his successor and the Board started for the coast; it was October 8 when the Board began its hearings in Seattle. Realizing that the task of getting the men back to work would be difficult, the Board asked five international presidents of unions involved in shipyard work to come to Seattle.

The public hearings lasted five days. The Board decided not to render a decision without holding further hearings in Portland and San Francisco. At first the shipyard workers of Seattle refused to return to work. The Board's fumbling in getting to Seattle and the further delays before a decision was rendered destroyed the last vestige of faith Seattle union men had in the Board. But after strenuous efforts and appeals to patriotism, the international presidents were able to get the men in the Seattle yards back to work on the old conditions.

After the termination of the hearings in the down-coast cities, the Board rendered a decision which outraged Seattle labor. The wages paid on June 1, 1916 were used as a base point, from which the Board granted a 31 per cent pay increase. The basic rate for skilled men was set at $5.25 for an eight-hour day. The Board stated the primary motivation in its award:

> The enticing of workers from one plant to another and from one city to another has had a demoralizing effect on the production of ships. The establishment of a uniform wage scale for the San Francisco, Columbia River, and Puget Sound districts will have a steadying influence. Therefore, since the cost of living in these districts is substantially the same, we have decided upon a uniform scale for them all.[36]

To make matters worse, not only were the wages established by the Board lower than the men in the western yards expected, but these wages became not minimum wages, as hoped, but maximum wages.

The Board did make an exception for Seattle in its policy of uniform wages. Having experienced the intense hostility of the Seattle shipyard unions when regional standards were discussed, the Board allowed the rate of $5.50 per eight-hour day—the prevailing wages Skinner and Eddy paid its skilled men—to become the pay standard of the Puget Sound district.

This did not satisfy the Seattle metal-trades unions. They claimed that using the 1916 pay scale as a bench mark was highly discriminatory, particularly against the unskilled and semi-skilled. Because these men were not as well organized as the skilled in 1916, unions representing them had contracts then which they later viewed as unsatisfactory. As these unions organized more Seattle shops engaged in non-EFC work, the 1916 scale had little relevance to the wages paid their men. The Metal Trades Council claimed that the EFC, by applying the 1916 scale in Seattle yards, forced the shipyard management in many instances to pay union workers $22\frac{1}{2}$ cents an hour less than their fellow unionists were making for comparable work outside the shipyards. On the other hand, a smaller group of unions, which had satisfactory contracts with the shipyards in 1916, received under the Macy award 60 cents an hour more than their unions could get for their fellow members in comparable jobs outside the yards.[37]

The Seattle metal-trades unions were dissatisfied with the Macy award for another reason. Even though Seattle shipyard wages were established in relation to the wages paid in other western shipyards, it became obvious that these wages were established in relation to those received by the men in eastern shipyards:

> . . . unlike the workers in other sections of the country the men of the Pacific Coast Shipyards had not profited by the awards of the Shipbuilding Labor Adjustment Board because wage scales in the West had been higher than in other parts of the country. In the general wage scale leveling process that inevitably accompanied the war the tendency of the board toward standardization resulted in much smaller wage increases in the West than in the East. Seattle, which had enjoyed a particularly high scale, was most adversely affected by this policy.[38]

The Board was not unmindful of the prevailing sentiment of the western shipyard workers. It feared that the men, particularly those in the Seattle and San Francisco yards, would go out on strike again unless further action were taken. As an expedient they hit upon a temporary 10-per-cent war bonus for the workers in the Pacific Coast yards. But this bonus, even when it was made a permanent addition to the base wage, was also looked upon by the Seattle shipyard workers as insufficient in relation to the raises in pay in the eastern yards.

The Seattle Metal Trades Council attempted to appeal the Macy Board decision. James A. Taylor, president of the Council and representative of the Pacific Coast Metal Trades Council, traveled to Washington, D.C., to present his case in person. An appeal board of the Emergency Fleet Corporation, composed of three labor representatives and three representatives of the Navy Department and Fleet Corporation, was especially constituted. In a vote after the hearing, the board split—the government men voting to sustain the award, the labor men to upset it. The deadlock was ruled as a rejection of Taylor's plea. Although he failed to get the Board officially to upset the Macy award, Taylor thought he had gained an important informal concession from Charles Piez—"the verbal understanding that unions may deal directly with employers if possible," as long as any employers' concessions did not increase the financial obligations of the EFC.[39] Piez made this commitment verbally to Taylor on two separate occasions: the first time in Seattle in July, 1918;[40] the second, after the meeting of the appeal board:

> . . . he asked me whether I would interpose any obstacle in case he attempted to enter into separate agreements with individual yards. At that time substantially all of the yards in the Puget Sound District were paying their men more than the Macy scale, although the Fleet Corporation had taken the position that it would not compensate for any increases beyond those specified in the Macy award. Recognizing this situation I told Mr. Taylor that, inasmuch as it was likely the Macy agreement would expire on March 31st, I would interpose no obstacles to any agreements between his crafts and the yards that he could amicably arrange for, but stipulated that in no case would the Emergency Fleet Corporation reimburse builders for any payments in excess of the Macy scale.[41]

Piez later confirmed this understanding in writing. But under the pressure of the Northwest Shipbuilders Association, he withdrew his consent for direct negotiations[42] and ruled that "the men were under agreement, not with the shipyards, but with the Emergency

Fleet Corporation not to strike and to accept the award of the Macy Board. . . ." [43] As the Seattle shipyard union leaders and men believed, he had double-crossed them.

Before Piez's arbitrary change of mind became known, Taylor and the Seattle Metal Trades Council operated on the assumption that they had permission to deal directly with Seattle shipyard management. They rightly believed that Piez's concession was just as valuable as the overturning of the Macy award, their original goal. During the war, Piez had prevented just such direct negotiations leading to wage increases by threatening to withdraw steel allotments from employers who would negotiate with their employees without the authorization of the Emergency Fleet Corporation.

The Seattle Metal Trades Council waited eagerly for news of the Armistice which would end the fighting, so that it could invoke its new authority of direct negotiation. "For more than a year [the Seattle shipyard workers] continued to work, although under constant protest against the fairness of the agreement, to which they stated they had not been a party." [44] Metal-trades representatives constantly stressed the point that the international officers of their unions illegally committed them to abide by the decisions of the Macy Board, since "according to the constitution of various craft unions, the International Officers of the various locals had no authority to bind their locals without a referendum vote." [45] The men continued to work, union officials pointed out, only because of patriotism; when the fighting stopped this would no longer need to be demonstrated.

Less than two weeks after the Armistice, the Seattle metal-trades unions decided to invoke the permission to deal directly with the Seattle shipyards' managements. In the last week of November, 1918, the unions put to a vote of their rank and file an authorization to strike.[46] According to the voting rules of the international unions affiliated with the American Federation of Labor, if an entire industry involving many crafts unions is to be struck, the strike must be affirmed by a majority of the crafts unions involved. In turn, two thirds of each local's membership must vote to strike. But a majority of all workers potentially involved in a walkout is not sufficient, for under this rule, smaller unions have power out of proportion to their membership. For example, among the locals then affiliated with the Seattle Metal Trades Council the Boilermakers' Local 104 had more members than the combined total of the other sixteen crafts involved. A negative vote by a coalition of nine minor unions could have thwarted the desire of an overwhelming majority of the men to strike. But this did not occur.

The vote was counted on December 10, 1918. On December 11, Bert Swain, secretary of the Metal Trades Council, announced that "the proposition to reject the Macy award, which carried with it authorization to the Pacific Coast Council of the Metal Trades to call a strike has been adopted by the requisite two-third majority in a majority of the unions affiliated with the Seattle Council." [47] He also stated that not only had a majority of the unions voted to strike,[48] but a majority of the total men voting as well. But the specific figures were kept confidential so that management could not offer a wage increase to only the smaller unions voting to strike and break labor's united front. This plan boomeranged, however. Labor's failure to be completely candid led to damaging charges—said by Council spokesmen to be management-inspired—that the voting was manipulated or the figures falsely reported. Later, Bert Swain ruefully admitted that the secrecy surrounding the vote was a bad tactical error.[49]

Backed by the strike authorization, the Metal Trades Council prepared to meet the management negotiators across the conference table. It set its demands at $8.00 a day for mechanics, $7.00 for specialists, $6.00 for helpers, and $5.50 for manual laborers. The labor negotiators did not intend that these demands be rigid; they were put forth only as a basis for negotiation.[50]

The position of the Metal Trades Council was not unassailable. There were a number of minor points in the conduct of its affairs that management could have seized upon as bargaining counters or propaganda themes. For example, the Metal Trades Council was sponsoring the Soldiers', Sailors' and Workingmen's Councils. This dubious project forced the Metal Trades Council to devote a disproportionate amount of time and effort to a secondary issue. The Council had made extravagant promises, such as raising $60,000 to help make the new organizations stable,[51] which, if kept, would have hindered its strike efforts.

There was difficulty on other questions of internal policy. The Council was unable to maintain control of allied trades during the negotiations and strike. Its first difficulty was with the electricians. On January 16, Electrical Workers' Local 46, already notorious for engaging in jurisdictional disputes with other crafts, called four hundred of its workers out of the shipyards to enforce a demand for a pay scale of $8.00 a day for electricians and $6.00 for helpers. Protesting vigorously that the electricians' strike was unauthorized and illegal, the Metal Trades Council claimed that it alone had jurisdiction in the shipyards.[52]

Another important claim of the Metal Trades Council, which would enhance its bargaining power if it could be enforced, involved the unions in the yards constructing wooden-hulled vessels. More than thirty-two hundred men who worked in the wooden yards were organized by the Puget Sound Maritime District Council and were not represented on the Metal Trades Council. The Metal Trades, however, claimed that it had the authority to make the wooden-yard workers participate in the proposed Metal Trades strike. The Maritime Council protested bitterly over the Metal Trades' "unauthorized attempts" to represent it.[53] But the wooden shipyard unions' protests were sabotaged by one of their own international officers. George F. Sanfacon, general international organizer for the Brotherhood of Carpenters and Joiners, stated in a telegram to Ed Rowan, business agent of the Shipwrights' and Joiners' Union, that he believed the wooden locals ought to be bound by the decisions of the Metal Trades Council.[54]

With great hopes for victory, the Metal Trades Council entered upon negotiations with the employers on January 16, 1919. They met with President David E. Skinner and General Manager David Rodgers of the Skinner and Eddy yard, J. Twohy of Seattle North Pacific Shipyard, and Edgar A. Ames of the Ames Yard. They were bitterly disappointed when Skinner, claiming to speak for the management group, offered a raise in wages only to mechanics; these skilled workers were promised an increase to $86\frac{1}{2}$ cents an hour. The employers' committee would not discuss a wage increase for the less-skilled and lower-paid groups.[55] After the labor negotiators interpreted the management group's action as a flat refusal to "accede to demands for a new blanket agreement," the Metal Trades leaders informally decided to put their strike mandate into effect.[56]

Union claims aroused a great deal of sympathy. After negotiations were broken off, Metal Trades Council's statements emphasized that its demands would most benefit the lowest-paid workers. Management's refusal to discuss wage increases for the lowest-paid groups seemed to bear out this claim. Initially this proved influential in molding the position of the local opinion makers. The Seattle *Post-Intelligencer* was favorably disposed toward union claims.[57] The Seattle *Star*, as late as January 22, stated that 60 to 70 per cent of the shipyard workers were receiving $4.60 per day. The *Star* thought it most commendable for the more skilled and highly paid workers who were offered a pay increase not to abandon their lower-paid brothers.[58]

The relative calm with which the issues were joined soon evaporated. Charles Piez re-entered the situation to upset the collective bargaining process. The fears of the leaders of the local AFL movement were confirmed. In their struggle to improve the wages of the shipyard workers and consolidate the war-enhanced power of the local AFL movement, they would have to contend not merely with local management but with the power and majesty of the United States government. Piez, taking the Seattle situation out of the hands of the Shipbuilding Labor Adjustment Board, sent a telegram to the shipowners, ordering them to stand firm before union demands under threat of the loss of their steel allotment.[59] To the embarrassment of Piez and the fury of local labor, the telegram was received by the wrong party: "Through the 'mistake' of a messenger boy one of these telegrams was delivered not to the Metal Trades Association [the employers] but to the Metal Trades Council [the workers]. The anger of the shipyard workers was thus directed against Washington. . . ." [60]

Charles Piez's motives for this action were an enigma to Seattle labor. Was he leading and the Seattle employers following, or was he put up to this act by the local shipyard owners? There were three schools of thought on the question in the labor movement. Many informed persons thought that some or all of the local employers sincerely wanted to come to an agreement with their workers. In fact, those who espoused this view said that the employers and employees were in reality working together to break Charles Piez's hold over the shipbuilding industry. Both sides felt that control of their activities from three thousand miles away resulted in arbitrary decisions which did not give proper consideration to local problems. Although the war was not legally terminated, the adherents to this view believed that local labor and management both moved in concert against Charles Piez before he could throttle their postwar plans. Harry Ault, editor of the *Union Record,* was convinced to the day of his death that the shipyard strike was tacitly approved by the employers, most particularly by the owner of Skinner and Eddy.[61]

The second interpretation was stated by William Short, president of the Washington State Federation of Labor. He thought that Piez was forced into opposition by the entreaties of Seattle shipyard management to stand firm on the Macy award. Converts to this view assumed that local management informed Piez that it could not absorb the cost of wage increases. All but a few small wooden yards were on "lump sum" rather than "cost plus" contracts.[62] Thus, unless the Emergency Fleet Corporation were willing to renegotiate the contracts, the local shipyards would not be able to pass the increased costs onto the United States government. With the wartime demand for ships ended, Piez would not, of course, consider renegotiation. Short stated that this was the action of the smaller shipyards over the protests of David Skinner. The Skinner and Eddy yards, Short felt, were sufficiently large and efficient to absorb the costs; the others were not.[63]

The final school of thought among Seattle labor on the cause of the hostility of the Emergency Fleet Corporation was the most popular but the least reputable. As previously stated, it was rumored and widely believed that Charles Piez was attempting to crush Seattle labor in order to protect his investment in the Hog Island shipyards in his home town, Philadelphia. The local shipyard owners acquiesced in his attempt, according to the rumor, because "Eastern" capitalists had bribed them with stock in eastern shipyards. It must be remembered that the working-men of Seattle were westerners who inherited the Populist belief in the long arm of "Wall Street." The westerner's constant fear of having his life manipulated by forces beyond his immediate control was an emotional attitude of considerable impact in shaping his actions. Seattle workingmen believed in the duplicity of Charles Piez. It conveniently explained those specific aspects of a complex situation which had meaning in terms of their lives.[64]

Later evidence indicates that the second theory has some truth, although Short was too uncritical of Skinner and Eddy's motives. The main reason that Piez moved against the strikers was his conviction that Skinner and Rodgers were manipulating the Seattle labor movement for their own ends. He had received considerable information from his own agents in Seattle that the other shipyard owners feared and detested the Skinner organization. According to Henry Marshall, Piez's special representative in Seattle, "other yards kept in perpetual turmoil for fear Rodgers will put through another secret agreement and again corner [the] labor market." [65] The secret agreement referred to was the 86½-cent-an-hour compromise offer, "made by Rodgers in an improper way which bound Duthrie Ames and Wiley. . . ." [66] The smaller plants, working together to prevent Skinner and Eddy from upsetting their postwar plans by cornering the labor market, pressured Piez to curb their larger rival.[67] Because he felt that the EFC would lose control over Puget Sound shipbuilding unless labor were stopped from "pyramiding of wages" through the encouragement of one company,[68] Piez responded to their entreaties. But this was not the only reason for Piez's strong anti-labor position. Basing his appreciation of the situation in part upon reports from his labor spies, he feared that the unsettled conditions in Seattle shipyards were being used by radicals for subversive purposes. These reports, documented by few facts but containing very strong opinions, all led to one conclusion: "the wage conditions is [sic] not the present issue, but radicalism versus conservation. . . . This is not an industrial, but a political upheaval." [69]

Northwest labor had neither time nor the inclination to delve into the niceties of the question of fault. Piez had publicly condemned the strike and had forced the yard owners into a position where granting higher wages would appear unpatriotic and illegal. James A. Duncan and other labor leaders feared that management's obstinacy augured a period of attempted "union-busting," backed by the prestige and power of the United States government.[70] The "progressives" and "conservatives," who realized that the war had vastly inflated the membership and influence of their organization, were apprehensive over the possibility of a full-scale open- versus closed-shop struggle. Their task in the immediate postwar period was to consolidate the position labor had won in the community; a struggle against the open-shop advocates and Charles Piez would make this difficult and perhaps impossible.

For evidence of local support for an open-shop drive they had only to turn to the vitriolic editorials of Edwin Selvin, editor-publisher of a local weekly business newspaper. Selvin espoused a full-scale drive by employers to replace union "agitators and malcontents who stir up trouble" with returned servicemen.[71] The Seattle *Times* recognized the dangers of such a program; while admitting that there was strong sentiment among "certain interests to establish 'open shop' conditions in this city," the *Times* stated editorially that "success for the movement fostered by these employers merely would strengthen the IWW and the Bolsheviki and would discredit the municipality's really capable labor leaders." [72] This was an acute observation, since the Wobblies hoped that with AFL job control destroyed, they could organize the workingmen of Seattle.[73] The shipyard unions, therefore, had to win this strike, and the rest of Seattle AFL labor was willing to stage a general sympathetic strike.

After the deadlock of the employer-employee conference of January 16 and the Piez telegram, there could be no turning back. On January 18, A. E. Miller, chairman of the conference committee of the Metal Trades Council, began distributing the formal strike notices to the managements of the various yards. The notices stated that all work in the shipyards was to cease on January 21.[74] The shipyard employers met immediately, but they made no decision regarding their position on the strike because not everyone had received the formal notices. Both sides were standing fast.[75]

The position taken by labor in the Seattle yards was viewed sympathetically by shipyard workers in other Puget Sound cities. Representatives of the Tacoma Metal Trades Council declared that they were in direct sympathy but had not yet decided to stage their own walkout. It appeared as if the situation in Seattle would soon be reproduced throughout the Puget Sound area.

The Seattle press was not unduly alarmed by the imminent work stoppage, but took the situation in stride. Clark Nettleton, president and publisher of the Seattle *Post-Intelligencer,* ruminated quietly on the fact that "In Seattle there will be a strike, and perhaps parades and disturbances, but life will flow along much the same." To him, the shipbuilding industry was not part of the "real" Seattle; it was a temporary wartime boost to the economy which, when the war had ended, would certainly be reduced in size and importance. In fact, he was not unhappy about the prospect of the diminution of the shipbuilding industry; during its short lifespan it had caused prices to rise and had hurt those not associated with the industry. Nettleton remarked, "We had a city before we had so many shipyard workers, and we will have one after some of them are gone." [76] The newspapers agreed unanimously that the Metal Trades Council had chosen a foolish time to strike. After all, they reasoned, the war had been won and the government would naturally require fewer ships. It was widely believed that the government would respond to the strike with an immediate sharp curtailment of contract shipbuilding, instead of the previously hoped for gradual decline.[77]

On January 20, the day after the formal strike notices were distributed to the employers, the text of the strike notice appeared in the papers.[78] Management still remained silent before the inquiries of the unions and the curiosity of the public.[79] According to the Metal Trades Council, however, the employers were busily at work behind the scenes.[80] The Council's representatives accused the employers of circulating rumors that the shipyard employees did not really favor the strike, but had been forced into compliance by their radical leaders. Foremen and other supervisory personnel began circulating petitions among the men requesting that a revote be taken on permission to strike. Management representatives conducted a straw vote at Skinner and Eddy; they claimed that 95 per cent of the men opted against the strike. The Metal Trades Council issued a formal statement denying the validity of the petitions and straw vote because they were circulated by the employers. It was also rumored that the Metal Trades Council had refused to put to a referendum vote a generous compromise offer of the employers: $5.00 per day for helpers and laborers and 86½ cents an hour for mechanics. The next day A. E. Miller called the whole thing an employers' trick. The employers, said Miller, had made no such offer.[81]

On the morning of January 21, silence fell over the shipyards. All work stopped. Men filed silently out of the gates. Although the unions with jurisdiction in the wooden yards claimed that the Metal Trades Council had no right to control the actions of their members, all the wooden yards except the McAtee Shipbuilding Corporation were struck. In all, approximately 35,000 men were out of work—25,300 in the metal yards, 3,250 in the wooden yards, and the remainder in allied trades.[82] The only employees other than supervisory personnel who did not respond to the strike call were the carpenters employed in the metal yards. They were not covered by the Macy award.[83] Clerks in all the yards were on the job temporarily to prepare the final paychecks. When this task was completed, they too filed out of the gates.[84]

The initial movement out of the yards was very quiet. According to the *Union Record,* the calling of the strike was "absolutely clean" [85]—no violence, no fuss, no crowds. In order to maintain this serenity, the Metal Trades Council turned down a request by some of the striking workers to hold a parade.[86] The solidity of Northwest union sentiment was enhanced by the calling of a similar strike in the Tacoma shipyards, which had, in fact, gone out a few hours earlier than the Seattle yards. Puget Sound labor was disappointed with its fellow shipyard unionists in Portland, however. Portland's Metal Trades people did not comply with the Seattle request that they join the strike.[87]

Calm lasted through the next day, January 22. Neither side made a new offer or even an effort to resume talks. Charges of worker opposition to the strike were still hurled at the union leaders by the employers.[88] The Metal Trades Council, preparing for a lengthy siege, requested the assistance of the Central Labor Council in arranging to feed the strikers and their families.[89]

On January 23 the calm was broken, but not by any event connected with the strike. The Three Hundred Forty-sixth Artillery Regiment of the Ninety-first Division arrived in Seattle, the first unit composed of local troops to return home from France. It was given a joyous reception. A thunderous parade put on by the conquering heroes occupied Seattle's attention.[90] Most of the citizenry enjoyed a one-day holiday and were far too busy to be cognizant of strike developments.

Those who read the inside pages of the newspapers were, nevertheless, able to get the news of strike developments. Some of it was disturbing. Labor, too, welcomed the men of the Three Hundred Forty-sixth Artillery home, claiming that the dough-boys cheered the strike headquarters of the Metal Trades Council as they marched by. Many of the soldiers, the *Union Record* claimed, were categorical in their refusal to be used as strike-breakers and were interested in joining the Soldiers', Sailors' and Workingmen's Councils after their discharge.[91] The Tacoma strikers hastily voted to form a Soldiers', Sailors' and Working-men's Council to aid the newly returning veterans. In the meeting at which this decision was made, speakers rose to castigate the employing class as "Wall Street curs." The organization committee was said to include Wobblies and Socialists.[92]

The strikers were displeased with the other important new development—a shift in rumors which they ascribed to management manipulation. The new line insisted that the strike was not for the benefit of the lowest-paid workers but rather for the benefit of the already well-paid skilled workers. The *Daily Bulletin* claimed that only ten men in all of the Seattle yards were receiving $4.16, the minimum wage for unskilled labor. The bulk of the men were paid $4.64 per day. For this large group, the unions were demanding a new wage of $6.00 per day, a pay increase of only $1.36. The skilled workers, who received $6.40

per day, were, according to the Metal Trades proposals, to get
$8.oo per day, a difference of $1.6o. According to the *Bulletin,*
these figures clearly demonstrated that the stated claims of the
strikers were fraudulent.[93]

All the propaganda speeches and leaflets moved no one. During
the next two days, neither of the protagonists made major efforts
to settle their differences. Seattle was becoming accustomed to
the situation and had prepared itself for a lengthy strike. The
employers still had "no statement to make concerning the situation." [94] The strike dragged on. On January 25 deadlock was so
complete that Henry White, commissioner in charge of the Seattle district of the Immigration Bureau and representative of the
Department of Labor, offered to mediate the dispute.

While the situation on January 24 and 25 seemed quiet to the
general public, union leaders began to grow apprehensive. A
number of events served to increase their anxiety. For one, there
was a possibility of a renewal of the influenza epidemic. In recent
weeks fifty-four new cases and four deaths resulting from the disease had been reported. With no current income, the strikers
would be hard-hit if it became necessary to pay medical expenses.
A movement to end the strike under these circumstances might
gain the support of the rank and file. Moreover, the "public
health" might give the authorities an excuse to interfere in the
striking unions' affairs. Dr. J. S. McBride, the City Health Commissioner, had already warned of the danger to public health if
large meetings were held during the strike.[95]

The second blow dealt labor was the suspension of credit to the
strikers. On January 24 the Seattle Retail Grocers Association
decided to discontinue credit for food purchases to the idle workers. The union movement immediately tried to soften this blow;
the Cooperative Food Products Association, owned by the Seattle
unions, promised to fill the gap by extending credit to the
strikers.[96] Later that same day, however, the new arrangements
did not seem very secure. The police had raided the offices of
the Co-op, ostensibly to look for an illegal cache of liquor. Labor
saw this as a crude attempt to annoy and harass the strikers, a
nuisance raid to prevent laboring men from putting their confidence in the Co-op's ability to feed them. The *Union Record*

claimed that the police, by their officers' actions during the raid, proved they were not looking for liquor: instead of searching the cabinets and storage bins, the raiding policemen went straight to the files and examined them carefully.[97]

Labor was clearly on the defensive. Another attack was aimed at striking shipyard workers the next day. David Skinner, previously thought by many members of the labor movement to be a fair and honest employer, stated in a wire to Charles Piez that "the majority of the workmen did not favor the strike but were forced into it by the radical leaders whose real desire was to disrupt the whole organization of society." [98] This charge, previously made before local audiences, was now presented to the national public. The nation, fed on bulletins from Charles Piez's office, began to feel that revolutionary radicals were in command of the Seattle shipyard strike. Labor was most furious over this charge because it was so difficult to refute. Moreover, several days after the beginning of the strike, labor was left stranded by the employers, who left Seattle on vacation. The strike leaders could only conclude that management had no intention of negotiating further and intended to starve them out.[99] Other items embarrassing to labor appeared in the Seattle newspapers at the time the shipyard officials left town. Letters to the editor by correspondents claiming to be members of the striking unions flooded the conservative Seattle journals. Most of them were antistrike in sentiment and reiterated Skinner's charges.[100]

The strike committee of the Metal Trades Council felt it necessary to find a convincing means to refute these rumors that the majority of the strikers did not favor the calling of the strike. For this purpose, a mass meeting of the largest striking union was held on January 26 in the Hippodrome Arena. The Boilermakers' Local 104, six thousand strong, voted unanimously to support the Metal Trades Council in its calling and handling of the strike.[101] The *Union Record* reported that this made liars of the employers and their hired rumor mongers.[102]

But management's antistrike propaganda had been effective. Charles Piez, still very much the czar of the government-controlled shipping industry, and V. Everit Macy, the chairman of the Shipbuilding Adjustment Board, came out publicly in favor of the position adopted by management. In telegrams to all the struck companies, Piez and Macy stated that the unions had violated their agreement with the government. To buttress their argument on the illegality of the actions of the Seattle shipyard unions, they claimed that the Boilermakers' International Union would not allow its Seattle local any strike benefits. Macy and Piez would stand by the Macy award and would approve no wage increases. They ordered the shipyard owners "to make no effort to resume operations unless the men were willing to accept the Labor Adjustment Board's decision." [103]

Officials of the Metal Trades Council immediately rebutted these charges. Bert Swain, secretary of the Metal Trades Council, denied that Piez and Macy were stating the true facts.[104] James A. Taylor, president of the Council, denied that the Boilermakers' International had refused to help. He emphasized that locals were not bound by the agreements of their internationals unless the agreements were accepted by a referendum vote of the locals; therefore, the international officers' compliance with the decisions of the Macy Board was illegal under union rules. Taylor claimed that the locals had abided by the dictates of the Board only because of the war emergency. But now the war was over, and this was a new situation. Taylor reiterated his claim that Piez had verbally agreed to allow the Seattle shipyard locals "the right to reach our own agreements with our employers, and stated that the Shipping Corporation would place no obstacles in our way." [105] Nevertheless, Piez ordered the local shipyards to prepare plans on canceling costs.[106] To bolster its shaky strike, the Seattle Metal Trades Council began to wire metal trades councils all over the country for support. After the general strike had begun, right-wing opportunists pointed to this effort to obtain support as a sign that both the shipyard and the general strike were part of a conspiracy.[107]

Seattle began to have second thoughts about the shipyard strike. As the Seattle *Times* stated, "the Emergency Fleet Corporation's intervention in the local shipbuilding strike has developed an entirely new situation." [108] And well might Seattle worry. On January 21, the secretary of the Tacoma Metal Trades Council proposed a general strike in sympathy for the shipyard workers, but Bert Swain denied that such action would be necessary in Seattle.[109] The next day, however, the Seattle Central Labor Council adopted a resolution, proposed by the Metal Trades Council, to call a general strike if the measure was approved by a referendum of local unions.[110] Seattle reacted quietly to this announcement, still unaware of the impending crisis.

IV

The Demand for
a General Strike .

At the regular weekly meeting of the Seattle Central Labor Council on January 22, 1919, the delegates adopted a resolution proposed by the Metal Trades Council: the Central-affiliated locals would poll their members on the proposal to call a general strike of all organized Seattle workers, in sympathy with the shipyard workers.

This decision, which would have momentous consequences for the Seattle AFL movement, was made in the absence of many of the regular leaders of the Central Labor Council and its associated craft unions. These men were in Chicago attending a conference called by the International Workers' Defense League to protest the imprisonment of Tom Mooney, a San Francisco AFL leader. Mooney had been convicted of murder in connection with the bombing of a Preparedness Day parade in 1916. Although his original death sentence had been commuted to life imprisonment by Governor William D. Stephens, Mooney's fate was bitterly protested by segments of organized labor, who believed his conviction was based largely on perjured testimony.[1] This conference, which assembled over one thousand delegates on January 14, 1919, decided that if Mooney were not granted a new trial by July 4, the delegates would arrange to have their locals call every organized worker in the land out on strike.[2] So a nationwide general strike was being discussed at the very time that Seattle workers were considering a city-wide strike.

Seattle was a hotbed of Mooney agitation. The Seattle Central Labor Council was one of three city centrals to endorse the holding of a special conference.[3] Among its twenty-five delegates were the best known of the local progressive and radical leaders— James A. Duncan, Harry Ault, Anna Louise Strong, Frank Turco, and William Coffey.[4] Two of them made an outstanding impression on the other delegates—Harry Ault, who, because of his literary skills and his prestige as editor of the only labor-owned daily in the United States, became secretary of the conference,[5] and Frank Turco, who, because of his pugnacious personality and tactics, became the chief nuisance.[6]

In Seattle, the absence of the twenty-five delegates was sorely felt; the Central Labor Council and many of its affiliated locals were in effect left leaderless. As a result, the meeting of January 22, during which the metal-trades men demanded a city-wide general strike, was a wild, tumultuous affair. Charles W. Doyle, acting secretary of the Council, found himself unable to maintain a smooth, orderly flow of business. He had to pound his gavel frequently to quiet the spectators in the packed galleries— Wobblies, according to the *Star*—who again and again disrupted the speeches on the floor by shouting, clapping, and singing.[7] The delegates themselves behaved only slightly better. There were emotional appeals for the Seattle labor movement to cast itself adrift from the AFL and reorganize on the industrial-union plan. Pandemonium broke loose when the Metal Trades Council requested the general-strike referendum. Only one significant protest was raised when the Council overwhelmingly voted to stage the referendum, and the protester—T. H. Bolton, president of the bakers' local—was barely audible amid the tumult.[8]

The noise and confusion of the meeting made a poor setting for serious discussion of the broad ramifications of this decision. Yet if the strike were to be successful, the delegates should have carefully considered, in particular, the purpose the strike was to serve. A. E. Miller tried to indicate the Metal Trades' view of this important question in his speech justifying the request for the referendum. He stated that the Metal Trades Council did not view the general strike as a jumping-off point for an immediate overturn of contemporary society. Rather, a general strike was necessary to insure the future existence of the metal trades—and all other Seattle labor organizations—within the framework of that society. He was not proposing a revolution but a "demonstration of [labor's] power" which would convince Northwest management of labor's will to survive.[9] He said the shipyard managements were attempting to destroy the shipyard unions. Miller emphasized his fear that once the metal-trades unions were destroyed or crippled, labor would have insufficient power to stave off open-shop drives in smaller trades and industries. A general strike was necessary, he felt, because without it the shipyard strike was doomed to failure. Management intended to starve labor into submission by sitting tight for several weeks and refusing to negotiate; finally it would make a wage offer that would be far below the demands of the Metal Trades Council. The shipyard unions—if any still held the confidence of their members—would be forced to accept. It seemed even more likely that individual workers, rather than the unions, would accept management's carefully timed invitation to return to work. A general strike, Miller hoped, would force management to return to the negotiating table immediately. Unfortunately for Seattle labor, Miller's attempt to state a definite aim for the strike was paid scant heed. His effort proved futile, as did all other attempts of Seattle labor leaders to impose some order on a runaway general strike.

By the following evening, support for a general strike began to snowball.[10] At their regular meetings, eight local unions either voted to strike or indicated that they favored the strike. Without dissent, the Building Laborers' Local, in a well-attended meeting, endorsed a general strike. The roofers passed the general-strike resolution with only one negative vote. The Hotel Maids' Local "was unanimously for mass action, but on account of the fact that the attendance was not large, a special meeting was called for Tuesday evening" to take a formal strike vote.[11] The unanimity of sentiment and the rapidity of assent astonished and mystified those Seattleites who believed they understood the internal workings of the labor movement. In the face of all expectations to the contrary, this sentiment continued to grow. At this early stage, however, the conservative local press could not conceive of labor resorting to the use of a general strike. The Seattle *Times* said editorially:

> A general strike directed at WHAT?
> The Government of the United States?
> Bosh!
> Not 15% of Seattle laborites would consider such a proposition.[12]

The press was not alone in presuming that labor would not make good its threat. Many Seattle employers (such as Charles W. Carkeek, president of the Seattle Master Builders' Association, who had maintained amicable relations with the unions) would not believe that these unions would violate their word by participating in a strike forbidden by their contracts.[13] All of the doubters were wrong—more and more locals quickly indicated approval of a general strike.

A special meeting of union executives was held January 27 to canvass their opinions on the advisability and practicability of calling a general strike. These officials were convened because they were not ordinarily delegates to the Central Labor Council, where the initial decision to put the general strike to a rank-and-file vote was made. The discussion revealed that their attitudes toward the strike were strongly influenced by their ideological affiliations within the labor movement. Thus the usual three-way split developed among the 120 men present. The radicals adamantly insisted that a general strike be called immediately. No delay was justified, they said, because the animus and ultimate aim of the shipyard employers—destruction of the entire Seattle AFL movement—were completely evident.

The progressives were more cautious in their estimate of the situation, although they too believed that Seattle labor's future required victory in the shipyard strike. While they approved of a referendum vote authorizing a strike, they believed that the regular leaders of Seattle labor ought to decide when to put it into effect. For tactical reasons, the progressives said, the results of the authorization vote should be leaked to labor's enemies via the newspapers. But the authorization should not be invoked until management announced, as expected, that the yards would reopen on the open-shop plan. If the threat were sufficient deterrent to prevent such a management move, the general-strike authorization could be quietly shelved.

Only the conservatives saw no reason for pulling all organized labor off the job. To them all contracts were ironclad. But like all legal-minded men, the conservatives did concede that extreme circumstances—such as the imminent destruction of the labor movement—might create a situation in which faith could be broken in good conscience.[14] They argued, however, that no extreme threat to the labor movement had been conclusively proved by the advocates of a general strike. H. F. Jones of the Building Trades Council, hoping to head off a reckless dash into a general strike, introduced. a resolution requesting that the Central Labor Council delay the referendum vote until local management made a definite open-shop move. But in arguing that a general strike was not called for under the circumstances, Louis Nash, president of Retail Clerks' Local 174, admitted that the cause of the shipyard strikers was just.[15] The resolution was voted down almost unanimously, at least in part because Nash had weakened the conservatives' case.

But whether or not they approved of the strike, the executives had no direct power to halt the referendum. While each could attempt to exercise his personal influence over his local's vote, the executives as a group, having rejected an appeal to the Central to halt the referendum, could merely prepare to handle a general strike. Thus they agreed that if by Sunday, February 2, a majority of the unions which had held referendums voted for a general strike, a mass meeting should be convened to make a definite decision. Three representatives from each union voting to strike would be given credentials admitting them to the floor of the Hippodrome Arena at eight o'clock Sunday morning. If only a small group of locals had completed their voting, however, the mass meeting would be postponed until a sufficient number of locals had turned in their referendum results. Before adjourning, the executives agreed that these arrangements were to be ratified by the Central Labor Council.[16]

By late the same afternoon, the Central Labor Council sat in extraordinary session to put its stamp of approval on the tentative arrangements made only hours earlier by the executives of the affiliated locals. After some torpid discussion of the institutional arrangements for coordinating a general strike—a subject on which most delegates had to claim ignorance—the Council turned its attention to the possibility of canceling the Sunday meeting if the locals lagged in holding their meetings and reporting their votes. In particular, the Central wanted definite news of voting progress within two days, in time for its regular Wednesday night meeting. The Council therefore set up a five-man *ad hoc* committee to work in conjunction with a similar committee of the Metal Trades Council to urge immediate action in the locals.[17]

As events soon proved, the committees were unnecessary. Most locals needed no urging. Even before the committees could effectively organize themselves, five more Seattle unions reported that their members had voted to strike: the Structural Iron Workers, the Newsboys, the engineers in the gas plant and the public schools, Carpenters' Local 1335, and Barbers' Local 195, in the "largest meeting the union ever held." [18] The committees received assistance from an unexpected quarter when a well-known opponent of labor unwittingly helped assure approval of a general strike. Edwin Selvin, who for weeks had been assailing Northwest labor in his weekly *Business Chronicle,* began inserting a series of full-page advertisements in the three nonlabor-owned Seattle daily newspapers.[19] According to Harry Ault, he first submitted an ad to the *Post-Intelligencer* which urged that the labor leaders be "hanged on the nearest telephone pole." The *Post-Intelligencer* was unable to accept Selvin's polemic, however, because its union printers, led by Alvaro Shoemaker, refused to set it in type.[20] Selvin then submitted a reprint of his editorial of January 25—only slightly less vicious but involving no direct incitement to violence—which the *Post-Intelligencer* published on January 28.[21] In it he proposed that all labor "agitators" be replaced on the job by returning veterans. Selvin advocated that employers turn Seattle, "the most labor tyrannized city in America" because it was "overrun by red-flag agitators in the guise of labor leaders," into a bastion of the open shop. Although union men were well aware of Selvin's views, his attempt to gain a mass audience helped convince them that the expected all-out effort to destroy organized unionism in Seattle had begun.[22]

Night after night, as locals held their meetings, votes for a general strike continued to roll in. Electrical Workers' Local 77, Millmen's Local 338, Leather Workers' Local 40, Hotel Maids' Local 528, and the jewelry workers' local all certified officially that their members were willing to strike.[23] But most significant were the results from well-established, conservative locals with strong craft traditions. To the astonishment of the Seattle *Times* man on the Labor Temple beat, they announced stunningly lop-sided pluralities in favor of a general strike. The six-hundred-man Cooks' and Assistants' Local 33 reported that its members voted five to one for a general strike. By a margin of sixteen to one, Housepainters' and Decorators' Local 300 came out in favor of striking. The men of the Green Lake Carpenters' Local 1335 also were reported to have voted "yes" by an unexpectedly large margin.[24] When a majority of the seventeen-hundred-man Teamsters' and Auto Truck Drivers' Local 174, the largest of six Seattle teamster locals, voted in favor of the strike proposition, it was a "virtual certainty" that, as the Seattle *Times* predicted, a general strike would be held. The *Times* also correctly prognosticated the immediate effect of the vote of Local 174: the five smaller teaming-trades unions quickly jumped on the strike-bound band wagon.[25]

On the evening of January 29, at the regular meeting of the Central Labor Council, twenty-four locals, or approximately 27 per cent of the locals eligible to vote,[26] reported that their members were willing to strike. The most recent affirmative vote reported, that of the forty-five-hundred-man International Longshoremen's Association local, although expected, confirmed the gloomy strike predictions of reporters from the nonlabor-owned press.[27] The reporters could hold out little hope to middle-class Seattleites that "sensible" and "patriotic" conservative union men would halt the march toward chaos. Only two of the many labor units reporting—Gas Workers' Local 15741 and the federal employees' local—opposed a general strike, and only the leaders of the federal employees, F. H. Newhall and E. G. Ellis, tried to persuade the other delegates that a general strike would tear down "twenty years of good work." [28] Thus there was little discussion of whether to hold a mass meeting on Sunday; the votes already reported had provided the answer.

Discussion at this meeting centered on the questions of when the strike would take place and how it would be conducted. While the debate on the floor was at times acrimonious, it was handled better than in the previous Council meeting, because the progressive leaders, returned from the Mooney Conference, were now attempting to resume control. Their efforts were complicated, however, by their radical colleagues who returned with them. Chagrined by a decision made during their absence, the radical leaders attempted to compensate by a display of verbal enthusiasm. With James A. Duncan again on the rostrum this was quickly cut short, but not before Frank Turco and a Council guest, William Spooner, secretary of the Oakland Central Labor Council, came to blows. [29]

The essential question of whether to hold the strike was out of the hands of recognized leaders of all ideological hues—the matter had gone too far. The radicals, who approved of the strike, could merely attempt to lead what had begun without them. The conservatives opposed a general strike under any circumstances, but their influence corresponded closely to their relatively limited numbers. While the progressives or Duncanites had neither ethical nor ideological compunctions against calling a general strike, most of them feared the consequences of the unrestricted use of so unusual a weapon. Many of them believed that some nonviolent but dramatic demonstration was necessary to counter the growing antilabor agitation in Seattle. They did not fear a general strike if they, the progressives, planned and controlled it, but a strike or demonstration led by any other group, they felt, would get out of hand.

The progressives faced what appeared to be an unsolvable dilemma. For the first time they had lost control of the movement; the rank and file seemed to have gone over to the radicals. The progressives could not stop the agitation for the general strike; and without risking loss of respect among the majority of laboring men, neither could they openly oppose it. But their lack of enthusiasm for the strike prevented them from making a strong bid to regain leadership in this moment of crisis. Instead, they chose to act as informal advisers to the elected strike leaders in an attempt to prevent them from blundering into rash or extreme acts.

This split vastly complicated the problem of setting clear and attainable goals for the strike. The conservatives totally opposed the strike and therefore were of no assistance in formulating its goals. The ends sought by the progressives were somewhat negative—to show sympathy with the shipyard workers without allowing the strike to become uncontrollable and, therefore, a threat to the labor movement itself. The grandiose expectations of the radicals indicated that despite their propaganda about general strikes, the radicals did not understand their own tactic.

The Wobblies were in part responsible for providing the idea. The general strike was the core of IWW ideology; if applied on a universal scale, it would be the cataclysm needed to destroy capitalism. But like all working-class anarcho-syndicalist movements, the IWW was anti-intellectual and direct-actionist. Thus the general strike was an emotional goal the conditions for which the true believer must strive to create, but which he declined to define with care. Beyond assuming that a well-organized strike could peacefully revolutionize society, the IWW gave little thought to the method of conducting a general strike or the nature of the world it would create.[30] Once the situation had been created and the workingmen had laid down their tools, Wobblies hoped that revolutionary spontaneity would finish the job. With these views, those borers who rose to positions of leadership within the Seattle AFL organization obviously were poorly equipped to lead a general strike. They hoped it would be the beginning of the revolution in America, but the Wobblies did not have the means to turn the strike into a revolution.

However vague the Wobbly concept of the general strike, the borers were at least pointed toward revolution as a specific goal. Not so the free-wheeling radicals. While they had no love for the capitalist system, they did not conceive of the upcoming general strike as a direct blow at the heart of capitalism. Their aim was multi-directed—to get back at *all* enemies of labor. How could there be a single target for labor's wrath with so many enemies—the government, capitalism in general, the shipyard owners, the slave-wage advocates of the open-shop movement? The free-wheeling radicals also wanted to reward their friends; in addition to assisting the shipyard workers in their strike, they would interpose the grievances of nonshipyard unions into a general-strike settlement.

This move was spearheaded in the January 29 Central Labor Council meeting by the longshoremen, barbers, millwrights, meatcutters, and waiters. All had old complaints about wages, hours, and working conditions, and their past experiences seemed to indicate that the action of their individual unions was ineffective. For example, the meatcutters' union had lost its closed shop the previous year when it was locked out after a strike. Others, such as the longshoremen, dissatisfied with a Henry White mediation award, opportunistically viewed the general strike as a way of reopening dead issues. The effort to inject other grievances into general-strike demands was heatedly opposed by the Metal Trades Council and metal-trades unions' representatives. They feared that the focus of the impending strike would be shifted from the shipyard strike to matters irrelevant to that cause. As Andy Mulligan of Boilermakers' Local 104 put it, the metal-trades people wanted "a clean-cut demonstration of the economic power of organized labor or call it off." [31]

Realizing, however, that some of the supporters of the scheme —particularly the free-wheeling radicals representing the longshoremen and barbers' unions—had significant following among the delegates, the Metal Trades Council attempted to offer a compromise. If the disgruntled unions dropped their immediate demands, the Metal Trades Council would offer them its full support once the shipyard strike was won. But the vagueness of the offer merely made the dissidents doubt its value, and consequently the millwrights' delegate made a formal motion that the demands of all unsatisfied unions be met as a condition for the settlement of the general strike. The motion was seconded by Herman Rose and then defended by Phil Pearl of the barbers in an impassioned speech. The progressives, trying to prevent further complication of an already confusing situation, lined up behind the Metal Trades Council; only then were enough uncommitted delegates mobilized to defeat the motion.[32] But this negative victory for the progressives merely indicated what the general strike would *not* accomplish. Labor's inability to state reasons and goals for the strike was the major reason for its subsequent collapse.

The crisis had been reached. The complacency of the local press evaporated as it became apparent that even many of the "responsible" labor men either were overwhelmed by rank-and-file support for the strike or themselves went along with it. Editorials and columns began to suggest that Seattle might soon face a situation experienced by no other major city in the United States. The journalists made it clear that they disapproved. "The Stroller," correspondent of the weekly *Argus,* viewed labor's attempt to stage a general strike as "chasing the pot of gold at the end of the rainbow." [33] If his assessment was based on the strike discussions at the Central meetings, his view was well founded. The *Post-Intelligencer,* among others, after plaintively reminding laboring men of how good Seattle had been to the AFL, saw the strike merely as a radical plot.[34] Newspaper editors began to believe that none of the real substantive issues in dispute was of sufficient importance to trigger a general strike. Logically then, they could only conclude that the strike was the deliberate beginning of an attempt to destroy established society.

For the first time many Seattleites took the general-strike threat seriously, and new mediation schemes were hastily proposed. On the assumption that local shipyard management would agree to bargain with labor if it were not bound by the rulings of the Emergency Fleet Corporation, O. S. Larson, president of the Scandinavian Bank and local representative of the War Labor Board, suggested that a labor-management committee prepare a joint complaint against the EFC for submission to War Labor Board or Department of Labor mediation. Until the complaint was acted upon, the shipyard workers should return to work.[35] The next day, Charles Piez wired his reply. The Emergency Fleet Corporation, he said, "cannot consent to outside mediation that would involve a revision of the decision of the Shipbuilding Labor Adjustment Board." [36]

In all probability Piez's quick negative response saved Larson from putting himself in a personally embarrassing situation. A statement by Henry White, the first mediator, had effectively shaken labor's faith in other would-be mediators. White was quoted by the Seattle *Times* as saying that the shipyard-strike vote was not honest and that the general-strike vote was probably also dishonest.[37] The *Union Record* replied with a violent attack on White's integrity:

> Who is this Henry White?
> White is the Commissioner in charge of the Immigration Bureau in this district. White is the man who controls the policy of the Seattle detention station where prisoners have been held for months under conditions that are an affront to decency and a slap in the face of democracy. White is the man who has denied jury trial to men held under charges that he knows will not bear the light of publicity; who has refused open hearings to prisoners whose friends were prepared to disprove the allegations of the authorities.[38]

Although the following day White claimed that he had been incorrectly quoted, his usefulness was at an end.[39] His blunder served only to strengthen Seattle labor's conviction that a general strike was required to ward off the hostile blows from its legion of enemies.

From across the continent, Charles Piez had again intervened in the shipyard strike. He publicly made clear what he had announced by telegram to Larson: "The decisions of this tribunal [the Macy Board] have been and must continue to be binding upon the Emergency Fleet Corporation and the workers alike. So long as the workers remain away from their posts the Emergency Fleet Corporation cannot treat with them." [40] Apparently Piez did not realize that his implacable stand merely heightened the strikers' determination and directed their ire away from local shipyard management and open-shop advocates, and toward the United States government. The Metal Trades Council issued only a routine announcement reiterating its well-known objections to the validity of the Macy Board's award.[41]

But Piez was not deterred. Operating on the assumption that the general-strike vote was forced on reluctant union men by their radical leaders, Piez believed that he could put the situation aright by communicating directly with the mass of shipyard workers. Hopefully, Piez thought, the men would return to work when they realized that their union officials had duped them. On February 3, the first of a series of full-page paid advertisements appeared in Puget Sound newspapers, carrying a statement by Piez to the shipyard workers. He urged the workers to return to their jobs in order to preserve the sanctity of contract. If the Macy award were not honored, Seattle unionists would be taking unfair advantage of other workers.[42] Piez found, however, that appeals to reason do not change the minds of committed men.

The second advertisement appeared the next day. It called the shipyard strike a "Colossal Business Mistake." [43] Piez warned the workers to consider the future shipping needs of the United States government. Shipyard wages, he indicated, were already high; if Seattle workers pressed their demands, the government might not choose to continue the building of ships. For the good of the industry, he pleaded for labor-management cooperation.[44]

The men did not respond with passion, but Upton Sinclair did. He wired Piez that he hoped no government money was used to pay for the advertisements: "If it is your personal money," said Sinclair, "all right. If it is mine, I protest with utmost vigor." [45]

But the shipyard strike was no longer the focus of attention for Seattle workingmen. They were already deep in preparations for a far more exciting adventure. Plans for the February 2 mass meeting were being completed. By the morning of the third, an official general-strike notice would appear in Seattle newspapers. There would be no turning back.

V

Crisis

THE uncommitted were becoming frightened and the committed more obdurate. Labor's determination to hold the February 2 meeting was a rude shock to complacent Seattleites. They had assumed that "American" leaders of the Seattle unions would never actually stage a general strike; it would merely be used as a vague threat to force further concessions in the shipyard strike. Having previously supposed that this strike would not concern it, the middle class was now particularly aroused. The complacency vanished. Although the purpose of the mass meeting was to decide whether to hold a general strike, most Seattleites considered the matter settled. Their thoughts now turned to possible consequences.

The press thought they would be catastrophic. Stimulating the already awakened imaginations of its readers, the Seattle *Times* reported in headlines that "Seattle Would Be Destitute in 48 Hours." [1] Food distributors and suppliers of other essential commodities predicted immediate shortages in the event of a complete labor tie-up. The most frightening report concerned the supply of fresh milk; it was predicted that available stocks would last only two days, then babies and hospitals would be forced to do without. Bakeries, said the *Times,* would soon run short of flour for bread. If the strike lasted longer than a few days, residents of Alaska would suffer terribly. By tying up ships in Seattle's harbor, the strike would cut the sea supply route to Alaska; the territory that Seattleites with serious jocularity claimed to "own" [2] would soon face outright starvation.

With adroit timing, Edwin Selvin inserted a new full-page advertisement in the major Seattle dailies, further inflaming the fears of the local populace. Selvin claimed that "the real cause of the strike is to loot the union treasuries";[3] venal labor leaders were simply using the strike threat as a smoke screen to cover their own self-seeking machinations. The closed shop, which gave these unprincipled men positions of unassailable power, was to blame, according to Selvin. The strike threat and the labor leaders' stranglehold over the city could be ended by a crusade for the open shop. The Selvin advertisement, by claiming that the strikers' cause was not legitimate, helped to transform a general dread of the strike into a demand that it be prevented.

Other citizens were concerned with averting the general strike, but unlike Selvin, they did not advocate action that would destroy labor's position in the community. These people still believed that the essential cause of the threatened general strike was a wage struggle in the shipyards. If this could be settled by bringing Seattle labor and management together to work out a compromise, they hoped the combined weight of the community and the directly interested parties would be sufficient to force its acceptance on the reluctant shipping czar, Charles Piez. Before labor had irrevocably committed itself to a general strike, the Permanent Labor Committee of the Seattle Ministerial Federation attempted to put pressure on Piez. This group wired Emergency Fleet Corporation headquarters that, in its opinion, the shipyard workers of Seattle were underpaid. It also stated that an acceptable settlement could be reached if the EFC would consent to raising the minimum wage in the yards to $5.50 per eight-hour day.[4] The committee also held a special meeting to hear testimony from shipyard workers on the strike situation.[5]

A second group, the Industrial Relations Committee, formed for the purpose of conciliating the protagonists in the shipyard strike. Because of the reputations of its acknowledged leaders, newspaper announcements of its formation again rekindled hope that the strike threat might be ended.[6] All three of its leaders—the Reverend Dr. Mark A. Matthews, James W. Spangler, and Judge George Donworth—were well-known and widely respected civic notables. Matthews, the pastor of the First Presbyterian Church, had become Seattle's best known clergyman for his leadership in an antivice crusade which lead to Mayor Hiram Gill's recall in 1911.[7] Spangler was president of the Seattle National Bank and vice president of the Seattle Chamber of Commerce and Commercial Club. The optimism of the press was not unjustified— these men had previously maintained good relations with the leaders of the local AFL organization, and presumably their efforts would be given serious consideration. Matthews and Jimmy Duncan were "good friends" who for years had "agreed to disagree." [8] During the days preceding the general strike, the two men were frequently in contact. Spangler was also highly regarded by labor. He had been a member of the Mediation Commission, appointed by President Woodrow Wilson to investigate the 1917 timber strike in the Northwest woods, which had submitted a report critical of the employers, much to labor's delight.[9] Equally important to its ability to engineer a settlement of the shipyard strike was the committee's advantageous position vis-à-vis Charles Piez. Local reporters thought that Piez could not dismiss out of hand a settlement put together by established men of wealth, position, and power, even if it did compromise his national shipbuilding program.

The committee swiftly organized for negotiations with the now deadlocked and adamant leaders of management and labor. Dr. Matthews arranged a meeting of himself, Duncan, and James A. Taylor, president of the Metal Trades Council. In the course of that meeting, Dr. Matthews mentioned that the committee would contact the international officers of the various shipyard unions and the government officials in order to find some basis for serious three-way negotiations among committee, labor, and management.[10] Meanwhile, other committee members began preliminary talks with A. E. Miller, the Metal Trades Council's chief negotiator, and David E. Skinner.[11]

The conciliatory efforts of the Industrial Relations Committee, however, were begun too late to show results that would warrant any attempt by labor's regular leaders to call off the mass meeting. It would, in any case, have been difficult for them to do so because of rank-and-file enthusiasm for a complete tie-up. Last-minute reports sent to the Central's secretariat showed more and more locals voting to go out. Contrary to the expectations of labor experts, the weak and recently organized streetcar workers' local voted to participate in the strike.[12] The laundry drivers, by a vote of 103 to 83, moved into step with the other teamster locals that had voted to strike.[13] Even the Seattle typographers, although prevented by their international from participating, reported an affirmative vote.[14]

Representatives of these unions were among approximately three hundred delegates who assembled early Sunday morning. Thirteen hours later the weary delegates left for their homes, convinced that they had adequately prepared for their venture into the unknown. Their satisfaction in organizing the strike was heightened by knowledge of the handicaps they had overcome. As a decision-making body, the group was too large and unwieldy to work with efficiency and dispatch. Moreover, most of the delegates (three from each striking local) were rank and filers who had little previous leadership experience. Finally, because the delegates were from such a wide variety of locals, they had rarely worked together; and because most of them were not personally acquainted, they had made no previous estimates of the qualities and capacities of the others.

The morning was taken up with accepting the credentials of delegates and organizing the committee. The documents of delegates from 101 locals were checked and, with only a few exceptions, accepted. Twenty-one unions represented on the committee were from the Metal Trades Council, the remaining eighty were other unions affiliated with the Central Labor Council.[15] The committee was formally constituted as the General Strike Committee and permanent officials were elected. Jack C. Mundy of the engineers' local, later president of the Central Labor Council, was president and Frank Turco of the Metal Trades Council was vice president.[16]

The first substantive decisions by the Committee, while most important, were made with little discussion: to take all responsibility for issuing a general-strike call and overseeing arrangements for the conduct of the strike. The delegates were convinced that the mandates from their locals required a strike; therefore, a formal strike vote was not taken in the Committee. Debate was necessary, however, before a definite date was chosen. The delegates decided that 10:00 A.M., Thursday, February 6 would be the most opportune time. The labor movements of Tacoma and Aberdeen, which had voted to go out in support of Seattle's general strike, had planned to order their men off the job earlier that day, but the Committee formally requested that they postpone their walkouts until ten o'clock.[17]

As they debated the problems they would face, the members of the General Strike Committee finally realized the formidable nature of their task. The unique nature of a general strike became apparent when the representative of the garbage-wagon drivers' local explained why his union had voted not to participate in the strike. Dr. J. S. McBride, Seattle Health Commissioner, had informed the drivers' union that if garbage for hospitals and sanitariums was not hauled, the local would be held responsible for violating a city ordinance. Since the union did not know if the General Strike Committee would allow any exceptions, they had voted not to strike.[18] After this report it became obvious that numerous exemptions would have to be made for basic facilities if the Committee did not want to prostrate the city.

Other difficult responsibilities were also discussed in sufficient detail to give the delegates an inkling of the important and delicate decisions they must make. One of the most troublesome issues of the strike was the question of shutting down the municipally-owned City Light plant. If the strike were to be complete, such a move was necessary. It would cause suffering, however, and perhaps panic. Discussion on the floor was inconclusive, and the question was not resolved. Although the newspaper reporters showed special interest in the fate of City Light, no announcement on it was released. Nevertheless, the newsmen managed to demonstrate to their readers that this was a key issue: they reported that Mayor Ole Hanson was waiting outside the convention hall for a report from union leaders on City Light.[19]

The Committee's inability to resolve the City Light problem and other issues, and the time already consumed by inconclusive discussion and debate, convinced many members of the General Strike Committee that their organization was simply too large and unwieldy; it could neither handle questions involving detail nor conduct sensitive negotiations. A smaller, tighter-knit organization with broad powers was needed to control the strike. An Executive Committee of 15 was set up and charged with the general responsibility of formulating strike plans. It was to co-operate with the strike committee of the Metal Trades Council. But perhaps its most important and certainly its most time-consuming job was passing on exemptions for unions, hospitals, individuals, and municipal departments in order to prevent chaos when most activities shut down. The decisions of the executive group would not be final. It was to be accountable to the General Strike Committee, which in theory could veto any action taken.[20] To reduce the work load of the executive committee, other sub-committees of the General Strike Committee were created to handle special matters, such as publicity, finance, and tactics. Finally, fifteen members of the General Strike Committee were appointed to the executive group. The selections were soberly and cautiously made; only two of the fifteen members had reputations as radicals.[21]

At the end of a long session the weary delegates voted to settle a number of minor matters. A resolution was passed to wire the President of the United States in the General Strike Committee's name to demand the removal of Charles Piez as head of the Emergency Fleet Corporation. In a burst of rank-and-filism, a resolution was passed to stop the salaries of all union officials and committeemen for the duration of the general strike. Finally, before adjourning until Thursday morning when the strike was to commence, the Committee adopted a strike slogan. After rejecting "We have nothing to lose but our chains and a whole world to win," the group decided that "Together We Win" was sufficiently vague to serve as the rallying cry in a movement whose goals were undetermined.[22]

Before the Sunday meeting of the General Strike Committee adjourned, its recently elected executive committee had already begun its deliberations. Only three full workdays remained before Seattle was to be struck. Time was precious: time to handle hundreds of requests for keeping essential facilities operating; to set up cafeterias to feed those who could not eat at home; to get fuel and laundry to hospitals, mail delivered, government cargo unloaded, milk stations set up in residential districts; time to secure emergency transportation and fire protection.

The executive committee immediately chose officers. Ben F. Naumann of the hoisting engineers was elected chairman and Tom Egan of the barbers was secretary. Since the fifteen members realized their committee had to make decisions on many disparate subjects, they decided to divide into subcommittees rather than exhaust everyone by acting only as a full committee. Exemptions were to be the major headache; therefore, three subcommittees were set up to deal with exemptions in the construction, transportation, and provisions trades. In addition, other subcommittees were created to handle miscellaneous exemptions, grievances, and general welfare. Although few of its members had previous experience in positions of responsibility, the executive committee realized that its efforts to bring some order to the strike would be worth little unless the strikers and general public knew of the committee's work and trusted it. For this reason, the committee announced that it would hold public meetings daily at 1:30 P.M. in the Labor Temple and would be available to anyone who wished to raise a question concerning the strike.[23]

On February 3 the official strike notice, signed by W. F. DeLaney, chairman of the publicity subcommittee of the General Strike Committee, appeared in the local press.[24] For most Seattleites the announcement was anticlimactic. But the *Union Record* was jubilant. Its headlines announced that "60,000 Will Walk Out" because it was necessary for "Charles Piez to be Taught a Lesson." To the *Record* the reason for the strike was simple: "People Revolt When Justice Can Be Had in No Other Way." [25] Labor's self-righteous rationale merely reinforced the convictions of the convinced. Those Seattleites without a direct interest in labor's cause were apprehensive, and only a slight amount of antilabor propaganda was necessary to push them to the brink of panic. The *Record,* aware of the problem, made a feeble attempt to win over small businessmen, which failed abysmally. The promise that if labor won the shipyard strike the union men would have $200,000 to $300,000 more per week to spend in their shops[26] did not overcome businessmen's fears that revolutionary workers would take over their property.

Handbills and fliers urging such a course, passed out by Wobblies and other radicals, were common along Seattle's waterfront and downtown streets. The shipyard strike noticeably increased the number of leaflets urging workers to confiscate the means of production.[27] After the decision for a general strike was announced, a radical dodger entitled "Russia Did It" hit the streets. Its author, young radical Harvey O'Connor, urged the workers to "take over the management of the shipyards." He continued:

> The Russians have shown you the way out. What are you going to do about it? You are doomed to wage slavery till you die unless you wake up, realize that you and the boss have not one thing in common, that the employing class must be overthrown, and that you, the workers, must take over the control of your jobs, and through them, the control over your lives instead of offering yourself up to the masters as a sacrifice six days a week, so that they may coin profits out of your sweat and toil.[28]

Public reaction was immediate and explosive. An operative of the American Protective League arrested two men for distributing the leaflet.[29] Suddenly the threat to the property system seemed real. Many Seattleites believed that "Russia Did It" was an official statement issued by the General Strike Committee. Although O'Connor's handiwork was quickly disavowed by the strike leaders, the impression that the general strike was the first stage of a revolution remained firmly fixed in the minds of many city residents.[30]

On February 3 everyone concerned with the strike was feverishly busy. The Industrial Relations Committee was making a last-ditch effort to avert the walkout of all organized labor.[31] But management, the metal-trades unions, and the EFC would not budge. While metal-trades representatives negotiated, their fellow workers on the executive committee strove to bring the general strike to orderly fruition. Monday morning the committee granted its first exemptions. It summoned a delegation of city firemen and asked them to remain on the job during the strike.[32] The committee also made basic decisions on transportation. To prevent the use of vehicles not specifically exempted, the transportation subcommittee had signs printed which read, "Exempted by the General Strike Committee." Attempts to break the transportation shut-down could thus be immediately spotted. This tactic proved to be a two-edged sword—it did assure control, but there was considerable public resentment, particularly when sacred cows of the culture, such as hearses and ambulances, had to carry the signs.[33]

The problem of fresh laundry for the city confronted the committee on February 3. It decided that organized labor would do no private laundry during the strike. To assure hospitals of a steady supply of fresh linen, the Washington Laundry—not the union-owned Mutual Laundry—would remain open strictly for the purpose of filling hospital orders. Its delivery wagons were also exempted. When the decision was announced, Seattleites inundated the laundries with dirty linen they hoped would be ready before the strike began.[34] So heavy was the rush that the laundry workers' local requested that the owners accept no more orders. When the owners proved cooperative, their workers petitioned the executive committee—successfully—for permission to remain at work a few hours after the general strike officially began, so that clothing already in the plants would not become mildewed.[35]

Not all problems were so easily solved. C. R. Case, head of the city's street department, appeared before the committee to request that the City Light plant be kept open, because the water supply of the Queen Anne Hill and West Seattle districts depended on electrical pumping apparatus. He also warned that enormous quantities of food in cold storage would spoil if the power plant were shut down and that "without the street-lights the city would be prey to lawlessness and disorder. . . ."[36] Whether to keep the power plant open was a decision the committee was not yet prepared to make. Case was merely told that a special hour would be designated during which the heads of city departments would be heard sympathetically.

City officials were not alone in warning that the general strike might have grave consequences. Some labor leaders told the committee that their locals would be harmed. If his men went out on strike, a spokesman of the Meatcutters' Union warned, his organization might be shattered.[37] Representatives of the Telephone Operators' Union made substantially the same claim.[38] In both cases the unions had recently lost bitter, destructive strikes, leaving their organizations considerably weakened. The meat-cutters, who had unsuccessfully attempted to inject their griev-ances into a general-strike settlement, reminded the committee that they had lost their closed shop. Only small, individually-owned butcher shops still employed union labor; striking these would not shut down the large markets which employed non-union labor. Thus, only union labor and employers friendly to the union would be hurt. The committee was forced to let both the meatcutters and the telephone girls stay on the job. A plan was effected, however, to reward labor's friends. The meatcutters, while staying on the job, would technically be on strike, and therefore would not be paid. The small shopkeepers were quite willing to deduct the cost of wages they did not have to pay from the price of the increased quantities of meat they expected to sell.

The tempo of executive committee business increased the next day. Speed in completing arrangements was all the more necessary because the Industrial Relations Committee had terminated its efforts to mediate between management and labor. The last possi-bility of averting the strike had passed.

During the morning, requests for exemptions poured in. Even the minimum requirements for sustaining a large municipality were numerous and varied, as the committee's minutes show:

> King County Commissioners asked for exemption of janitors to care for City-County building. Not granted.
> F. A. Rust asked for janitors for Labor Temple. Not granted.
> Teamsters' Union asks permission to carry oil for Swedish Hospital during strike. Referred to transportation committee. Approved.
> Garbage Wagon Drivers ask for instructions. Referred to public welfare committee, which recommends that such garbage as tends to create an epidemic of disease be collected, but no ashes or papers.
> The retail drug clerks sent in a statement of the health needs of the city. Referred to public welfare committee, which recommends that prescription counters only be left open, and that in front of every drug store which is thus allowed to open a sign be placed with the words, "No goods sold during the general strike. Orders for prescrip-tions only will be filled. Signed by general strike committee."
> Communication from House of Good Shepherd. Permission granted for transportation committee to haul food and provisions only.
> Port of Seattle asks to be allowed men to load a government vessel, pointing out that no private profit is involved and that an emergency exists. Granted.[39]

A second request of the Port Commission, headed by labor's friend, Robert Bridges, was granted. The cold-storage plants owned by the commission would be kept in operation by Electrical Workers' Local 46.[40] Labor tried not to hurt its friends.

With the strike a certainty and the tempers of all groups in the city frayed, the committee had to arrange to keep public order. The municipal police were not striking, but control over them rested in City Hall, which had not yet announced a firm position in regard to the strike. To avoid giving Mayor Hanson an excuse to use the police as strikebreakers, the committee formed a group— a labor War Veterans' Guard—to prevent union men from committing any provocative acts. With union men thus kept in line, the committee stated that it would be unnecessary for the city to add extra policemen for the duration of the strike.[41] The Guard was to be headed by Frank A. Rust, head of the Seattle Labor Temple Association and well known locally as a labor conservative. Volunteers for the Guard were solicited through an advertisement in the *Union Record,* as well as through the local Soldiers' and Sailors' Council.[42] Three hundred men responded. Armed only with white ribbons and their ability to talk, persuade, and cajole their "fellow workers," this group saw to it that not a single striker was arrested for a breach of the peace.[43]

The committee also heard some bad news. Pressmen's Local 39 announced that the members, in a delayed vote, had refused to endorse the strike.[44] The pressmen were undoubtedly influenced by the typographers' local, which decided to abide by its international's refusal to allow it to participate in the general strike. As a result, the strike would not close down the major nonunion-owned dailies, which could operate without scabbing. Two of the three major Seattle newspapers—the *Star* and the *Post-Intelligencer*—announced that they would take advantage of the opportunity.[45] This was a blow, but the committee stuck to its policy of keeping the *Union Record* closed. Interference from other internationals, objecting to their local affiliates' participation in the strike, was to cause the committee many anxious moments. A few days earlier, T. V. O'Connor, president of the International Longshoremen's Association, wired the forty-five-hundred-man Seattle branch that he would rescind its charter if it took part in the general strike.[46] But the local—one of the strongholds of general-strike agitation—was too firmly committed and finally chose to defy the international. Thus the loss of a key group was narrowly averted.

The executive committee, for all its judicious solutions to hundreds of detailed problems, essentially failed to face up to its main responsibility: to decide where the strike was leading. Like its parent body, the General Strike Committee, the executive committee was primarily concerned with questions of strike tactics, that is, how effectively to shut down Seattle without causing anarchy. But if the strike were to achieve any positive goal, some responsible persons or group within the labor movement had to formulate a coherent set of demands, fall-back plans if these demands were rejected, and a basic decision on the length of the general strike.

While this lacuna was not evident to the members of the executive committee—as a result either of inexperience or the heady air of mass action—it was glaringly obvious to the regular progressive and conservative leaders of Seattle labor. Previously inhibited by fear that their lack of enthusiasm for the general strike would lose them control over the movement, the progressives now realized that they had to act if the movement was not to shatter itself in a blind, self-destructive rush. Jimmy Duncan, Harry Ault, Frank Rust, and Bill Swenson (a progressive, sometime member of the Typographers' Union, and a salesman of typesetting machinery) informally mulled over the dilemma in Duncan's office on February 4, two days before the strike was to begin.[47] They agreed that, although sentiment among the mass of union men for an unlimited general strike was stronger than they had suspected, any attempt to carry it out would be suicidal.

If a general strike were staunchly opposed by the remainder of the community, they believed it could have only three possible results: planned revolution; spontaneous, violent revolt due to frustration; or capitulation as a result of threatened starvation or force. An unlimited general strike could be used as a revolutionary instrument, as they were well aware. But Duncan, in assessing both the mass of union men and the strike leaders, stated, "there was not a revolutionary thought in anybody's mind," [48] that is, in anybody's mind who counted in the Seattle AFL movement. The first possibility was dismissed by the four men. The second—a spontaneous outburst—could happen. If it did, state or federal troops could easily crush the unarmed union men of Seattle. Even if violence could be prevented, an unlimited general strike was extremely unwise because it would be a contest between, as Duncan put it, "the people on Capitol Hill and the people in Rainier Valley to determine who had the most food in the larder and coal in the basement." [49] The working-class people of the Valley, who had smaller financial reserves, would naturally feel the economic pinch first.

Although none of these four men was officially responsible for the general strike, they were obligated to act. They had to see that a publicly-announced time limit be placed on the strike—preferably twenty-four or forty-eight hours, but even a longer period would do, so long as a limit was announced. It was absolutely necessary to assure the public that the general strike was merely a gesture of protest and to forestall countermeasures against labor which an outraged citizenry might demand. A limited general strike might even do some positive good, the four agreed. First, it could dramatize the plight of the shipyard workers and help arouse public opinion on their behalf. Second, if the shipyard strike were settled on favorable terms—aided by the general strike—this might demonstrate to those who were thinking of supporting a general open-shop drive that labor was too deeply entrenched in Seattle to budge.

The four chose the conference committee of the Metal Trades Council as the logical group to sponsor a plan to limit the strike before the three-hundred-man General Strike Committee. First they called in Bert Swain, secretary of the Metal Trades Council; when he saw that their position was "only common sense," they went before the conference committee.[50]

The discussion lasted from 2:30 in the afternoon until 7:30 in the evening. The proponents of a definite time limit faced considerable opposition from committee members, particularly John Von Carnop, who feared that anything less than unlimited support would destroy the morale of his machinists' local. However,

John Ballinger, an influential member of the conference committee, finally joined the pro-limitation forces and carried a majority of the committee with him. The best way, the metal-trades men thought, to get a favorable decision from the General Strike Committee was to have its own tactics subcommittee make the limitation proposal.

With the aid of the telephone operator at the Labor Temple, most of the members of the tactics subcommittee were assembled by 9:30 that night. The necessity of limiting the strike then had to be debated before this second group. The members were generally neutral toward the idea and needed a good deal of convincing. The little group arguing its case thought progress was being made, but at 12:30 A.M., A. E. Miller burst into the room and completely destroyed their efforts. As Bill Swenson reported it, Miller said: " 'It's all off.' I turned to him and said: 'What is all off.' And he said, 'Any proposition coming from the Metal Trades Council or Conference Committee of the Metal Trades Council suggesting that a time limit be set upon the strike.' " [51] As a result of the withdrawal of Metal Trades Council support, the attempt to limit the strike quietly expired before the tactics subcommittee.

Later Duncan and his friends learned what had caused their agreement with the metal-trades men to collapse. While they were arguing their case before the tactics subcommittee, the Metal Trades Council met to vote on the position adopted by its conference committee. Bert Swain had been delegated to explain and defend the recommendation to limit the strike. He barely had time to introduce his proposal when Frank Turco jumped to his feet, shouting, "Who the hell sold out here?" [52] Swain wilted under the barrage, and the case for limitation went virtually undefended.[53]

While the involved negotiations to limit the strike were taking place, Mayor Ole Hanson was also busy. He too was talking about the effect of the general strike upon Seattle. Both adroit and sophisticated in his analysis of the power and motives of the striking unions, he told his audience of Spanish-American War veterans that "I do not anticipate any serious disorders or outbreaks. It is a mistake to charge to union labor the wild rantings of men who hate the American Federation of Labor as bad as they hate us [*sic*]." [54]

Seattle badly needed such messages to restore the confidence of its people. As the day of the strike approached, apprehension grew apace. Thousands were firmly convinced that the strike was a deliberate attempt to begin a revolution. General strikes were unprecedented in the American experience, but too many Seattleites had read in their newspapers of the world-wide revolutions, uprisings, and putsches not to fear that their turn had come. Even those who believed that Seattle labor was incapable of deliberately fomenting a revolution feared that the general strike would get out of hand and degenerate into widespread chaos, rioting, lawlessness, and bloodshed. The Seattle *Star* reflected the overwhelming feeling of the Puget Sound public. Once the major nonlabor-owned daily, read by union men and usually sympathetic to their views, the *Star* now bolted completely and issued a warning of impending disaster in a page-one editorial:

> This is plain talk to the common-sense union men of Seattle.
> You are being rushed pell-mell into a general strike. You are being urged to use a dangerous weapon—the general strike, which you have never used before—which, in fact, has never been used anywhere in the United States.
> It isn't too late to avert the tragic results that are sure to come from its use.
> You men know better than any one else that public sentiment in Seattle—that is, the sentiment of the 90% of the people who are not directly involved in the wage dispute of the shipworkers—*is against a general strike*. You know that the general public doesn't think the situation demands the use of that drastic, disaster-breeding move. *You know too, that you cannot club public sentiment into line, and you know too, that no strike has ever been won without the moral support of the public.*
> The people know there is a decent solution of the issue at stake. And the issue at stake is merely a better wage to the average unskilled worker in the shipyards. To a large extent public opinion is with these unskilled workers now, but public opinion will turn against them if their wage issue brings chaos and disaster upon the whole community unnecessarily. Seattle today is awake to the fact that she is on the brink of a disaster, *and Seattle is getting fighting mad*. The people are beginning to visualize the horrors that a general tie-up

will bring. They see the suffering that is bound to come and *they don't propose to be silent sufferers.*

Today Seattle resents this whole miserable mess. Seattle resents the insolent attitude of the shipyard owners; Seattle resents the verbosity of Director General Piez, whose explanation does not explain, and just as emphatically resents the high-handed "rule or ruin" tactics of the labor leaders who propose to lay the whole city prostrate in a vain attempt to show their power. Let us not mince words. A general strike cannot win unless one of two things happens. Either the shipowners and Piez must yield or else the workers must be able to control the situation by *force.* The latter method no doubt would be welcomed by the agitators and the babblers of Bolshevikism. But the latter method is bound to be squelched without much ado and you decent union men of Seattle will be the sufferers then. *A revolt— and some of your leaders are talking of a revolution—*to be successful must have a countrywide application. There isn't a chance to spread it east of the mountains. There isn't a chance to spread it south of Tacoma *and today 50% of the unions of Tacoma have turned down the proposition for a general strike.*

Confined to Seattle or even confined to the whole Pacific coast, the use of force by Bolsheviks would be, and should be, quickly dealt with by the army of the United States. These false Bolsheviks haven't a chance on earth to win anything for you in this country, *because this country is America—not Russia.*[55]

Responsible citizens could not be satisfied with a mere protest against their fate; the possibilities of violence seemed all too real. While editorial writers were predicting violence, a group of men who considered themselves both responsible and practical was meeting to prevent such an occurrence. Two hundred delegates from thirty-six local organizations gathered on the evening of February 4 to form an organization known as the Citizens' Committee. On hand were delegates from women's groups, commercial organizations, professional associations, civic organizations, fraternal lodges, and religious, humanitarian, and service groups.[56] After passing a resolution calling for law and order, the delegates elected an executive committee empowered to do something practical toward that end. As chairman they elected A. J. Rhodes, president of the Seattle Chamber of Commerce and Commercial Club.[57] As events were soon to show, the Citizens' Committee was not entirely an impromptu organization. It had a direct link with the now defunct Industrial Relations Committee. Two of the latter's spokesmen—the Reverend Mark A. Matthews and James W. Spangler—now became Rhodes's publicly acknowledged assistants. Previously unable to settle the shipyard strike by mediation, they now had powerful backing which considerably enhanced their voices in the events of the immediate future.

As if to justify all that newspapers, civic luminaries, and ordinary citizens feared about the strikers' motives, the *Union Record* on February 4 published what was to become the most famous document of the general strike—Anna Louise Strong's editorial, "No One Knows Where." This editorial was seized upon by opponents of the strike as proof that labor meant to confiscate private property and begin a revolution. Miss Strong said:

> There will be many cheering and there will be some who fear.
> Both of these emotions are useful, but not too much of either.
> We are undertaking the most tremendous move ever made by LABOR in this country, a move which will lead—NO ONE KNOWS WHERE!
> We do not need hysteria.
> We need the iron march of labor.
> LABOR WILL FEED THE PEOPLE.
> Twelve great kitchens have been offered, and from them food will be distributed by the provision trades at low cost to all.
> LABOR WILL CARE FOR THE BABIES AND THE SICK.
> The milk-wagons and the laundry drivers are arranging plans for supplying milk to babies, invalids and hospitals, and taking care of the cleaning of linen for hospitals.
> LABOR WILL PRESERVE ORDER.
> The strike committee is arranging for guards, and it is expected that the stopping of the cars will keep people at home.
> A few hot-headed enthusiasts have complained that strikers only should be fed, and the general public left to endure severe discomfort. Aside from the inhumanitarian character of such suggestions, let us get this straight—
> NOT THE WITHDRAWAL OF LABOR POWER, BUT THE POWER OF THE STRIKERS TO MANAGE WILL WIN THIS STRIKE.
> What does Mr. Piez of the Shipping Board care about the closing down of Seattle's shipyards, or even of all the industries of the northwest? Will it not merely strengthen the yards at Hog Island, in which he is more interested?
> When the shipyard owners of Seattle were on the point of agreeing with the workers, it was Mr. Piez who wired them that, if they so agreed—

HE WOULD NOT LET THEM HAVE STEEL.

Whether this is camouflage we have no means of knowing. But we do know that the great eastern combinations of capitalists COULD AFFORD to offer privately to Mr. Skinner, Mr. Ames and Mr. Duthrie a few millions apiece in eastern shipyard stock.

RATHER THAN LET THE WORKERS WIN.

The closing down of Seattle's industries, as a MERE SHUTDOWN, will not affect these eastern gentlemen much. They could let the whole northwest got to pieces, as far as money alone is concerned.

BUT, the closing down of the capitalistically controlled industries of Seattle, while the WORKERS ORGANIZE to feed the people, to care for the babies and the sick, to preserve order—THIS will move them, for this looks too much like the taking over of POWER by the workers.

Labor will not only SHUT DOWN the industries, but Labor will REOPEN, under the management of the appropriate trades, such activities as are needed to preserve public health and public peace. If the strike continues, Labor may feel led to avoid public suffering by reopening more and more activities.

UNDER ITS OWN MANAGEMENT.

And that is why we say that we are starting on a road that leads—NO ONE KNOWS WHERE! 58

This was an artful document. The mays, mights, and humanitarian sentiments expressed by Miss Strong were later important in saving her from a conviction for sedition. More important, however, was the fact that this editorial was the major statement in justification of the general strike. But, although it ran a full page, Miss Strong never mentioned what the goals of the strikers were, what their terms were, or against whom the strike was directed—shipyard owners, eastern capitalists, open-shop advocates, all Northwest employers, the United States government? Did the editorial mean revolution? The real message of this confusing editorial was the total confusion among the strikers over their aims—no one did know where!

But the Seattle public was now convinced it knew where—straight to revolution. Miss Strong's mention of "the taking over of POWER by the workers" confirmed their worst fears. Her references to the ability of the workers to manage and possibly open industries under union control were read by the Seattle public as the definitive plans of the General Strike Committee. With this editorial, Anna Louise Strong destroyed the possibility that anyone would negotiate with labor to settle the strike. Now no individual or group would demand anything less than labor's unconditional surrender.

Publication of the editorial was, according to Harry Ault, a terrible blunder for which he had to accept responsibility. It had been written two or three days before its appearance in print. When Ault first saw it, he would not approve it for publication because he feared the editorial might be interpreted as a call to revolution.[59] But because he was working a twenty-hour day at the time, it slipped in when he was too tired to check his copy carefully.[60] Ault realized soon after its publication that the editorial succeeded only in aiding those opponents who were deliberately trying to impress upon the public an image of the general strike as a revolution. In this, it succeeded all too well. The Seattle *Post-Intelligencer* reprinted "No One Knows Where" the next day with no editorial comment; none was needed.[61]

Now thoroughly convinced that they would be caught in the middle of a revolution, the people of Seattle saw in other newspaper stories only confirmation of this belief. The report of a meeting of the Soldiers', Sailors' and Workingmen's Council was alarming. Although this group was only indirectly connected to the labor movement through the sponsorship of the Metal Trades Council, the public had difficulty in distinguishing its utterances from the official pronouncements of the General Strike Committee or its executive group. The newspapers reported that the Soldiers', Sailors' and Workingmen's Council frankly claimed revolution as a goal. Its constitution proclaimed it part of a world-wide insurrectionary movement, advocating release of all political and military prisoners and protesting the invasion of Russia. Rumors abounded that the formal organization of the Soldier', Sailors' and Workingmen's Council immediately before the general strike was not fortuitous. Many citizens thought this group would attempt to take over the city government after the first revolutionary blow was struck.[62]

Equally alarming was the report of a labor meeting the next day. Although not sponsored by the local AFL, the meeting attracted an audience of eight hundred at the Odd Fellows Hall to listen to the harangues of "labor agitators." Sam Sadler, the

Socialist, advocated that the working class arbitrarily confiscate food supplies and declare a rent moratorium. Vincent Brown, himself a "two-card man," defended dual unionism in an impassioned speech. In triumph he announced to the crowd that the "radical element" was in control of the Hope Lodge of Machinists.[63] The people of Seattle were disposed to believe him.

With opinions of the nature and purpose of the general strike now firmly set in their minds, Seattleites made last-minute provisions to cope with its consequences. The city prepared for a state of siege. People scurried about, each intent upon gathering together sufficient supplies to sustain his family in all foreseeable emergencies. Business was brisk for Seattle merchants. If a revolutionary proletariat had confiscated retail stores, it would have acquired, in most cases, bare, empty premises.

Store shelves were emptied the day before the strike: grocery shops were reported completely out of staples; patent medicines, bandages, and other supplies were hard to find; druggists reported a last-minute demand for prescription renewals; hardware stores also prospered in the panic—goods ordinarily of interest only to those contemplating a prospecting trip to Alaska were now grabbed up by stay-at-home Seattleites, particularly emergency oil stoves and kerosene lamps. Another item in which Seattle shoppers showed an abnormal interest was guns; the supply lagged far behind the demand. Numerous Seattle families sat behind closed blinds and locked doors on the night of February 5 cleaning rifles, shotguns, and pistols, with fathers instructing wives and teen-age sons in their use.[64]

Anxious housewives also had other tasks to perform. After assuring themselves that the head of the house had ordered the coal supply replenished in time, the women filled bathtubs, jugs, pots, and pans with water so that their families would have an emergency supply which would last for several days. If the strikers were going to shut off City Light, they reasoned, why not city water? It was better to be prepared.[65] The wealthy prepared for the strike by packing. Many of Seattle's better known families found early February a convenient time to take a midwinter vacation.[66]

The newspapers put out their last pre-strike editions. The *Union Record* wasted its last opportunity to calm the fears of the people of Seattle. Even if Harry Ault was no more omniscient than anyone else in the labor movement about the direction of the strike, he ought to have attempted to undo the damage of the "No One Knows Where" editorial. A strong statement on the nonrevolutionary aims of the strikers might have helped labor's cause. Instead, the *Record* merely lashed out again at Charles Piez.

The *Star*, however, did not waste its opportunity to sway public opinion, earning in the process the sobriquet bestowed upon it by its former labor friends—"the Shooting Star." The editorial of the previous day—"Stop Before It's Too Late"—while bitterly critical of labor leaders who hoped to lead the men astray, expressed belief in the justice of the shipyard unions' wage claims. But the front-page editorial of February 5 had no soothing words of sympathy for labor's cause. Having failed to persuade Seattle's laboring men to cancel the general strike, the *Star* could only conclude that the strikers were intent upon fomenting revolution:

UNDER WHICH FLAG?

The general strike is at hand. A general SHOWDOWN—a showdown for all of us—a test of Americanism—a test of YOUR Americanism.

As the Star stated yesterday, this is no time to mince words. A part of our community is defying our government, and is, in fact, contemplating changing that government, and not by *American methods.* This small part of our city talks plainly of "taking over things," of "resuming under *our* management."

We call this thing that is upon us a general strike, but it is more than that. It is to be an acid test of American citizenship—an acid test of all those principles for which our soldiers have fought and died. It is to determine whether this is a country worth living in and a country worth dying for. The challenge is right up to you—men and women of Seattle.

Under which flag do you stand? [67]

It was this editorial, the *Star* later claimed, which helped rally the people to oppose the revolution. Many Seattleites agreed that the *Star*'s blunt warning was of central importance in making them realize they had to face up to and defeat the "Bolshevists."

One of the other two major dailies followed its lead. On February 5 the *Post-Intelligencer,* while expressing regret that the community was to be burdened by a complete work stoppage, did not attack the motives or goals of the strikers. It was still convinced that Seattle labor was striking to support the economic demands of the shipyard workers. The next day, however, after the *Star*'s appeal to patriotism, the *Post-Intelligencer*'s editorial line was reversed; now it too saw red.

Within the strike movement, the executive committee was struggling to complete the last of its pre-strike preparations. Inundated with work, it had to remain in continuous session from early morning until after three o'clock the next morning. The sheer volume of exemption requests to be processed again prevented— or gave the committee an excuse to avoid—the making of basic decisions on strike strategy. Instead it tidied up the details. On Wednesday, for example, the committee heard from a representative of the Trade Printery. He wanted permission for his shop to remain in continuous operation because it was printing strike materials for a number of locals. Instead, he was asked to turn his plant over to the committee for the duration of the strike. But the executive group had first to reject a subcommittee recommendation that the organization use the facilities of the Equity Printing Company, because it was too well known as printer for the IWW and other radical organizations.

Other exemptions—although numerous—were more routine. School janitors were ordered to respond to the strike call rather than, as their delegate requested, be exempted to keep the school plants running. Auto drivers received permission to carry "mail only" on the Des Moines Road. In addition, the auto drivers' representative was informed that his organization could dispatch vehicles on emergency call for hospitals and funerals if the request were first routed through his own union headquarters.[68]

In the middle of the day, the committee stopped considering exemption requests to hear a delegation from the Seattle Ministerial Federation, which had come to plead for a last-minute postponement of the strike. They argued that a week-long "cooling off" period would permit sufficient time for reasonable men peacefully to settle the dispute which lay behind the general-strike call. Although their organization held membership on the Citizens' Committee, the ministers assured the committee that they believed in the justice of the shipyard unions' economic demands.

As proof of their sincerity, they submitted to the committee resolutions that had been passed by their organization and sent to President Wilson and Director General Piez. After listening to the delegation's presentation, the executive committee politely turned down its request. As consolation, the ministers "were given a rising vote of thanks." [69] (There were others, however, who were not so appreciative of the Ministerial Federation's gesture. Seattle's smart set who read the *Argus* saw the city ministers characterized as "sloppy sentimentalists." [70])

The most important problem for which the executive committee had to find a solution was saved for late that night. It was the thorniest and had been saved for last because the committee could not envision any satisfactory solution. But whether the city's power plants would be in production at ten o'clock Thursday morning was a matter which depended at least in part on the committee's decision. In order to avoid an open clash with municipal authorities, the committee invited Mayor Hanson to join this discussion. He arrived at the Labor Temple after midnight and remained closeted with the committee until 3:30 A.M.

The strikers' apparent determination to shut down both the privately-owned Puget Sound Traction, Light, and Power plant and publicly-owned City Light was extremely damaging to labor's image in the community. City Light—which supplied electricity to Seattle's residential districts and therefore touched the practical reality of everyday convenience, comfort, and even safety—became *the* major issue on which Seattleites judged the strikers' intent. Labor, instead of appearing as the wronged party in the public eye, now appeared, at best, as an omnipotent force demanding its own way whatever the cost. At worst, its threat to turn off all city light and power appeared to Seattleites as the first step to revolution.

Leon Green, business agent of Electrical Workers' Local 77, caused the furor over City Light. A mysterious man not long in Seattle and supposedly a Russian national, Green stated that he intended to pull all union workers out of the City Light plant; no exemptions would be made to provide power for hospitals, food-storage facilities, streetlights, or any other "private and public enterprise which depend[ed] on 'juice.' " [71] He told reporters the reason for a complete shutdown: "We shall place the city in such a position that the strike will last but a few short days." [72] And he reiterated the substance of this message many times in the week before the strike.

Understandably, this position caused a wave of revulsion over the methods supposedly adopted by the strikers. A week of open bickering between Green and civic officials served only to heighten public fears. When James Delmage Ross, head of City Light, was first apprised of Green's stand, he replied with a statement indicating the perils for Seattleites if electrical power were shut off:

> I am not prepared to say what we will do but we are going to see that the street lights are maintained. To cut off the street lights would open countless opportunities for robberies, and burglaries. The strikers themselves ought to be as much interested in preventing such a condition as anybody else, yet when I asked Leon Green, business agent of one of the electrical workers' unions, to exempt the city light men, he refused to consider it. He said there would be no exemptions.[73]

When Green repeated his demand for a complete shut-down to Mayor Hanson, Ole excitedly called him an "alien, slacker, Bolsheviki and IWW."

More in hope than knowledge, Hanson also told Green that "he was not running the city light department." [74] Neither Hanson nor Ross realized that Green was quite incapable of making good on his threat; it was a bluff. Green's Local 77 was composed of outside line men and meter men; he had no jurisdiction over the organized laborers affiliated with Local 46, who worked inside the plant.[75] And the engineers—the only group essential to the plant's operation—were unorganized.[76] Even the organized men inside the plant were no longer controlled by the Electrical Union officials. Both Green and Andy Heller, a representative of Local 46 and member of the executive committee, were physically expelled from the meeting of City Light department employees at which the general-strike vote was taken. The men then decided not to strike.

Green was furious. He charged that the meeting had been engineered by Ross and Hanson in a deliberate effort to double-cross him. In his anger he claimed that the vote was invalid because the meeting was packed with clerks masquerading as electrical workers. To put pressure on the inside men to reconsider their stand, he threatened to have them expelled from the Electrical Workers' Union.[77] He also put up a bold front which made even those who should have known better believe he had the power to shut down the light plant: he had his own captive Local 77 pass a resolution stating it would insure that all power plants, public and private, remain closed during the general strike.[78]

Green's boldness shook the confidence of both Ross[79] and Hanson.[80] Ole, widely underestimated locally as an erratic clown with a not overlarge amount of backbone,[81] displayed a certain shrewdness. Force, he realized, would probably make labor more obdurate and be useless besides, if Green's men were really willing to sabotage the power plant and lines. Yet civic notables and his own municipal department heads were pressuring Hanson to take a strong stand. He held them off while he tried to persuade the regular leaders of the Central Labor Council to keep City Light running. Two days before the strike, he brought Jimmy Duncan and Charles Doyle, business agent of the Central Labor Council, together for lunch with Thomas Murfin, head of the public utilities department, and C. B. Fitzgerald, a member of the City Council. Duncan recalled that during the luncheon Hanson pressed him on City Light:

> Mr. Hanson himself brought up that subject. He said to me in that conversation, "Jim, Jim, won't you please give me my light"; "Jim, Jim, now come on and be a good sport"; "won't you please give me my light"; "I need that light"; "I don't give a damn about the street car company"; "Jim, Jim, come on, be a good fellow and give me my light." . . . Mr. Hanson kept on repeating that stuff . . . over and over again. It was a repetition for practically an hour while we were seated at lunch.[82]

Duncan indignantly turned down Hanson's plea, telling him that

> I was in no way responsible, and that I couldn't do anything in the matter; that there was a committee of 300 appointed to take charge of all matters pertaining to the strike; that there was an Executive Board functioning under the direction of the committee of 300, and that the best I could do would be to get him in touch with the committee of 300; that that was the best I could do for him, and that I would willingly do that.[83]

While Duncan was technically correct—he was not responsible —he probably could have been more helpful. If Duncan had openly backed Hanson's proposal, his prestige might have helped get a favorable decision from one of the responsible committees. His refusal probably was not the result merely of fearing to put his prestige on the line. In all likelihood, tough Jimmy, whose own mode of operation was open and straightforward, instinctively backed away from a man who operated by indirection and whose manner was whining and obsequious. Since Duncan realized what was at stake in the City Light issue, this was a decision he later should have regretted.

But Hanson, knowing Duncan's general position in the Seattle labor movement, did not accept Duncan's claim of powerlessness. He walked into Duncan's office the next day (February 5) to renew his effort. To get rid of him, Duncan set impossible terms. He told Hanson he could get the general strike called off if Hanson would do one favor in return: since the shipyard strike was called for the purpose of raising wages 10 per cent, if the cost of living could be lowered by a comparable figure, the shipyard strike could be called off without forcing management to grant a wage increase. All Hanson had to do was somehow get the cost of living to drop 10 per cent. Hanson purportedly replied "I think I can do it," left the office, and never returned.[84]

To find labor allies, Hanson went to the offices of the *Union Record* to feel out the staff members on the City Light question. Years later, Anna Louise Strong recalled his attempt to persuade her to help line up the *Record* for City Light. He expressed such admiration for the cut and pattern of her dress that he asked where she had bought it so that he could buy an exact copy as a present for his wife! [85] Again, Hanson failed. He could only make whatever preparations possible without the assistance of local labor leaders. As a precautionary measure to prevent a complete breakdown in case Green could make good on his threat, J. D. Ross organized a group of six volunteers—engineers from the Western Electric Company—who could if necessary take over the most essential operations in the plant.[86]

The members of the executive committee knew about these preparations of the city government. What they feared were other unknown preparations Hanson might have made to keep the power plant operating. They realized the City Light issue provided a convenient excuse for disgruntled citizens to demand that Hanson take more drastic measures. City Light was a problem they would have to solve. But like Hanson, they were unsure of their ability to control the situation. The demand to black out the city completely had come from Green and his Local 77. If they decided to allow part or all of the plant to operate and Green defied them, how could they force Green's men to carry out the order? The executive committee too was ignorant of Green's bluff. Besides, Green's announced position, however harsh, did make good tactical sense. A single measure which could cripple a city might force the opposition to terms quickly. Control of City Light was too powerful a weapon to be given up lightly.

On the other hand, the committee members did not wish to harm City Light permanently. Like their fellow Seattle unionists, they had a strong emotional and ideological affinity for this government-owned public utility.[87] And if City Light as a public utility could be shut down as easily as a privately-owned company, one of the major arguments for public ownership—impartial and continuous service for all the people—would be undercut. Furthermore, J. D. Ross, both as public official and person, was respected by labor men.

The executive committee moved cautiously. On Wednesday morning, after discovering a gap in its plans, it requested that the electrical unions allow sufficient power to be manufactured to operate the city's fire-alarm system. (Earlier, the committee had exempted the organized firemen from participation in the strike. But without the alarm system, their effectiveness would be sharply cut.) The committee also appointed a special subcommittee to work quietly in conjunction with the conference committee of the Metal Trades Council to find a solution to the entire vexing problem of City Light.

This combined group worked together to pressure the electrical workers to modify their stand. They met with a three-man negotiating team from Local 77. At first, the electricians remained adamant. But the representatives of the metal-trades unions, for whose benefit the general strike was being called, convinced the electricians to give way partially. They agreed to allow the City Light plant to operate on the condition that a committee sit in the plant to decide on each exemption individually. A. E. Miller, chairman of the conference committee, then invited Mayor Hanson to participate in the talks between his group and the electricians. But Ole would have none of the scheme. He insisted upon complete, normal power production.[88] Nevertheless, he agreed to hear the arguments of the electricians' exemption committee, hoping to convince its members of the need for full operation of the power plant. This discussion was almost immediately stalemated when Hanson insisted upon sufficient power to operate the streetlights and the electricians refused.

When word of the breakdown reached the combined committee working on the City Light problem, this group believed it necessary to assure Hanson that the light department would not completely collapse. Although the members were unsure of controlling the electricians, they requested that a representative of the Engineers' Union inform Hanson that the engineers would be able to keep enough of the City Light plant in operation to supply power for hospitals and other public facilities.[89]

But the city was still in a precarious position. The full executive committee had procrastinated too long; it now had to make a definite decision on City Light. This was the purpose of the midnight meeting on the eve of the strike. All the interested parties —the electrical workers' negotiators, the members of the Metal Trades' conference committee, and Mayor Hanson—were invited to participate. Hanson saw no reason to come, but Frank Rust persuaded him to make one final effort for the sake of "conservative progressive labor." [90] After prolonged discussion he still insisted upon full operation of the City Light plant. Before Hanson left at 3:30 A.M., he announced that he would prefer to run the light plant with union labor, but if necessary would invoke martial law and run it with soldiers. The executive committee knew that Hanson's answer was final. It finally decided to override the objections of the electricians, who capitulated quietly and promised to accept the decision. A representative of the committee informed Hanson that, with the face-saving exception of commercial service, the light plant could operate at full capacity.[91]

Ole Hanson, however, had other plans. The time to reach a compromise agreement had been two days earlier when he approached Jimmy Duncan. One hour *before* the midnight meeting at the Labor Temple he had decided to give in to the powerful pressure of civic groups and his subordinate officials and attempt to suppress the strike.[92] Ole now knew which way to jump. He had sworn in extra police. He had "kept the phone hot" between his office and the Governor's, requesting the services of the National Guard. But Henry Suzzallo, president of the University of Washington and wartime chairman of the State Council of Defense, and Vaughn Tanner, state attorney general, who had informally taken over the duties of ailing Governor Ernest Lister, telephoned Secretary of War Newton Baker for federal troops.[93] The two men feared that the one untrained regiment of state troops that had not been federalized would not be sufficient to control the potentially explosive situation in Seattle.[94] Authorized by Baker to take personal charge,[95] Major General John F. Morrison, Western Department Commander, ordered elements of the First Infantry, Thirteenth Division, to be dispatched to Seattle and Tacoma.[96] At 2:30 A.M., February 6, he notified the governor's office of the orders he had just issued.[97] The opponents of labor's move into the unknown were ready.

VI

Strike

"Streetcar gongs ceased their clamor; newsboys cast their unsold papers into the street; from the doors of mill and factory, store and workshop, streamed 65,000 workingmen. School children with fear in their hearts hurried homeward. The life stream of a great city stopped." [1] So Ole Hanson described Seattle on the morning of February 6, 1919. It was as if the city were acting out Jack London's inspired description of a general strike:

> The effect on one's sensibilities was weird, depressing. It seemed as though some great cosmic thing lay dead. The pulse of the land had ceased to beat. Of a truth the nation had died. There were no wagons rumbling on the streets, no factory whistles, no hum of electricity in the air, no passing of street cars, no cries of newsboys—nothing but person who at rare intervals went by like furtive ghosts, themselves oppressed and made unreal by the silence.[2]

The quiet was unnerving; urbanites are unaccustomed to silence. An hour after the strike began, an automobile backfire downtown drew a huge crowd—people wanted to witness the beginning of the shooting they were sure would mark the first stage of the revolution.[3]

The desire for news "was a need almost greater than that for food." [4] Rumors spread easily. It was said that the strikers had blown up the city's water-supply dam. Two hundred Bolshevik gunmen were supposed to have been imported from Chicago by Seattle's revolutionaries. Ole Hanson, another story went, had been assassinated. Reports of water and food poisonings, dynamiting, shootings were whispered about. It was said that the strikers had already begun to confiscate private property.[5]

Fear that the strikers intended to deal harshly with the rich caused an exodus of those who could afford to leave the stricken city. Portland hotels were reported to be filled with well-to-do Seattleites. The Pacific Steamship Company abandoned Seattle as a port of call for both freight and passenger ships.[6]

In contrast to the disquietude of other Seattleites, the strikers themselves were jubilant. They were impressed—if somewhat awed—by the demonstration of their own real power. They had shut down the city; things were going well; for the moment this was enough, with no need to think what would happen next. They were moving in fine, disciplined fashion, even if they did not know where they were going.

More than sixty thousand organized AFL workers laid down their tools when the ten-o'clock whistle blew. They were solidly supported by other working-class organizations. The segregated Japanese unions joined the walk-out with the approval of the General Strike Committee, which (magnanimously!) allowed the segregated unions to send nonvoting delegates to its sessions.[7] The IWW was also eager to cooperate. With their usual *élan*, thirty-five hundred Wobblies walked off the job. Although the General Strike Committee was glad to increase the number of strikers, it was somewhat fearful that the revolutionary Wobblies would create disorders which would be blamed on the regular labor movement. But the Wobblies promised to behave—no demonstrations, no soapbox speeches, no baiting of opponents. Any Wobbly who disobeyed this order, IWW headquarters announced, would be rushed out of town by his own fellow "Wobs." [8]

In addition to the strikers, forty thousand other workers were off the job on Thursday morning. Some feared to find themselves downtown in the midst of a revolutionary uprising. Others were out of work because their employers could see no reason to open their premises: no one was in the mood to patronize downtown shops, theaters, or restaurants. But most of the absentees were simply unable to get to work because public transportation facilities were completely shut down; no streetcars, either publicly or privately owned, ran the first day of the strike.[9]

Seattle was in a coma, but it was not dead. The essential parts were operating. Although some inside and outside men had struck the City Light plant, it could still produce power at full capacity.[10] The operation of the city's hospitals was unimpaired. Telephone operators, exempted from striking by the executive committee, still put through all calls. Cold-storage plant engineers, also exempted, were on the job preventing large stocks of food from spoiling. Although sixteen of Seattle's eighty-eight public schools closed voluntarily, school janitors remained at their posts contrary to the orders of the executive committee.[11] Butcher shops and food markets remained open. Government employees continued to handle government business; for them striking was an offense punishable by imprisonment. Three newspapers— the *Post-Intelligencer,* the *Star,* and the *Daily Bulletin*—were able to print abbreviated editions, but they had to be given away at the plants. When newsboys were sent out to hawk copies, the reaction of the crowd was hostile, and to prevent violence, members of the War Veterans Guard sent the newsboys back to the plants with their papers unsold.

Even more remarkable to labor than its ability to shut down the city was the orderliness with which it was done. Not a single striker or antistrike partisan was arrested on any charge related to the strike. In fact, the usual police docket of about one hundred cases a day fell to about thirty during the strike.[12] The Seattle chief of police was impressed, and so was the commander of the Thirteenth Division, Major General J. D. Leitch, whose troops were on the way to suppress the disorders that never happened.[13]

Labor's record of good conduct was in large part due to the effective operations of the three hundred men whom Frank A. Rust had hastily inducted into the War Veterans Guard. They served without legal authority, carried no weapons, and wore only a white armband to identify themselves. Labor later claimed that Mayor Hanson offered to deputize them, but the offer was refused by the executive committee because it was convinced that persuasion would be more effective than force in preventing the outbreak of violence.[14] Left unsaid was the committee's realization that, if deputized, the Guard would take orders from City Hall and not the Labor Temple. In any case, the War Veterans Guard's key assumption—"people want to obey the law if you put it to them reasonably"—worked during the general strike.[15]

Perhaps the presence of federal troops after the first day contributed to labor's peaceful conduct. Guardsmen dispersed crowds before they grew too large to be controlled. They convinced union men loitering downtown to go home. They advised their fellow workers to treat their time off from work as a holiday to be enjoyed, but without alcoholic refreshments—the Guard also persuaded bootleggers to cease distributing their illicit wares for the duration of the strike.[16] Supplementing the efforts of the Guard were the blandishments published in the General Strike Committee's *Strike Bulletin* urging workingmen to obey the Guardsmen, to stay out of arguments and fights, and not to listen to or spread rumors.[17]

The machinery of the strike, so hastily arranged by the executive committee, was astonishingly successful, bogging down in only a few spots. Initial mistakes were quickly corrected. No one starved or lacked heat; no children had to do without milk; no sick or injured were denied hospital care. Strikers and those who could not eat at home were fed in union-run soup kitchens, or "feeding depots," as Duncan called them.

Labor propaganda had implied that one of the aims of the strike was to teach the workers how to manage business themselves; the executive committee and certain unions had a thorough lesson indeed in managerial techniques—and problems. The distribution plans of the milk-wagon drivers were elaborate. At first the union planned to allow the dairies to operate normally, but the Milk Dealers' Association did not want to operate at full capacity with the unions completely controlling transportation of their product. The employers wanted to keep only downtown supply points open. After consultation with Jimmy Duncan, the drivers' officials decided to supply fresh milk straight from the farm, pure but unprocessed, to thirty-six grocery stores throughout the city's residential areas. These milk stations were open from 9:00 A.M. until 2:00 P.M. Milk was sold for cash only, and each purchaser had to supply his own quart bottle.[18] The Dealers' Association, however, was allowed to operate one dairy to pasteurize milk for the city's hospitals. On the first day of the strike, the milk supply sold out early; by the third day, when all minor problems had been ironed out, the milk stations were selling as much milk as the public would buy. The drivers would have made a profit if they had not promised to absorb the cost of milk wasted in the strikers' "feeding depots." In the end, the drivers lost $700.[19]

Establishing the feeding stations was a far more difficult task. Locations had to be found, number of diners estimated, food purchased, equipment borrowed or bought, transportation problems solved. Many restaurateurs offered free use of their facilities; with their workers almost 100 per cent organized, they saw no possibility of remaining in normal operation. But because it would have been unfair to open some restaurants and not others— and this might have led to difficulties in signing union-shop contracts after the strike—the culinary workers' unions decided to use large public halls where available. Only in outlying districts were restaurants used. The provision-trades section of the General Strike Committee, responsible for feeding the strikers and the public, opened eighteen and later twenty-one eating places, among them the Longshoremen's Hall, Labor Temple, Zero Pool Hall, the city jail, the old Masonic Temple, and the Moose Hall.[20] The meals, cooked in central kitchens and transported in large vats to the feeding stations, cost union members 25 cents, and the general public 35 cents. The menu was usually beef stew or spaghetti, occasionally steak or pot roast, with vegetables, coffee, bread, and butter on hand.

Problems cropped up on every side. One minor, albeit touchy, problem of human relations arose: Ed T. Levi, president of the provision-trades section, noted that it went against the grain of his "high-toned waiters to handle grub in big metal barrels, with tin plates." [21] More vital was the impossibility of planning for circumstances beyond control. Originally it was announced that diners in the feeding stations would provide their own utensils, but most of those who wanted a meal forgot their plates. Dishes and utensils then hastily had to be acquired. Dishwashers, originally not planned for, had to be recruited. There was no way accurately to estimate the number of meals needed, except by experience. As a result, food was overstocked; much of it was left over after the strike or spoiled. The Metal Trades Council, which had promised to accept financial responsibility for the feeding stations, lost $6,000–$7,000. Central locations for cooking seemed, in the planning stage, to be the most efficient mode of operation. But the transport expenses proved higher than estimated, costing the Metal Trades Council $1,500 for trucking alone.

But these problems too were short-lived; after the first day, when many went hungry for lack of dishware, the organization began to take shape. By the last day of the strike, thirty thousand meals a day were served without a hitch.

While the strikers were grappling with their problems, others were also busily making arrangements for the strike. At 1:30 P.M., Thursday, February 6, Brigadier General John L. Hayden left Camp Lewis, outside Tacoma, for Seattle with eight staff officers. Arriving at 3:15 P.M., he immediately issued an order assuming command of all United States troops in Seattle and vicinity. He set up headquarters in the United States Marshal's office in the Federal Building, and after conferring with Admiral J. H. Glennon, commanding officer of the Thirteenth Naval District, took over command of 950 sailors and marines. Quickly, he met with Mayor Hanson, Police Chief Joel S. Warren, the heads of the different federal departments in the city, the representative of the Emergency Fleet Corporation, and the heads of the gas company and the privately owned Puget Sound Traction, Light, and Power Company to get advice on how he should dispose his troops. On the basis of this advice, Hayden sent one battalion of the First Infantry to Fort Lawton as a reserve; another battalion and a machine-gun company to be quartered in the State Armory (with permission of state authorities); and smaller detachments to guard the Navy Pier, Ballard Locks, and several power-distributing centers of the Puget Sound Traction, Light, and Power Company. The troops themselves, arriving from Camp Lewis at one o'clock Friday morning, were dispersed to their prearranged

Courtesy of University of Washington Library

Workers outside Skinner and Eddy yard during shipyard strike.
Volunteer policemen receive firearms in preparation for strike.

Courtesy of Seattle *Times*

James A. "Jimmy" Duncan   Ole Hanson
Harry E. B. Ault   Anna Louise Strong

billets directly from the train station. Every soldier was issued 120 rounds of live ammunition. The men in the armory were on orders to maintain a constant state of readiness, but to remain inside the armory unless specifically ordered out for duty. The troops sent to guard the power stations were ordered not to mount a guard outside, but to remain in the stations to act as a reserve for the civilian watchmen.[22]

Although the troops were carefully kept in the shadow, labor was aware of their presence. But labor did not know what the military's powers or intentions were. Would martial law be declared? Would the troops fire on strikers at the first sign of a union incident, or merely protect government property? Labor never found out. But when Major General John F. Morrison, Western Department Commander, arrived on Saturday morning to supervise the operations in Seattle, one point became clear. He informed a delegation of labor leaders that only he had the power to invoke martial law. Mayor Ole Hanson's threat to do so had therefore been a bluff. Morrison did not, however, reveal any further information about his orders for handling the Seattle situation.

Labor's uneasy uncertainty about the army's possible actions probably had a subtle restraining effect on the strikers' decisions. Most contemporary observers hostile to the strike regarded the army as the city's savior. Some more friendly to labor argued that the presence of the army was totally unnecessary, since labor's nonviolent record during the strike was evidence of wholly peaceful intentions.[23] But to this argument must be added the fact that only the first day of the strike—before the troops arrived— is an adequate measure of labor's conduct without threat of reprisal; and that first day was a day of exuberance. Later days, when labor realized that shutting down the city would not bring victory, would have been a truer test; but then the army was present.

Nevertheless, labor's peaceful record is still most remarkable, considering the provocations by the city government which might have led to unplanned outbreaks of violent strife. Ole Hanson was organizing his own army. Six hundred extra policemen were added to the regular city force for the duration of the strike.

"Clubs by the hundreds [were] distributed among the volunteer police." [24] They also received firearms when available. Machine guns were placed at strategic locations in downtown Seattle. The volunteer police were in reserve ready to be called up when needed by the regular police; twenty-four hundred special deputies, many of whom were young and irresponsible, were sworn in, armed, and turned loose on the city, usually with no instructions from the authorities. For them, the strike was part lark and part opportunity to demonstrate how to save the world from bolshevism. Appeals for recruits went to fraternities, the Reserve Officers Training Corps unit, and other male organizations at the University of Washington. Some were hired by businessmen to guard their properties. As one former deputy put it twenty-eight years later, "it was a wonder that some darn fool kid with bullets in his gun didn't blow somebody's head off." [25]

When the General Strike Committee met at noon on the first day of the strike, it was not concerned with the measures taken by the city government, or any other question of major significance to the fate of the strike. The need for basic policy decisions on the goals for, and terms of, settlement of the strike would soon be startlingly evident; but on February 6, the General Strike Committee was not prepared to make them. This was particularly unfortunate for the strikers because the executive committee had considered itself responsible only for exemptions and the coordination of the strike machinery. Thus, no individual or group existed for making strategic decisions.

The General Strike Committee displayed no awareness of this lacuna, its members were too intoxicated by the success with which the strikers shut down the city. That meeting was generally occupied with discussion of decisions already made by the executive committee or of interesting but minor sidelights. Although its members haggled over the executive committee's handling of the City Light issue, the General Strike Committee was on the whole satisfied with the work of its subsidiary and turned over a number of exemption requests to it.[26] After some discussion, the General Strike Committee decided to permit the Japanese unions to participate in its deliberations without vote. The more radical members of the Committee were drawn into a debate on whether the Wobblies' Red cards should be accepted in the "feeding stations." Until the Wobblies' complaint became known to the Committee, only holders of AFL cards were being charged 25 cents a meal; Wobblies, like all others, had to pay 35 cents. As fellow workers cooperating in the strike, the Wobblies' advocates claimed, they should be charged the same price as AFL cardholders for meals. They won their case.

Perhaps the complacency of the General Strike Committee was related to the lack of concrete action, so far, of the city government. Hanson's measures appeared to be only preparations for possible labor violence; on that first day the Mayor had made no move to break the strike.

That first blow would descend late Friday. Hanson issued a direct challenge to labor and threatened that he would intervene forcibly to counter any labor initiative:

> By virtue of the authority vested in me as mayor, I hereby guarantee to all the people of Seattle absolute and complete protection. They should go about their daily work and business in perfect security. We have fifteen hundred policemen, fifteen hundred regular soldiers from Camp Lewis, and can and will secure, if necessary, every soldier in the Northwest to protect life, business and property.
>
> THE TIME HAS COME for every person in Seattle to show his Americanism. Go about your daily duties without fear. We will see to it that you have food, transportation, water, light, gas and all necessities. The anarchists in this community shall not rule its affairs. All persons violating the laws will be dealt with summarily.
>
> Ole Hanson, Mayor[27]

This proclamation was printed on the front page of a free issue of the Seattle *Star,* distributed throughout the city in trucks and cars guarded by armed policemen, some of them equipped with machine guns.[28] This statement for local consumption contained no direct indication that he considered the strike a revolution to be suppressed. Nor did Hanson cite any specific action that labor had taken to justify opposition to the strike.[29] He was full of generalities. But, on February 9, for the local representative of United Press, Ole became more specific. Just in time for the nation's Sunday newspapers, Seattle's Mayor decided that the general strike was a revolution:

The sympathetic revolution was called in the exact manner as was the revolution in Petrograd. Labor tried to run everything. Janitors and employees in schools were called out, everything was stopped except a few things which were exempted.

We refused to ask exemptions from anyone. The seat of government is at the City Hall. We organized 1,000 extra policemen, armed with rifles and shotguns, and told them to shoot on sight anyone causing disorder. We got ready for business. They knew we meant business and they started no trouble.

I issued a proclamation that all life and property would be protected; that all business should go on as usual. And this morning our municipal street cars, light, power plants, water, etc., were running full blast.

This was an attempted revolution which they attempted to spread all over the United States. It never got to first base, and it never will if the men in control of affairs will tell all traitors and anarchists that death will be their portion if they start anything. Law and order are supreme in our city.

Let us clean up the United States of America. Let all men stand up and be counted. . . . We refuse to treat with these revolutionists. Unconditional surrender are our only terms.[30]

The startling news that Mayor Hanson would not "treat with these revolutionists," however, was not released locally, probably because too many Seattleites knew it was a flat, bald lie. Ole's great deeds in suppressing the strike had not yet been performed. Politically wise, Hanson knew he had to treat with the revolutionists if he was to get them to end the strike peacefully; violent suppression without attempting to cajole his opponents into surrender was alien to the mayor's nature. He telephoned James A. Duncan on Friday morning and said: "Jim, this strike has got to be called off by noon." [31] But Duncan, who was not the man to surrender meekly, even if he could have done so, informed the Mayor in formal tones that the authority to control the strike was out of his hands. In any case no one could call off a strike of this magnitude in a few short hours.

When Hanson realized that Duncan could not be budged, he asked Jimmy to bring the executive committee to his office for a conference. Duncan replied that he would transmit the Mayor's message, but thought it unlikely that the whole committee could come because of the press of business. And indeed, the executive committee voted to send a representative delegation of six labor men—Duncan, Martin Flyzik, head of the state miners, A. E. Miller, Hulet Wells, John Von Carnop, and Jim Taylor. Regular leaders of Seattle labor, these men were chosen for their general knowledge and negotiating experience and skill. When the men arrived at City Hall, Hanson greeted them with a barrage of accusations. Specific members of the labor delegation were accused of holding Red cards. The whole Seattle labor organization, Hanson said, had come under the control of the radicals.

Although Hanson had worked himself up into a highly emotional state, he still had sufficient control to vary his bargaining techniques. He asked if the city government could do anything to bring about an adjustment of the strike. If the strike were called off, he would volunteer to lead a delegation to Washington, D.C., to fight for more money for the lowest-paid shipyard workers. If the strike were *not* called off by eight o'clock on Saturday morning (a new deadline, since the old one was less than an hour off), he threatened to impose martial law on the city.

At the mention of martial law, it was the labor men's turn to get aroused. In the name of the delegation, Duncan hotly stated that labor had absolutely nothing to fear from martial law because it was not performing any illegal acts. Duncan also implied that if martial law were declared, all the public utilities presently operating would be shut down. Labor had kept them open because the strike as it was presently organized made them feel responsible; with martial law, the Mayor would have to be responsible for operation of the utilities. Flyzik stated that if martial law were declared, his miners would also go out in sympathy. Then Duncan taunted Hanson with the possibility that he could not carry out his threat, implying that the soldiers might refuse to act as strikebreakers. There are two versions of the next exchange. Duncan's account, reiterated many times, was:

"By G___," said the mayor, "if they are not loyal I want to know it."
"If you want to see the streets of Seattle run with blood to satisfy your curiosity about loyalty, we don't," replied Mr. Duncan.[32]

According to Hanson, it went like this:

[Duncan said:] we don't want to make the test [of the soldiers' loyalty]. I told him nothing would please me better than to have the test come.[33]

But for all of Duncan's pugnacity, he realized that labor must face up to the alternatives Hanson had offered. Eventually labor would have to capitulate, but Hanson's offer to go to Washington if the strike was called off was no better than previous peace offers labor had received. Both O. S. Larson and the Ministerial Federation, in conciliation attempts, had offered to support labor's appeal to the federal government if labor would not strike— and had been turned down. Now labor had struck, and the terms of settlement were no better than if the effort had not been made. But Duncan still hoped that the surrender could at least be arranged on more generous terms. Unfortunately, neither he nor anyone else really knew what terms would be acceptable to the rank and file of Seattle labor.

The general strike was ostensibly a sympathy strike with the shipyard workers. But that motivation had long since faded into the background for those nonshipyard workers who voted to go out. Too many subconscious feelings—fear, apprehension for the future, intensive in-group solidarity and out-group hostility— were present for conscious, rational demands to be formulated. And even if more generous terms could be worked out in this negotiating session, labor's delegates had no certain knowledge that any specific settlement would be acceptable to their followers, who could refuse to return to their jobs. The more obdurate laborers might resort to violence. Of even greater concern to these regular leaders was the fact that labor's failure to accept a compromise peace would shatter the internal unity of the labor movement. Duncan's only hope—and it was a slim one—was somehow to obtain better terms from the Citizens' Committee, which had an interest in preserving civic harmony. He therefore asked Hanson to arrange a meeting with the latter group for that afternoon.

Labor faced uniformly hostile public opinion. Led by the Seattle *Star*, the press condemned the strike as a revolution. All the newspapers published during the strike advocated no compromise with labor until "loyal Seattle workers" or the public authorities had purged Seattle unions of radical influences.[34] Labor's feeble efforts to destroy this revolutionary image through strike bulletins failed utterly. Only if a group of civic notables were willing to work with labor to find a satisfactory solution (and the rank and file to accept it), could this solution possibly be imposed on a hostile Seattle public.

With this desperate hope, the labor delegates reappeared at Hanson's office at three o'clock. The faithful Spangler, Reverend Matthews, and four other members of the Citizens' Committee arrived. For an hour Hanson and the two delegations struggled to work out a formula acceptable to all parties. The labor leaders would try to settle the strike, but they needed better terms to offer the General Strike Committee. They left the formulation of these terms to the Citizens' Committee. Spangler, though personally amenable to settling the strike, felt he could not commit his organization. He could probably determine the Committee's opinion by eight that evening; another meeting was therefore arranged for that hour.

The five hours between meetings was sufficient for the Citizens' Committee to arrive at a position, and it dashed the few lingering hopes of the labor delegates. Spangler reportedly said:

> Well, gentlemen, I do not think it is necessary for us to sit down or make ourselves comfortable in any way. Our stay will be very brief. . . . Our people have come to the conclusion that this is a revolution, that we cannot have any dealings with revolutionists.[35]

Later, A. J. Rhodes reiterated this stand for the public. He stated that "Seattle has defeated an attempted Bolshevik revolution." [36] With its powerful backing of civic, cultural, fraternal, business, and humanitarian organizations, the Citizens' Committee—and not Ole Hanson, as he bombastically claimed—sealed the fate of the general strike.

Learning the Citizens' Committee decision before it was announced to labor at the eight-o'clock meeting, Hanson knew what he had to do. He took the same stand as the powerful Committee —the strike was a revolution and no terms but unconditional surrender could be offered. Hanson had played a waiting game. Now he would have to appear more willing to crush the strike forcefully. But canny Ole still left himself some room to maneuver. He issued his antistrike proclamation to the newspapers in time for copies to be on his desk for the evening meeting with the labor delegation. The proclamation contained no specific promise of what the city government would do if the strike were not called off voluntarily, but only gave assurances to the people of Seattle that City Hall would maintain essential services and prevent violence. Hanson no doubt hoped that the labor leaders to whom he showed newspaper copies would be sufficiently perceptive to discern the inevitable next step he would have to take if labor did not voluntarily capitulate. When Duncan and his colleagues remained obdurate, Hanson was forced into taking the next step. Early in the evening of February 7, he sent his secretary to the Labor Temple to read a formal notice to the executive committee:

> To the Strike Committee:
> I hereby notify you that unless the sympathy strike is called off by 8 o'clock tomorrow morning, Saturday, February 8, 1919, I will take advantage of the protection offered this city by the national government and operate all the essential enterprises.
> Ole Hanson, Mayor[37]

Hanson had been under intense pressure to prevent or break the strike for at least a week. Business leaders particularly were incensed over his noncommital position during the formative stages of the strike. Most businessmen believed that Hanson was actually to blame for the outbreak of the strike. If he had taken a firmer stand earlier, they thought, strike sentiment among the nonshipyard workers would not have snowballed.[38] The pressures mounted during the first two days of the strike. Delegations from organizations that held membership in the Citizens' Committee besieged the mayor's office. Often the delegations were extremely large, such as the 250-man group of Elks who came to offer Hanson their support and assistance if he would firmly wipe out radicalism.[39] Spokesmen of business groups released statements to the newspapers "demanding that the city be put under martial law." [40]

But Ole was wiser than the businessmen who urged him forcefully to prevent the strike. He understood that the mood of

Seattle labor was beyond prediction. There was as good a chance of violence as of peaceful acquiescence as a response to attempts to forbid the general strike. From the beginning, no worker "knew where" the strike would lead, and he could find out only by staging it. But after learning how easy it was to close down a major city, their ardor was gone. Many of the strikers began to realize that the general strike led nowhere. Hanson's demand to call off the strike came when the strikers were psychologically vulnerable.

Hanson's timing was more likely the product of his political cautiousness than conscious planning. As he analyzed the forces involved on both sides of the strike, he probably realized that either faction could destroy his political career. Since he had not been the candidate of business groups, Ole had little incentive to yield completely to their demands if it would involve losing a large segment of the voters who had swept him into office. While not sponsored by labor, Hanson had previously maintained good relations with its leaders and comfortable majorities in working-class districts. It was unlikely that the business community could in the future replace the labor votes that Hanson would lose if he took an antistrike stand. But he knew that if business pressure became too great, or the strike were maintained too long, he would have to act. Ole probably saw in the strike an opportunity to avoid his dilemma by rising above local politics altogether. He could become a national hero. The situation was tailor-made to put his name on the front page of America's newspapers. Hanson turned against his former supporters under circumstances that were not likely to do him any personal harm.

Public acclaim came quickly to Ole Hanson. After his proclamation appeared in the *Star,* his office was overcrowded with individuals and delegations offering congratulations. According to the *Daily Bulletin,* the men who noisily filled his office came spontaneously to "assure him of their undivided support." Ole made a brave speech urging them to return to their normal occupations. "Run EVERYTHING," he said, "this thing has gone far enough. This is the end." His remarks were "enthusiastically cheered." [41]

Hanson's actions infuriated labor. Rather than weakening la-

bor's resolve to go on, he strengthened it and destroyed the position of those labor leaders who had been urging their more
adamant brothers to end the strike. No labor man could quietly
accept being forced back to work. Now labor held out, as Charles
Doyle said later, just to spite Hanson.⁴² His deadline for stopping
the strike at eight o'clock Saturday morning would *not* be met.⁴³

Eight o'clock came and passed; the General Strike Committee
took no action on Hanson's ultimatum. But cracks had begun to
appear in the solidarity of labor's position. Many union men
began to realize that without extreme action, the continuation
of the general strike would win them nothing. Most of them did
not think of themselves as revolutionaries, but how could they
explain the charge away if they stayed off the job much longer?

The first to break, on Saturday morning, were the streetcar
men. Although full service was not restored—only six cars ran—
it was possible for residents of the Ballard district to get downtown. By Saturday afternoon, other union workers had returned
to their jobs. Some restaurants, barber shops, and retail stores
had reopened for business. The Bon Marche, one of Seattle's
large department stores, informed its Seattle customers—via the
Portland *Oregonian*—that its doors would be open on Saturday.⁴⁴
The privately-owned Puget Sound Traction, Light, and Power
Company plant was back in full operation. Another private transportation company, Stone and Webster, had restored partial service on its streetcar lines after 3:30 P.M. Saturday.⁴⁵

Pressures to end the strike were mounting. The city govern-
ment, while not daring to interfere with the AFL strike leaders,
served warning of possible future action by beginning to arrest
Wobblies. Walker C. Smith, a Wobbly spokesman and editor of
The Industrial Worker, was jailed for distributing the leaflet
"Russia Did It." ⁴⁶

The press, now that the foundations of the strike were shaky,
heaped opprobrium and scorn on the strikers with renewed vigor.
The papers were beginning to sense victory for the antistrike
forces and would consent to no compromises. The *Star,* of course,
led the pack with its editorial, "There Can Be No Compromise
on Americanism." ⁴⁷ The *Star*'s importance in the suppression of
the general strike cannot be exaggerated. The forces opposed

to the strike rallied around this journal, and it provided them with a voice to intensify the already aroused fears of the people of Seattle.

The message of the *Star* was quickly taken up by other papers. The weekly *Argus* outdid even its mentor, claiming that the general strike was run by "muddle-headed foreigners," the "scum of the melting pot of hell," for their own purposes. "This riffraff from Europe" were trying to revolt against the American form of government and, in the process, were attempting to "terrorize the community." The *Argus* advocated the forceful suppression of the strike by soldiers from Camp Lewis who had not had the opportunity to go overseas to make the world safe for democracy and should therefore be given the chance to make the United States safe for democracy: "This thing has got to be fought to a finish right here in Seattle." [48]

Even the business paper, the *Bulletin,* viewed the strike with more perspective than the *Star* and its satellite. While the *Bulletin* was totally opposed to the strike, it did make some effort to differentiate between labor in general and its radical elements. The general strike, according to the *Bulletin,* was a revolution, engineered by the radicals and Wobblies, into which the large mass of innocent laboring men had been involuntarily drawn. Radicals like Leon Green, Hulet Wells, and Anna Louise Strong, who were "fighting for the control of labor and the power to intimidate capital and the taking over of industry and the government," were using the shipyard wage dispute as a blind to cover their own motives and bring the organized labor movement behind their efforts. W. L. Kidston, editor of the *Bulletin,* was convinced that once the radicals had been suppressed, the wage dispute could be settled by compromise.[49]

Seattle labor was under pressure to end the strike from other sources. The general strike was a serious embarrassment to the American Federation of Labor. Its most immediate effect on the federation was to slow down an organizational drive in the eastern steel industry. The steelworkers' international had signed a contract with Bethlehem Steel but reportedly was unable to sign with any other major company because of the news from Seattle.[50] When informed of the plans of their Seattle locals to use the unprecedented general strike, many of the international officers began to take fright. Telephoned and telegraphed orders forbidding Seattle locals from participating poured into the Labor Temple. Some international officers quickly entrained for Seattle personally to prevent their locals from going out, but only those of the printing trades were successful. After the strike began, even more international officers arrived in Seattle to add to the vocal demand that the strike be stopped. The early return of the streetcar men and teamsters was due in part to on-the-spot pressure from these men. When the international auditor of the teamsters, Mr. Briggs, was denied a hearing by the General Strike Committee and the Central Labor Council, he ordered the teamsters back to work. Briggs claimed he might have acted differently if he had been shown a little courtesy.[51] As a result of the general strike, the Seattle Central Labor Council was severely censured by the American Federation of Labor for "alleged 'un-American' motives." [52]

Another indication that ardor for the strike was waning was the resumption of publication on Saturday by the *Union Record.* Belatedly the executive committee realized that closing the *Record* had been an important tactical error which had deprived labor of an instrument for communicating with both the strikers and the frightened middle class. The strikers had no reliable means of receiving authoritative statement from their leaders. Although fifty thousand copies of the *Strike Bulletin* were handed out during the strike, the distribution system was fitful. The *Strike Bulletin* never reached enough of the strikers regularly to seem authoritative. Nor did it impress the middle class, because it was not familiar to them, as was the *Union Record.* As a result, with only the *Star, Post-Intelligencer,* and *Daily Bulletin* publishing, all newspaper comment on the strike was hostile. The decision to resume publication of the *Union Record* was correct, but came too late to restore the sagging morale of the strikers or the confidence of the public.

Even as they were allowing Hanson's deadline to pass without action, the executive committee realized that the strike was in trouble. More and more locals were defecting. Many of the regular labor leaders were advocating that the strike be stopped simply to cut labor's losses. At last the committee realized that the success of the strike depended upon their making decisions on goals and negotiating terms. They had lost the confidence of the public, which had a firm, unchangeable conviction that the strike was the beginning of a revolution. Now the only alternatives were to stage a *real* revolution, to abdicate control and allow extremists to indulge in violence, or to capitulate. The choice was capitulation. By a margin of thirteen to one (with one absence), the executive committee voted to request that the General Strike Committee end the strike at midnight that day, Saturday. That afternoon, a long resolution was written for presentation to the General Strike Committee:

WHEREAS; the unparalleled autocratic attitude of Charles E. Piez, General Manager of the Emergency Fleet Corporation, in refusing to permit the shipyard employers and employees of this community to enter into a mutually satisfactory agreement as to wages and working conditions (which would not add to the government cost one penny) so aroused the indignation of all unionists in Seattle as to cause them to express that indignation through the medium of a general strike; and

WHEREAS; on the 7th day of February, 1919, the Executive Strike Committee was in session deliberating upon the advisability of calling off said strike on the ground that its object had been fully attained through the unprecedented demonstration of solidarity and the encouragement to the workers in other ship building centers to further co-operate; and

WHEREAS; the ill-advised, hysterical and inexcusable proclamation of Mayor Ole Hanson tremendously embarrassed the committee in carrying out its plans, by reason of the fact that it suggested coercion; and

WHEREAS; martial law has been suggested and threats made to throw the military forces of this nation in the balance on the side of the employing interests; and

WHEREAS; thirty thousand shipyard workers have been on strike for a period of sixteen days, and sixty-five thousand workers have been on strike for a period of three days without so much as a fist fight or any other minor disturbance, now therefore be it

RESOLVED; that we recommend that the Executive Committee for the general strike, recommend that the general strike, excepting the shipyard workers, be called off at 12 midnight, Saturday, February 8th, with the understanding that all persons who went on strike return to their former positions, holding themselves in readiness to respond to another call from the General Strike Committee in case of failure to secure a satisfactory adjustment of the Metal Trades' demands within a reasonable length of time; and, be it further

RESOLVED; that Organized Labor of this community express to Mayor, and all others, its deep regret at the action taken, and announce that as law abiding citizens they have no fear of martial law or any other acts of intimidation used by those presumed to represent the public, but who in reality are representing only one class; and, further be it

RESOLVED; that we take this opportunity of expressing to the strikers our deep appreciation and admiration for the splendid spirit and order maintained under the most trying and aggravating circumstances.[53]

Because of his reputation within the labor movement, the executive committee asked James Duncan to present the resolution before the General Strike Committee that afternoon and argue on its behalf. Since Duncan was not a member of the General Strike Committee and was not entitled to speak on the floor, the executive committee requested that Robert Proctor, president of the Central Labor Council, appoint Duncan a special representative of that body to the Committee. Until that moment, Jimmy's participation in the strike had been wholly unofficial.

In the General Strike Committee, furious debate over the proposal raged until after four the next morning—well past the resolution's suggested midnight deadline for ending the strike. Duncan's initial presentation was greeted favorably; he was confident that the resolution would pass. But, after a supper recess, the delegates were sharply hostile. One longshoremen's delegate had stated before dinner that "Brother Duncan always gives us sane advice. If we follow him we can't go wrong." Afterward, he took the floor to register his change of heart: "Since I came back from supper, I've seen the light. . . ." [54] He, like many others, had been pressured by the more adamant rank and filers of their own unions during the recess.

Duncan began again from scratch to retrieve his advantage. He was joined by Harry Ault, who gave a two-hour speech—the longest he ever recalled making—trying to convince the men that continuation of the strike would be fruitless.[55] Members of the executive committee also spoke for the resolution. All to no avail. The resolution was overwhelmingly rejected; the strike would continue.[56]

The General Strike Committee's reason for continuing was the technicality that it did not know whether it was empowered to call off the strike without express permission, by vote, of the unions that had originally opted for a general strike. At another meeting, convened in the cellar of the Labor Temple by the IWW and other radicals excluded from the General Strike Committee, the reason was different but the decision was the same: the general strike was part of the class war and should be fought to the very end.[57]

A quiet Sunday helped to splinter the resolve for continuing the strike of many inactive strikers. It was a day to think; a day when there was no pressure to return to work; a day when it was not necessary to resist calling off the strike because of pride; a day to wonder when one's income would begin again. A number of locals held meetings to give the rank and file a chance to vote on whether their unions should continue to support the general strike. In most cases the militants lost. The big adventure was over; it was time to earn some money. In only two meetings did the members decide to continue the strike—the longshoremen's and the cooks'.[58]

On Monday morning there were significant gaps in the ranks of the strikers. The Seattle *Post-Intelligencer* triumphantly reported that "5 of Union Labor Units Vote to Return to Employment Today." [59] The strike would continue without the streetcar men, jitney drivers, barbers, garbage drivers, auto drivers, and teamsters.

The *Union Record*, however, would not admit defeat. It rationalized the defections by stating, "while one or two organizations have taken action ordering their members back to work on the theory that it was necessary to keep them intact, the effort to create a general stampede has signally failed." In reporting the morning's meeting of streetcar men, which approved their executive board's decision to return to work, the *Record* emphasized the car men's pledge to go out again if called upon by the Central Labor Council.[60]

When the General Strike Committee assembled on Monday morning, its members had had a chance to circulate among the strikers, and they had not found solid sentiment for continuing the strike. This attitude was reinforced by the appearance of representatives of unions that had gone back to work and wished to explain their action. The streetcar man was contrite and stated defensively that his union was forced back by its executive officer, working under orders from the international.[61] Before they had made their decision, they had asked Jimmy Duncan (who had helped organize them) whether they should return to work, explaining that the streetcar company had worked out a plan for restoring normal service by Monday. The company had promised the union not to discriminate against or fire strikers if they returned when the company requested. Duncan told them to make their own decision; his only advice was to act as a unit—he was afraid that if some men went back and some stayed out, the organization would be shattered.[62]

Other locals had similar tales. The teamsters explained that all the locals in the teaming trades had been sent back to work by the Joint Council of Teamsters. The representative of the lady barbers was embarrassed to relate that the members of her union were defying their executive committee and had returned to work surreptitiously. The newsboys were again selling papers on the orders of their executive committee, which took its decision illegally without a quorum. The barbers were also back at work; led by the radical Phil Pearl, they had been in the forefront of general-strike agitation, but did not explain their action.

Again Duncan, at the urging of the executive committee, argued for setting a time to end the strike. One hour after he made his request, the General Strike Committee (minus the shipyard workers, who were excluded from voting) accepted a new resolution prepared by the executive committee. It specified that the strike was to end on Tuesday, February 11, and that those local unions that had returned to work were to come out again so that all members of organized labor could return together:

> Whereas, this strike committee now assembles in the midst of the general understanding of the true status of the general strike; and
> Whereas, the Executive Committee is sufficiently satisfied that

regardless of the ultimate action that the rank and file would take, the said committee is convinced that the rank and file did stand pat, and the stampede to return to work was not on the part of the rank and file, but rather on the part of their leaders.

(However, be it understood that this committee does not question the honesty of any of the representatives of the general movement.) Therefore be it

Resolved, that the following action become effective at once, February 10, 1919:

That this strike committee advise all affiliated unions that have taken action to return their men to work, that said unions shall again call their men to respond immediately to the call of the rank and file until 12 noon February 11, 1919, and to then declare this strike at a successful termination, and if developments should then make it necessary that the strike be continued, that further action be referred to the rank and file exclusively.[63]

Response to the second strike call was spotty. The auto drivers and newsboys went out again in order to enhance labor's solidarity. On Monday evening the teamsters also voted to rejoin the strikers, but not all of them complied on Tuesday morning. The barbers and streetcar men would not go out again. The latter union explained that its executive committee could not be gathered in time to make a decision because they were working. The streetcar men who worked on the city-owned line, however, had another "excuse": Ole Hanson had threatened to fire any municipal streetcar worker who responded to the second call.[64]

At noon on Tuesday, all organized workers except those who worked in the shipyards had returned to their jobs. It was all over. Seattle could go, as the *Star* urged, "Full Steam Ahead." [65]

VII

Aftermath

THE FIRST major general strike in the United States ended quietly at noon on February 11, 1919. Somewhat sheepishly, Seattle's workers returned to their jobs in shops, factories, mills, hotels, warehouses, and trolley barns. The strike had been a failure, and they all knew it. In the days ahead they were to learn that it was worse than a failure—it was a disaster. Now, they were glad simply to return to work, leaving their fellow workers in the shipyards still out on strike.

I

Those who had had a hand in crushing the strike were delighted with the results of their actions. Congratulations poured into the offices of Mayor Ole Hanson and the editor of the Seattle *Star*. Among the hundreds of letters on the editor's desk was one from the Mayor himself: "Your paper saved Seattle. Your editorials before the revolution came drew the line between the Bolsheviks and patriots. . . ." [1] Others wrote to praise the courageous action of the *Star* in publishing its editions of February 7 and 8, which had to be distributed with police protection. The *Star* modestly published a full page of such messages on February 12, the day after the strike ended.

But the idol of the public, the subject of a torrent of adulatory messages, was Ole Hanson. A new American hero had been created, a man who (as he diffidently proclaimed and was widely believed) had singlehandedly crushed a Bolshevik revolution, a giant who could be held up as an example of how a patriot, armed only with courage, could prevent the ruination of the American way of life!

Local journalists quickly had to re-evaluate Hanson. Before the strike he had hardly been considered the type who would act heroically under any circumstances. He was widely regarded as a clown, a buffoon, an opportunist, a man who had gained office only because his rivals offered poor competition. In praising Hanson's actions during the strike, the weekly *Town Crier* profusely regretted its former opinion of Hanson as clown. As recompense, it ran a front-page picture of Ole, his rotund wife, and their eight children, labeled "9 Reasons Why He Insisted Seattle Remain an American City." ² The *Argus* too had to backtrack. While stating that it usually did not agree with Ole politically, it had to admit that "he made good in this emergency. He showed the country how to handle strikes in order to avoid disorders and riots." ³

Hanson's name was splashed across the headlines of the nation. The obscure forty-five-year-old mayor had overnight become a figure of national renown. Newspapers and magazines featured flattering articles. His past, as the reporters knew it, was dissected to discover the key to his courageous behavior. The New York *Times* billed Ole as "a man of force, direct and democratic in his methods." ⁴ Telegrams by the sackful, many from distant points, littered his office; opened in front of reporters, they were published and further enhanced the Hanson myth. Surrounded by telegrams, reporters, and flowers, Ole loved it all. His statement that the strike was an unsuccessful Bolshevist revolution, and that he was principally responsible for its failure, is Northwest lore that has persisted.⁵

The prevailing (Hanson) view of the strike in 1919 disconcerted the liberal, progressive, and left-wing supporters of labor. In the words of Charles T. Hallinan, executive secretary of the American Union Against Militarism:

> This Hanson is getting unendurable! As you know, he is making red-hot speeches everywhere against what he calls "Bolshevism" and he is filling the middle class with the profound conviction that all they have to do is to beat labor over the head, a la Hanson, and all

will be well. He is getting lots of publicity. I haven't heard him speak
but you can feel his influence everywhere—big stick stuff. He is
stiffening enormously the whole line of reaction.[6]

Hallinan and George Hampton, director of the Farmers' National Council (a union of farm organizations to work on reconstruction), thought Hanson a "four-flusher" who should be shown
up.[7] That job descended on Robert Bridges, president of the
Seattle Port Commission, who delivered speeches in strategic
cities attempting to refute Hanson's version of the strike and
his role in it. In Washington, D.C., Bridges stated that "the only
revolution we had was in the mayor's office while he was present.
We are sorry, for the mayor is a good advertiser, and a good
fellow, but he has lost his head entirely."[8] But the job of deflating Hanson could not be done in 1919.

Seattleites were relieved that they had escaped the danger of
revolutionary terrors and were concerned that no similar situation should ever arise again. Congratulatory messages to Hanson
and the newspapers were liberally dosed with exhortations to
continue the agitation against the revolutionists while they were
on the run. Ole Hanson voiced their feelings when he stated:
"Labor must clean house. Seattle may forgive, but it cannot
forget." [9]

The press insisted that the Seattle AFL rid itself of radicals.
The *Star* urged labor to purge its leaders—even though these men
were in many cases opposed to the general strike—and urged
"no compromise." [10] The *Bulletin,* too, consistent with its editorial line throughout the strike, hammered away at radicals within
the labor movement. Labor's reasons for the general strike—
sympathy for and solidarity with the shipyard workers, Charles
Piez's adamant position—were mere excuses to cover the machinations of radicals bent on upsetting society. The strike was clearly
the fault of the radicals harbored within the Seattle AFL movement, according to the *Daily Bulletin.* The more sophisticated
Argus summarized its attitude toward the strike, the strikers, and
the strike's results epigrammatically: "They struck for sympathy
—and didn't get it." It also characterized its publishing rival
the *Union Record* as "the rainbow paper—red and yellow." [11]
The *Town Crier* indulged in some amateur history, comparing

the technique of the general strike with Prussian ruthlessness and militarism and finding no essential difference.

Of all the charges hurled at labor, the aspersions on its patriotism hurt most. Laborers had not struck for what they considered adequate wages throughout the war; and, as Harry Ault noted, unions invested thousands of dollars in government war bonds.[12] Labor men also served on the King County Council of Defense.[13] But this did not stop the *Town Crier* from adding its voice to the cries for labor reform.

In reforming itself, however, labor was to get some diligent assistance from public authorities. The United States government began arresting editorial staff members of the *Union Record* on charges of sedition immediately after the strike was over. City officials issued a warrant for the arrest of Leon Green and began to round up Wobblies in large numbers. Anna Louise Strong was informed of her impending arrest over the telephone by her *Union Record* editor, Harry Ault, who asked her to come to the office to surrender with the rest of the staff. She was charged with the responsibility for the "No One Knows Where" editorial which had so frightened many Seattleites. The boilermakers soon turned over their Liberty Bonds for Miss Strong's bail. But the charges did not stick. According to her autobiography, the sedition charge against *Union Record* staff members was dropped when local Democrats complained to their friends in Washington, D.C., that the arrests would shift Seattle's labor vote to the Farmer-Labor Party in the 1920 elections.[14]

The end of the Seattle general strike was the beginning of a long odyssey for Anna Louise Strong. She complained bitterly to the famous muckraker Lincoln Steffens some months later that Seattle labor was tearing itself apart, with various factions all blaming each other for the disaster. Steffens felt a trip to Russia, "where issues were clearer," would benefit Miss Strong and renew her faith in proletarian causes. Anna Louise went to the new Soviet Union on a Quaker relief mission and was indeed impressed by what she saw. She stayed on in Moscow to become one of the most important English-speaking apologists for the Communist cause. In 1930 she established the Moscow *Daily News*, the first English-language newspaper in the Soviet Union.

Two years later, she married Joel Shubin, a Soviet agricultural expert. In the middle and late thirties, her numerous books glorifying the revolutionary people she came to love made her name known to readers in the western world. Her greatest influence as a journalist came from her reporting of the Spanish Civil War and China's titanic efforts to throw off the Japanese invader—those tragic events which led up to World War II—and later, that war itself.

Miss Strong's reward for defending Bolshevik revolutionaries, Spanish Loyalists, and Chinese Communist guerrillas was arrest and deportation from the Socialist motherland in February, 1949, just thirty years after the Seattle general strike. A victim of the schism between Stalin and Tito, she was characterized by the Soviet news agency Tass as a "notorious intelligence agent" and scheduled for speedy deportation. Return to the United States did not ameliorate her legal difficulties. American officials hinted that the Soviet arrest was a ruse to sow confusion in the West. Arriving in New York at the end of February, 1949, Anna Louise Strong Shubin was immediately handed a summons to appear before a federal grand jury investigating communism.[15] Again she left the country, this time for another new Communist state, China. Almost eighty, she has since lived in Peking, making public statements and writing articles defending Chinese action in the Tibetan revolt and excoriating American imperialism in Southeast Asia.[16]

Another warrant issued in Seattle in February, 1919, was for the arrest of the mysterious Leon Green, who had threatened to close down City Light during the strike. Green, however, did not oblige the authorities by surrendering. The police could trace his movements only until February 9, after which he was never again seen in Seattle.[17] Rumors of his whereabouts did get back to the city. Both James A. Duncan and Hanson believed that he was hiding in Chicago in 1920.[18] Years later, Seattle laborites heard that Green had turned up in the Soviet Union and been denounced to Soviet officials as an *agent provocateur* for management during the Seattle strike.[19] Harry Ault was positive of this. He stated that a Russian emissary asked him to clear Green in order to save his life.[20] To most Seattleites in 1919, Green—with his unknown origins, his short, controversial stay in Seattle, his outspoken advocacy of a complete shutdown of the city no matter what the cost, and his mysterious disappearance—seemed not to be management's agent, but rather a Bolshevik operative sent to Seattle specially to foment revolution.

The failure to convict Anna Louise Strong and the disappearance of Leon Green left the authorities without a prominent participant in the strike to use as whipping boy. Other well-known strikers could not be charged with any specific illegal act. The authorities therefore took the opportunity to wage a full-scale offensive on the IWW and other local radicals, always fair game for an outraged populace. According to the *Star,* Prosecutor Fred C. Brown intended "to arrest all IWW members" on grounds that they were to blame for the general strike.[21] The police raided and shut down the IWW hall at First and Columbia and the Socialist party headquarters. The Equity Printing Plant, which handled much of the local IWW propaganda and which was owned by local workers' groups, was raided and closed, and its manager was arrested. (Later, under police supervision, it was allowed to reopen.[22]) Thirty-nine men, including thirty-one IWW's, were held by the police for questioning. They were screened and interrogated, and it was announced that twenty-seven would be held because their alleged leadership in the strike was illegal under the recently passed Washington State Criminal Syndicalist Act.[23]

At the request of the imprisoned men, the Central Labor Council quickly came to their defense. A committee, sent by the Council to investigate the charges, decided that an "invasion of fundamental rights had taken place" and recommended that the Seattle AFL organizations assist in the men's defense. But little aid was necessary; Brown had no proof connecting the men with leadership in the strike. Brown therefore attempted to bring them to trial on the grounds that the personal *views* they had expressed were prima-facie guilt of criminal syndicalism. This first indictment was thrown out of court, and the judge required that the prosecutor produce specific *acts* during the general strike with which he could charge the men.

The first Wobbly, James Bruce, was brought to trial on these more specific charges before Judge Walter M. French on May 19, 1919. The prosecution, however, did not even try to press specific charges; instead, it alleged that Bruce advocated the forcible overthrow of the government. An IWW journal taunted that "the prosecuting attorney blandly admitted that he had no case against James Bruce." [24] The jury was of the same opinion; on June 5, it brought a verdict of not guilty.[25] Charges against the remaining defendants were dropped. Bruce's acquittal and the dismissal of charges against the others, according to the Wobblies, gave the IWW a clean bill of health as a legal organization, with full right to recruit openly.[26] Nevertheless, the Seattle police were undeterred in their campaign to cripple the operations of the local IWW organization. On June 23, within a week after the IWW's had reopened Seattle headquarters, the police raided a meeting and closed down the hall. The Wobblies howled, "Seattle Cossacks Commit Another Outrage," and continued their meeting in a vacant lot.[27]

In addition to action against the *Union Record,* there was one other punitive measure taken against the AFL by Seattle city officials: discipline of workers who struck the City Light plant. No striker who qualified under civil service was fined. But men who had remained at work and were promoted retained their new jobs; supervisors who had struck had to forfeit these positions for lower-paid jobs. Those strikers who had returned to work by Saturday morning, February 8, lost their vacations for that year; those who returned later took a fifteen-day layoff in addition. On the other hand, J. D. Ross wanted to reward those who had "helped him" in the emergency. One of his memos read:

> Mr. Kilbourne at 125 Lee Street helped us during the general strike, working all night on the job, and for that reason we extended his time of payment at his residence until June 1st. Please see that June 1st is the correct date and remind me of it at that time and if the bill is not paid, it will then be cut out and no extension granted as I think we have done our part a little better than Mr. Kilbourne.[28]

Seattle labor's position was made even less secure by the treatment it received from the American Federation of Labor. The

AFL Executive Council repudiated the general strike and severely censured the Seattle Central Labor Council:

The general strike inaugurated by the Seattle Central Labor Council was an undertaking in violation of the rules and regulations of the American Federation of Labor. The greater number of the local unions did not have the approval or sanction of their international unions and did not receive their moral or financial support. Born in a spirit of insubordination, disregardful of all rules and regulations adopted by trade unions for orderly procedure . . . this strike was from its inception destined to die an early death.[29]

Considering Samuel Gompers' well-known distaste for sympathetic strikes and for organizations favoring industrial unionism, such a reaction should not have been unexpected.[30] And relations between Duncan and Gompers had never been too friendly.[31] But the stand might not have been quite so harsh had the AFL not felt obliged to prove its patriotism. Although conservative in leadership and organization, the parent federation was constantly attacked by the press for harboring radicals. The AFL not merely condemned the general strike, but took credit for ending it:

It was the advice and counsel and fearless attitude of the trade union leaders of the American International Trade unions and not the United States troops, or the edicts of a mayor, which ended this brief industrial disturbance of the Northwest.[32]

At first, Seattle labor belligerently replied to its critics that it was fully competent to handle its own affairs and that any interference was unwarranted and unnecessary. The *Union Record* replied to other papers' "clean-house" editorials: "Let it be known once and for all that the labor movement will continue to handle its own affairs without assistance from the *Post-Intelligencer,* the *Star,* or any other mouthpiece or time-serving tool of Big Biz." [33] But defiance could not compensate for the knowledge that the general strike had been an unmitigated disaster for labor. The results, in the long run, were exactly what labor had hoped to avoid by striking: the encouragement of bitter factional struggles and jurisdictional disputes within the movement and the erosion of Duncanism, the growth of a powerful and determined open-shop movement, and the destruction of labor's economic hold on Seattle. In the words of Bert Swain, "it was fully twenty years before labor recovered from the unfortunate effects of the strike . . . and labor has been paying a pretty stiff price ever since." [34]

The most evident result of the strike to workingmen themselves was the shattering of Duncanism—that tendency for men of all opinions in Seattle labor to work together in hopes of "slowing up the radicals and speeding up the American Federation of Labor." The radicals and conservatives took more extreme positions; and the progressives, without the cooperation of left and right, were left hopelessly in the middle.

Soon after the general strike, the various radical wings made different assessments of the results. According to the Wobbly "two-card men" in the AFL, while the strike did not accomplish the immediate goal of demonstrating labor's power over the ship-yard owners and United States government, it did mobilize Seattle laboring men—and mass mobilization was the first step to revolution. Seattle had "started the ball rolling" for a whole wave of big strikes—in British Columbia, in the steel industry, in the coal mines. [35] The borers, wanting to press this advantage, set out to win absolute control of the Seattle AFL. The free-wheeling radicals, on the other hand, were appalled by the cost of the Seattle general strike to the labor movement. Radical in doctrine, they were still committed to the welfare of the *Seattle* labor movement. Men such as Phil Pearl of the barbers and Percy May of the longshoremen could not bring themselves to support further mass-action schemes because they felt such schemes would totally destroy organized labor in Seattle. [36] As a result, after the strike most of the free-wheeling radicals abandoned the radical position on key issues, leaving the borers in control of the left.

The conservatives maintained an "I-told-you-so" attitude toward the strike; the disaster they had predicted had indeed occurred. They were no longer willing to tolerate the presence of revolutionary radicals in the same labor movement with them. Seattle labor should revert to doctrines and practices associated with the AFL as a whole—more direct responsibility of a local to its international than to the Central Labor Council, more control of the local over its own affairs, and sharper jurisdictional lines to divide it from other trades.

The progressives, who had dominated the Seattle labor organization through mediating the extremes, now found their central position untenable. The strike had taught them that Seattle labor would destroy itself if they allowed radical demands for extreme measures to get out of hand. The progressives did not, however, want to eliminate the radicals or to drop the radical ideas they considered sound. But the radicals would not now be content with a subordinate position in the Seattle AFL, nor would they allow others to select which of their ideas were "sound." Thus, the progressives were often forced to vote against the radicals, alienating them further and widening the split between left and right. While trying to maintain their middle way, the progressives were forced on key issues to join the conservatives. Increasingly, the borers disliked Jimmy Duncan and attempted to upset his leadership.[37]

As a result of polarization of left and right, a bitter struggle for control broke out within the Seattle labor movement. One conservative, Ed Levi of the cooks, commented as follows:

> The worst feature of the labor movement in Seattle is the fact that there are two distinct labor movements fighting each other, and to make it still worse, both of the groups belong to the A. F. of L. and naturally both groups meet on the floor of the Central Labor Council, and what has been the result? The I.W.W. group distrusts the real A.F.L. group, and places all obstacles in the way of the A. F. of L. group that they conceive of. They interfere in any plan that we propose, and not only that, they slander the A. F. of L. members whenever they get a chance.[38]

The internal battles immobilized Seattle labor. The struggle was carried on in all important AFL organizations in the city. Every Wednesday night the factions exchanged bitter and futile words in the Central Labor Council. Vital business, such as the direction of on-going strikes, was neglected; striking locals were "left to fight it out alone." [39] Resolutions were offered urging the Central to expel all disrupters—radical, conservative, IWW, Minuteman, or American Legionnaire.[40] The teamsters' local passed a resolution condemning the Central and urging that, if it were to be of any use at all in the future, its meetings be held behind closed doors.[41]

Although the borers never succeeded in gaining control of the Central Labor Council, there were sufficient Wobbly delegates to disrupt its proceedings and prevent it from acting effectively.[42] The Wobblies tried to take over the movement by several measures; for example, gaining control of the delegations that Seattle locals sent to the AFL state convention at Bellingham in 1919. Their plan was to achieve sufficient voting strength to force William Short, president of the state Federation of Labor, out of office. Then they wanted to stampede the convention into voting the state federation out of the AFL. But their effort to "get" Short failed. Contrary to radical expectations, Boilermakers' Local 104, the largest single local and one on whose votes they had counted, voted solidly for him.[43] The borers almost succeeded in their second aim. Instead of forcing a vote directly on remaining in the AFL, they played on still heavy support for industrial unionism and introduced a resolution to submit a referendum to the rank and file on organizing the state labor federation on the "One Big Union" plan. This resolution was passed—much to the dismay of the AFL Executive Council, which threatened to revoke the charter of the state federation and its affiliates if the referendum went to the rank and file. To avoid this dire punishment, state federation officials introduced a motion in the Seattle Central Labor Council to rescind the referendum. With the support of Seattle conservatives, progressives, and most free-wheeling radicals, the motion passed and effectively killed the measure.[44]

The struggle for control was also waged in important Seattle trade councils and key locals, most of which were already rent by dissension over the failure of the general strike. The conservative officers of many locals affiliated with the Building Trades Council feared that the old organization was susceptible to radical control, and they threatened to withdraw their organizations from the Council unless it were reorganized and new officers elected.[45] They also pressed for the suspension from building-trades locals of all holders of IWW cards. The progressives voted for reorganization, but, still Duncanism-oriented, they would not eliminate the two-card men from the trade.[46]

The huge Boilermakers' Local 104 was also experiencing a power struggle. Fist fights were virtually regular features of its meetings. The borers were out to unseat President J. P. Martin, a well-known conservative. Secret union information was fed by borer members to a Wobbly publication and used to embarrass the boilermakers' AFL leadership. But Martin fought back successfully, maintained his leadership, and managed to counterattack by attempting to eliminate all two-card men from the union.[47] The conservative leadership demonstrated further disdain for the borers—it supported political action (a direct blow at the antipolitical principles of the IWW) and donated money to the Grand Army of the Republic to purchase American flags for Seattle schools.[48] But the conservative triumph was not wholly beneficial to Boilermakers' Local 104, for the victors now tried to impose craftism on a local which recruited virtually *all* metal workers except machinists, even to the extent of splitting the union—the skilled boilermakers demanded a separate charter; the mechanics tried to break away from their helpers.[49]

Radical-conservative struggles also took place in other important unions; radicals unsuccessfully attempted to upset the leadership of Duncan and John Von Carnop in the Hope Lodge of Machinists and to gain control of the longshoremen's union. On the other hand, Electrical Workers' Local 46 denied employment to workers found to be carrying Red cards.[50]

Another electrical workers' union, formerly Leon Green's Local 77, felt the disastrous effects of the strike and the turbulent poststrike condition of labor. Green's scheme to throw Seattle into darkness destroyed the reputation of his local with both the Seattle populace and the union's international. Almost immediately, the international revoked the local's charter. When most of the members working in City Light and the telephone company dropped their cards, Local 77 was virtually put out of business. The business agent who replaced Green threatened to affiliate the local with the IWW unless AFL recognition was reinstated. But the few remaining members rejected this proposal, fearing that they would be isolated.[51]

One important motive for the general strike had been fear that management was about to start a virulent antiunion, open-shop drive. Ironically, the strike gave this movement great momentum, and less than a month after the strike, the Associated Industries of Seattle was formally organized. The Associated Industries' historical version of its own founding was stated five years later by Roy John Kinnear:

> Labor unions, though ostensibly organized for the purpose of protection, advancement and welfare of the laboring man, had drifted into control of the radical, the un-American, the charlatan who, obsessed with the idea derived from his vision of super-power and control of Government, was ready to direct labor into paths leading to extreme conclusions *the end of which no one knew.*
> Therefore it was apparent that organized opposition was essential. The welfare of Seattle demanded it. The Associated Industries was created and immediately began to function [my italics].[52]

Composed principally of corporate members, the organization's avowed purpose—to destroy labor's closed shop—was frankly stated by Frank Waterhouse, the first president of Associated Industries:

> Understand, the Associated Industries of Seattle is by no means opposed to trade or labor unionism or to organized labor; but it is unalterably opposed to the closed shop, which system means that a working man cannot seek a job unless he belongs to some particular union, and an employer cannot employ. We are for the open shop, the fair, square American plan of industry which permits the union man, as well as a non-union man, to find a job.[53]

This group expected to accomplish its aim by several tactics: (1) insisting that its members not sign closed-shop agreements, (2) using its concerted economic power to force other employers not to sign such agreements (for example, withholding supplies from employers who would deal with organized labor), (3) assisting companies and industrial associations financially to enable them to defy organized labor, and (4) infiltrating the labor movement with spies and *agents provocateurs* to provide accurate intelligence and sow disharmony.[54] Since Frank Waterhouse, a steamship-line executive, was also a past president of the Seattle Chamber of Commerce (before it amalgamated with the Commercial Club), he was able to form a united antilabor business front.

(The chamber's committee on labor relations justified its support of the "American System" [open shop] by its memory of the general strike.[55] Edwin Selvin, whose advertisements had helped provoke labor to strike, was a member of this committee; its report must certainly have been for him a labor of love.[56])

Labor's first indication that a full-scale economic war was impending occurred in October, 1919, when William Short proposed to Frank Waterhouse that their organizations hold a joint conference to work out plans for adjusting disputes. Waterhouse would have none of it. He replied that Associated Industries would not meet with union representatives because they did not recognize the unions as the sole bargaining agency of their employees.[57]

Established as it was, when the unions were faction-ridden and confused because of the general strike, Associated Industries caught labor at a great disadvantage. How to respond to the challenge was a matter of fierce dispute within organized labor. The radicals wanted to use every opportunity to hit back at Associated Industries, and they opposed all plans for fighting management proposed by the conservatives and progressives. The radicals were so obstructive in the Central Labor Council that the conservatives and progressives finally found it necessary to create another organ which would be more effective in fighting Associated Industries. All presidents, secretaries, and business agents of Seattle locals met to map anti–Associated Industries strategy. They formed a separate group, not under the control of the Central, whose function was to coordinate labor's response to Associated Industries—the Committee of 15, with Duncan, Rust, James A. Taylor, Bert Swain, and Ed Levi as its major members. Their purpose was to gain supervision over strikes in progress and to prevent any other strikes in the immediate future. They hoped to counter Associated Industries' action by facing each of the individual members of that group with a united labor opposition. For this project they needed a war chest, which they promptly sought to fill. Half the funds would be used to fight Associated Industries directly, the other half would go to the *Union Record*.[58]

But the Committee of 15 could do little to win the strikes in progress. Since most committee members felt that the strikes were being run on an unsound basis and that the radicals had induced the strikers to hold out for exorbitant pay demands, the radicals bitterly resented the Committee's intrusion. With the backing of Associated Industries, the building, printing, and tailoring trades employers fought the strikes and were unwilling to compromise until they had destroyed the closed shop in those trades. The Master Builders Association was particularly incensed at labor; before the general strike, it had expressed confidence that the building-trades unions would not break their contractual promise and engage in a sympathetic strike. On February 7, 1919, members of the Association expressed their disappointment by opting for the open shop.[59] The strikes lingered for weeks (the tailors were out for seven weeks). Finally all three collapsed from lack of economic support, and the men went back to an open shop.[60]

Following this initial success for Associated Industries, the Waterfront Employers' Association began an open-shop drive. To protect itself from irate Seattle longshoremen, the Association had its own force of armed men. In this struggle the local longshoremen did not have the assistance of the international. The employers reportedly had the tacit consent of the international officers, who felt that the locals had given ample provocation for this punishment.[61]

Labor bitterly protested the activities of Associated Industries. William Short wrote a pamphlet "exposing" its nefarious machinations (about which Associated Industries had already been informed by one of its labor spies).[62] But the Committee of 15 could not retaliate effectively. Rather than counterattack as planned, the Committee could only struggle to keep the Seattle AFL's losses to a minimum.

To compound the Committee's already pressing difficulties, in the summer of 1919 the IWW set out to create its own rival unions in industries where the AFL had been strongly entrenched. The Wobblies were determined to break the Seattle AFL. They began to recruit Seattle shipyard workers for the Shipbuilders' Industrial Union No. 325; longshoremen for the Marine Transport Workers' Union No. 8; workers in the building trades for Construction Workers' Industrial Union No. 573; and hotel and restaurant employees for Hotel, Restaurant and Domestic Workers' Industrial Union No. 1100. The orthodox Wobblies, who would not bore into rival organizations, refused to accept the borers' assumption that the Seattle AFL, in its unsettled condition, could be converted from within; they were going to smash it from without. In Associated Industries they found an effective ally. As Wobblies analyzed the situation, the only reason the AFL had a tight hold on the Seattle economy was the closed shop. Without an AFL card, it was difficult to get work. Once Associated Industries had broken the AFL's closed shop in important industries, the men would no longer have an incentive to hold AFL cards. Moreover, they would feel resentful toward the AFL unions that had failed to protect them. The Wobblies hoped to move in and organize the former members of the shattered AFL unions. Thus, the Wobblies, who had been aided and frequently protected by the Seattle AFL, did nothing to assist the Committee of 15 in its struggle against Associated Industries. Instead it sat back and watched Associated Industries do "good work for the I.W.W." [63]

But the IWW organizational drive, though carried out with typical Wobbly enthusiasm, was short-lived. It could not succeed. First, while many employers would have preferred not to deal with any labor organization at all, if it came to a choice, they chose to deal with the AFL unions rather than the Wobblies. After the war, when jobs were scarcer, management could afford to be selective.

Second, the AFL did not allow the Wobblies to lure away its men without a fight. Boilermakers' Local 104 established gate check-off systems at the shipyards and other metal-trades establishments to make sure the entering men carried AFL cards. Those with Red cards were reported and promptly fired. Although the IWW complained bitterly as Wobblies were lopped off Seattle payrolls, Local 104 continued to enforce the check-off system, despite the attempts of the well-known two-card man, Vincent Brown, to have it stopped. [64]

Third, by the spring of 1920, Seattle's wartime industrial boom was over. Jobs were hard to find; and the Wobblies, last hired and first fired, were virtually eliminated from Seattle as an organized labor force. With the closing down of the shipyards, the Wobblies, most of whom were single men without ties, simply drifted away. One Wobbly gave this peroration for the IWW in Seattle:

> The I.W.W. are pretty well scattered now in Seattle. Some of our members are "pie card artists," and therefore they have to move when work shuts down. But I don't believe our membership has gone down any, for once a wobbly always a wobbly. You can't make a capitalist out of him. So, if we don't show our strength here in Seattle, it is shown somewhere else. At the present time it is in Butte, Montana, and soon it will be in the harvest field. With the dying of the industrial business here in Seattle, the activities of the labor movement died. The active workers went to places where active industry prevails, and Seattle is once more left in the hands of the real reactionary movement. The only organizations that have any pep left are the metal trades organizations. They are still on the map, while the Central Labor Council voted to interest itself in church work.[65]

By 1921, Seattle had become an industrial ghost town. The enormous war industries—particularly the shipyards—built with such extravagant haste, closed down because they were unable to convert their facilities to produce goods for a peacetime economy. In 1919, Seattle had 1,229 manufacturing establishments; by 1921 the figure had dropped to 907. From a 1919 record of 40,843 industrial workers making $63,395,000 in wages annually, Seattle in 1921 could support no more than 13,699 industrial workers making $19,142,000 a year. By 1921 Seattle had retrogressed almost to the point of its pre-war economic position—there were only 10 per cent more industrial workers than in 1914.[66] Not until World War II did Seattle recover its World War I position.

Inability to convert to peacetime production, of course, was not a phenomenon exclusive to Seattle. Throughout the country, employment figures in the metal-trades, machine-products, and shipbuilding industries dropped more than 39 per cent. Union membership, nationwide, dropped precipitously because of the closing of war industries and the ensuing 1921 depression. And 60 per cent of the decline was concentrated in metal-trades, transportation, and shipbuilding industries.[67]

Local citizens would not believe that Seattle's economic decline was in a sense a part of this national trend. The only psychologically satisfactory explanation was that the general strike had ruined the city economically. Their adoption of the strike as scapegoat was a result of high, if exaggerated, hopes for making permanent the wartime industrial boom. Seattleites had long dreamed of their city as a major industrial center, and World War I had presented an opportunity to turn dream into reality. But the war industries had to convert to the production of goods marketable in a peacetime economy if this expansion were to be permanent. Successful conversion depended upon a gradual tapering off of government shipbuilding contracts, however, to provide local management with enough capital and time for the change. But continuation of government shipbuilding was a decision beyond Northwest control.

As a direct result of the strike, the Emergency Fleet Corporation, in keeping with its warning, suspended all construction on vessels being built in Seattle yards. The inevitable next step would be cancellation—if the shipyard strike were not settled. Once the sympathy strike was over, the shipyard owners desperately strove to prevent the government from taking this next step. They wanted their yards in operation again, with or without AFL cooperation, and they had planned to reopen the yards on Wednesday morning, February 19, on the open-shop plan, hiring ex-servicemen in lieu of those union men who would not return to work. But Piez's suspension order did not merely suspend the government's obligations; it also required that the yards remain closed until the unions forced their men to return at Macy-scale wages. Piez would not allow the employers to reopen, wiring his Northwest representatives that he would not permit any alterations of Macy-award conditions, even in favor of management.[68]

The shipyard strike dragged on. Although internally divided over continuing the strike, the shipyard workers persisted in their unequal and now unsupported struggle with Charles Piez until March 17. By then it was too late. In April, contracts for the construction of twenty-five vessels were canceled by the EFC. The bottom had dropped out.

By summer of 1919, after the government orders were canceled, thousands of shipyard workers had been laid off by Seattle shipyards. In November, Skinner and Eddy, giant of Seattle shipbuilders, closed down Yard Number 2. By the beginning of 1920, Skinner and Eddy employed only eight hundred men—compared to six to eight thousand during the wartime peak—and those who remained worked for reduced wages.[69]

The metal-trades unions were decimated by the closing of the shipyards. The membership of Boilermakers' Local 104 was cut by two thirds. The shipbuilding laborers' local, formerly a thousand-strong, was reduced to fifteen die-hards with $7.00 in the treasury in the spring of 1920.[70] It was a long, cold winter. One old union man described it thus:

> By the end of January we will have conditions in Seattle like we never had before. The yards are laying men off by the hundreds. Every day the army of unemployed is getting bigger and bigger right along. . . . We have to sit tight until some readjustment takes place and more men go to work. In the spring most of the farmers will be going back to the farms where they belong. Then our old-time union men will be able to get a job, but now the rube who is willing to do anything for his boss gets all the jobs and the old-timers are left out in the cold.[71]

But labor still had hopes that the yards would reopen. The workers maintained skeleton organizations in the shipyard unions. Labor's optimism was based on the plans of David Rodgers, general manager of Skinner and Eddy, to convert part of the equipment of the Skinner and Eddy yards to the production of civilian goods. He resigned from Skinner and Eddy in August, 1919, and in the spring of 1920 he attempted to purchase its Number 2 yard. Rodgers claimed to have $46,000,000 in orders, which he hoped to start filling as soon as the yards could be put into production. He expected to hire six thousand men with a $10,000,000 annual payroll. This meant that unemployed AFL men would have jobs, with a boss who was approved by the shipyard unions. They expected Rodgers to operate the yard on a closed-shop basis, but even if he could not, Boilermakers' 104 would still be willing to work for him.[72]

But Rodgers' attempt was blocked by Associated Industries. Yard Number 2 had been leased by Skinner and Eddy, who had allowed the lease to lapse; it was not Skinner's to sell. Rodgers could have acquired it with sufficient funds, and he complained bitterly in advertisements submitted to the Seattle *Times, Post-Intelligencer, Star,* and *Union Record* that Associated Industries had successfully prevented bankers from lending him the money. (That group went so far as to contact Judge Elbert H. Gary to dissuade him from selling Rodgers steel.) This last failure to reopen the shipyards was a bitter blow to labor.[73]

Nor did Skinner and Eddy survive the termination of the government-sponsored wartime shipping boom. In attempting to close the books on its shipbuilding program, the government alleged that it was owed more than $9,300,000 by Skinner and Eddy because of overpayments to that company for contracted work done. To recover the sum, the government legally tied up the corporation's assets and sued for the money. When it won its case, Skinner and Eddy was effectively put out of business—another blow to labor and Seattle's economy.[74]

II

Defeated economically, suspected by most of Seattle's nonlabor public because of the general strike, the Seattle AFL tried to recover its position by entering into politics. To hostile Seattleites, the general strike had been a revolution, and they felt that its failure had rendered labor powerless. Political activity was the last method of retaliating against this impression available to organized labor.

Labor's move into 1919 politics did not begin propitiously. One month after the general strike, Seattleites expressed their distaste for the city labor movement by defeating all three of the labor-sponsored candidates for the City Council. Officially the city elections were nonpartisan, but everyone knew that Robert Proctor, Ed Levi, and C. H. Gallant were labor men. By an average margin of almost eight thousand votes, conservative incumbents were re-elected.[75] Although even Ole Hanson characterized the labor candidates as "decent, fairly conservative labor men," they were linked with the strike in the minds of the voters and the press.[76]

Labor was concerned with what it considered a smear, but the progressives and conservatives in the movement rationalized the defeat by claiming that too few workingmen knew or exercised their political responsibilities. Nor, they felt, was labor at that time well organized to function politically. The progressives and conservatives intended to remedy this lack in the next big municipal election, with hopes of vindicating the general strike that they originally had not approved. After the strike was over, even these original opponents began to feel a conscious pride in their organizational efficiency, which had made the strike possible and peaceful. They also vehemently defended the nonrevolutionary character of the strike. Therefore, over the protests of the antipolitical radicals, the Seattle labor organization threw itself into a campaign to organize the Triple Alliance—a coalition of the state AFL organization, the railroad workers, and the state Grange. Enormous effort was expended by the Seattle branch to create a solidly organized political machine, with emphasis on voter registration, a central file of party members, and a system of block captains.[77]

The first test of the machine was the December, 1919, elections for members of the Seattle School Board and Port Commission. The Triple Alliance candidates for the School Board lost by an average of ten thousand votes; the candidates for Port Commission were defeated by narrower margins.[78] But labor was undismayed; the new Triple Alliance had scarcely had time to get activated. They hoped to do better in the mayoralty election of March, 1920, which would be the big test of the Triple Alliance's effectiveness. Victory would provide sweet revenge, since labor would then take over the mayor's office recently vacated by Ole Hanson.

Seattle labor, the biggest third of the Triple Alliance, wanted the strongest candidate possible. Since the campaign was to be a direct defense of the nonrevolutionary aims of the general strike, a labor leader who would be so recognized in the officially nonpartisan election was desired instead of a "wishy-washy liberal." But it was also necessary that he be acceptable to all except the most radical wing of Seattle labor. The obvious choice was James A. Duncan. Although the radicals were no longer Jimmy's ardent admirers, he was still the only progressive who commanded their respect at all. The radicals did not ever actively support the campaign, but at least they agreed not to sabotage it. For them, the 1920 election would be another demonstration of the futility of political action as a labor weapon.[79]

Duncan did not want to run; his wife was against it, his health at the time was poor.[80] But the pressure was intense, and Triple Alliance spokesmen were able to convince him that he was the only man. Flattered, he accepted and plunged into the campaign. The February primary would narrow the field to two finalists, and Duncan believed he needed a broader base of support than labor; therefore, he concentrated his efforts on getting his name before the nonlabor public. But Duncan, being Duncan, put himself frankly on record on every issue. Not only did he defend the general strike, he even advocated the unionization of the fire and police department and the rigid enforcement of Prohibition.[81] He also attacked the opponent he considered stronger, president of the City Council and Acting Mayor C. B. Fitzgerald. Duncan's tactic was to appear personally before as many rallies and meetings as possible, in order to counteract what he feared would be slanderous treatment from the Seattle press.

The primary campaign turned into a personal feud between Duncan and Fitzgerald. The third strong candidate, Hugh M. Caldwell, a Republican lawyer and recently discharged army major, quietly campaigned on the theme of eliminating political rule at City Hall. Fitzgerald raked up all the old charges that the general strike had been a revolution and even attacked Duncan for submitting an anticonscription resolution to the Seattle Central Labor Council before Congress had passed the draft act.[82] He said that Duncan would be able to enact revolutionary measures legally as mayor. Duncan responded by offering to debate Fitzgerald on the issue of the general strike at any time before any audience; Fitzgerald refused to debate, and Duncan was left to shadowbox. But he tried to answer the charges of nonpatriotism nonetheless. At one point he said:

> The old gang says that the fight is Americanism vs Duncanism. I tell you that Americanism and Duncanism are the same thing. I studied Lincoln and tried to follow his ideals but I want to say that so doing got me into lots of trouble because it is not safe to follow his ideals at present. They just mock the great emancipator when

they mention his great name. . . . But we are going to redeem his fair name and that very soon.[83]

To everyone's surprise, Fitzgerald was eliminated in the primary. He now threw his support to Caldwell, and Caldwell, in his month-long campaign against Duncan, picked up where Fitzgerald had left off. He too impugned Duncan's patriotism and attacked the revolutionary intentions of the organization Duncan headed. Responding with the tactics he thought had been successful in the primary, Duncan relied on personal appearances at election rallies—sometimes six or seven an evening—at which he specifically answered Caldwell's accusations. Again he offered to debate with his opponent; again the response was negative.

As election day drew closer, the Triple Alliance and its union supporters spared no effort to sweep Duncan into office. The block captains were registering union men right up to the deadline. Letters and other campaign literature were sent to the faithful and to potential supporters. Some Triple Alliance campaign workers specialized in getting out the minority vote—Negroes and Nisei—reputedly solid for Duncan. Speakers were sent to drum up interest among the remaining workers in the shipyards. The opposition came in for some attention too. Longshoremen were ordered to attend Caldwell's meetings to "talk it up for Duncan." [84]

At Triple Alliance headquarters on election night, the election workers, so confident of Duncan's victory, watched the returns with growing dismay. Before the night was over, it was clear that Duncan had lost by some seventeen thousand votes out of eighty-seven thousand cast.[85] It was a Caldwell landslide. Caldwell received the largest majority of any candidate for mayor to that date.

At first, Duncan supporters could not believe that the vote count had not been tampered with; Percy May and Harry Ault bitterly complained that the only way Duncan could have lost was for the opponents to have stuffed the ballot boxes. Later, when the honesty of the election was no longer questioned, Duncan and his supporters consoled themselves with their "moral victory"; this campaign was a splendid beginning to the political efforts of the Triple Alliance. Given the relative immaturity of the organization, Duncan's primary victory and thirty-four thousand votes in the election were really all they should have expected.[86] Duncan was proud that he had received more votes in defeat than Ole Hanson had in winning the previous election.[87] But the labor men of the Triple Alliance could not admit to themselves that the people of Seattle had turned out in force in 1920—88 per cent of the registered voters voted—to defeat the general strike and the men who stood behind it.[88]

III

For one week in February, 1919, the newspaper headlines throughout the country screamed, "Revolution in Seattle!" The theme was familiar—Americans were becoming accustomed to reading about upheavals, revolutions, and putsches—but the location was an ominous novelty. The Seattle general strike seemed to signify that it *could* happen here. The American people, situated comfortably in untouched cities, towns, and farms, could no longer feel isolated from the dangerous events that followed in the wake of the World War. The Seattle general strike helped condition the American people to accept extreme measures against aliens, dissenters, and left-wingers, in what would become a year-long, fanatical Red scare.

Two months after the general strike, it appeared that revolutionaries were again about to act. On April 28, 1919, a small brown parcel, sent to Mayor Ole Hanson and left on a table in his office, began to leak acid. Upon investigation, the parcel was found to contain a defective home-made bomb. The next day another recipient of a similar brown package was not so fortunate. It exploded in the home of ex-Senator Thomas W. Hardwick of Georgia, blowing the hands off his maid and injuring his wife. In New York City, a post-office clerk read about the bombing and remembered that he had set aside sixteen similar packages for insufficient postage. Frantically he returned to the post office and was able to stop their shipment. A hasty bomb-hunt in post offices around the country resulted in the discovery of eighteen more of the brown packages. The addresses seemed to have been chosen more for prominence than for any ideological position; politically they ranged from liberals to extreme right-wingers.

There was another wave of bombings on June 2; explosions occurred simultaneously in eight cities, including the Washington, D.C., home of United States Attorney General A. Mitchell Palmer. Although the selection of the bombing victims was again eclectic, the coordination of the explosions seemed to indicate a well-laid revolutionary plot. What evidence could be discovered about the bombings pointed to a small group of deranged anarchists. But to the public, the beliefs and tactics of one segment of the left was assumed to be characteristic of all. Public opinion held that the bombings were the work of a large united group of radicals collectively called Bolsheviks. The public could distinguish only one color—red.[89]

The spring of the bomb scares also saw a noticeable rise in the number and importance of strikes and other labor difficulties. Having been released from wartime regulations, labor now sought more aggressively to find its place in the postwar world. In March, 1919, the month after the Seattle general strike, there were 175 major strikes throughout the nation; in April, 248; in June, 303; in July, 360; in August, 373.[90] Americans were nervous about the rise in labor demands; strikes, particularly violent strikes, looked suspiciously like revolts to a people well convinced that Seattle had been a revolution.

Another general strike, just across the border in Winnipeg, Manitoba, in May, 1919, and more prolonged and violent than Seattle's, confirmed American suspicions about the specter of bolshevism. The issues at stake were the right of collective bargaining, the eight-hour day, and, most significant, industrial unionism. When the iron-industry shopowners refused to deal with the Metal Trades Council, the other city locals went out in sympathy. With all organized labor striking, the Winnipeg workers decided to effect a previous decision of the Western Labor Conference to organize Canadian labor along the "One Big Union" principle.

Winnipeg labor held out for six weeks, paralyzing the city. The strike committee completely replaced the elected government as the locus of public decision-making. One reason for the length of the strike was the allegiance to the strike committee of a large number of ex-soldiers, who had been used as strikebreakers in other postwar strike situations.

The long duration of the strike and the frightening "One Big Union" idea alienated people in both the United States and Canada. Winnipeg's conservative citizens, determined to prevent labor from winning, formed a powerful antistrike group called the Committee of One Thousand. The dominion and provincial governments, urged by the local committee and convinced that the Winnipeg strike was inspiring walkouts in other Canadian cities, decided to act. Although the strikers had not attempted to impose their demands by force, violence now erupted as Royal Canadian Mounted Police and troops from eastern Canada were brought in to break the strike. Strike leaders were arrested in the middle of the night. The movement collapsed by June 30.[91]

Was this Seattle all over again? There were superficial similarities: both were begun by Metal Trades Councils in appeals for solidarity; both were called according to AFL rules regarding strikes; both were run by large general-strike committees empowered to make decisions on the strike; both had executive committees of fifteen men which actually dealt with substantive issues because of the unwieldiness of the large committee; both tried to close down all local newspapers including the labor journal; both placed exemption cards and stickers on vehicles exempted by the executive committee; both were blamed on radicals; and finally, both were orderly—Seattle completely and Winnipeg until "special police" were imported.

The Canadian press charged that these similarities were not a coincidence, that "radical leaders, failing in Seattle, had come to Canada to try their luck and that the strike in Winnipeg had been financed and led by radical labor groups from the United States." [92] But, with the exception of James A. Duncan, who complied with the Seattle Central Labor Council's request that he investigate the Winnipeg situation on his way east to the 1919 AFL Convention, no person involved in the Seattle strike was ever proved to have associated with the one in Winnipeg.[93]

In the fall, three major strikes and a bloody shooting affair which echoed the Seattle strike of the previous winter further alarmed the American people. On September 9, 1919, the Boston police struck for higher wages, better working conditions, and the right to unionize—and left the city unprotected. (What better proof that labor was radical and subversive of society?) There was violence in the streets of Boston, but Governor Calvin Coolidge quickly and uncompromisingly dismissed the entire force and suppressed the ill-advised strike. Later that month, the steelworkers struck against an industry which had stubbornly resisted unionization. This strike too ended disastrously—the 275,000 men who walked out of the steel mills under William Z. Foster's leadership failed to gain any concessions and were forced to return to work after three months. Twenty lives and $112,000,000 in wages were lost during the struggle. The miners fared somewhat better. Despite a temporary court injunction, 394,000 coal miners struck for higher wages. When the temporary injunction was made permanent by a federal court, John L. Lewis, head of the United Mineworkers' Union, ordered his men back. But wildcatting took place, and Lewis and other leaders were cited for contempt. The strike finally ended when the Federal Fuel Administration offered the strikers a 14-cent-per-hour temporary wage increase. With this financial incentive, the men could return to work gracefully, and an arbitration commission began investigating the miners' case for a permanent wage increase.[94]

Then on Armistice Day, 1919, attention was jolted back to the Northwest. In front of the IWW hall in the lumber town of Centralia, Washington, four American Legionnaires in a patriotic parade were shot down by Wobblies. The Legion claimed that the men had made a rest halt in front of the hall, but the IWW had supposedly heard that the Legionnaires intended to raid their hall. Armed Wobblies were stationed inside and outside the hall. It has never been proved whether the first IWW shots came before or after the Legionnaires had begun to storm the hall; but the local populace was outraged, and vigilante mobs began to round up all Wobblies they could find. Wesley Everest, a Wobbly exserviceman, shot and killed a Legionnaire while fighting off the mob. Everest was arrested, but was confined for only a few hours before a mob dragged him from the jail, emasculated him, and hanged him from a railroad bridge.[95] So hysterical was the re-action to Centralia that when the Seattle *Union Record* asked that judgment on responsibility for the incident be deferred until all facts were known, the United States government seized the newspaper plant, banned its issues from the mails, and arrested its editor and two directors.[96] It was not a year to call for rea-soned, calm judgment of unpopular causes.

Public outrage had its effect on official policy. In November, 1919, United States Attorney General A. Mitchell Palmer, one of the bombing victims and hitherto a staunch progressive and Wil-sonian, launched a vigorous campaign against aliens and radicals —all those he feared as threats to the values of a solid, middle-class America. With a $500,000 increase in his budget, Palmer set up a special antiradical division of the Department of Justice under J. Edgar Hoover. On November 7 the first radical aliens were arrested in simultaneous raids in cities across the country. Hoover's men, and particularly the "Red Squads" of cooperating local police forces, handled the prisoners brutally, making no effort to conceal bruises and lacerations. Many were arrested il-legally; too often the unfortunates rounded up were held in-communicado in filthy, overcrowded jails. Deportations were accomplished with astonishing speed, the Labor Department co-operating. On December 21, 249 anarchists (many of them philo-sophical anarchists with no record of violence) were deported to the Soviet Union on the army transport "Buford." During 1919, some five thousand warrants for arrest were issued; about six hundred "Reds" were deported. Early in 1920, the interest of the Justice Department shifted from anarchism to communism. On January 20, simultaneous raids in thirty-three cities rounded up some four thousand alleged members of the Communist and Com-munist Labor parties.[97]

In this mood, the American people were eager to learn how to whip bolshevism. Ole Hanson of Seattle had such advice, and he was not going to pass up the opportunity to give it. Six months after the general strike, on August 28, 1919, Hanson handed in his resignation as mayor of Seattle. Within the next year, he made more than a hundred speeches in cities and towns across the

United States under the auspices of the Redpath Lecture Bureau. His version of the Seattle general strike was a rabble-rousing insistence on "Americanism" and "law and order" before chambers of commerce, women's clubs, American Legion posts, school teachers' groups, and church organizations. To veterans he stated that the only way to assure that they did not "fight the good fight in vain" was to insist upon "deportation, incarceration, annihilation" of all radicals, socialists, Wobblies, anarchists, and enemy aliens.[98] Informed while on tour that a bomb had been addressed to him in Seattle, he responded by attacking the government's attitude toward bombers as "weak, vacillating, and changeable. . . . I trust Washington will buck up and . . . hang or incarcerate for life all the anarchists. . . . If the government doesn't clean them up, I will." [99]

Hanson's attacks directly impugned the loyalty of American organized labor, including the AFL. Labor leaders were conscious that Ole was harming their public image and making it more difficult for them to maintain their wartime gains. In mock seriousness, the Chicago Stockyards Central Labor Council claimed that Hanson was "a disease, a plague, that Seattle has turned loose over the country." [100] Samuel Gompers tried to defend his organization from Hanson's attack; the revered head of the AFL had in the past complained of radicals in his organization, but he would not tolerate such a charge from an outsider. But Gompers was not prepared for Hanson's response, which was particularly vicious and personal: "As to your attack on me, I care nothing, I realize that you are old and feeble, and as the body weakens, so does the mind!" [101]

Ole also turned author, telling his story of beating the Reds in Seattle and giving his prescription for accomplishing the same thing nationwide "in United States English of one or two syllables." [102] His book, *Americanism Versus Bolshevism,* and his several articles on the same theme were all part of a campaign of self-publicity. For Ole Hanson had taken to heart the possibility mentioned by the editor of *The Unpartisan Review:* "How would it do to add to your list of candidates for president in 1920 the name of Ole Hanson?" [103] Ole seriously hoped that by making enough

noise he could capture the Republican nomination. His candidacy
was thus described by the IWW:

> Ole Hanson, the crazy clown who resigned as Mayor of Seattle is
> preaching revolution. He wants to summarily drive the present gov-
> ernment out of office for its sympathy with the "reds." Some rascal
> put the presidential bee in his bonnet and he can't get rid of it.[104]

But Hanson was deceiving himself. By the time of the Republican convention of 1920, the Red scare was waning, and Ole,
whose entire platform was excoriation of the Red menace, was
never seriously considered. The nomination and the presidency
went instead to the less fanatic and more amicable Warren
Harding, who shared the country's growing boredom with witch-
hunts—"Too much has been said about Bolshevism in America,"
said Harding.[105] Hanson returned to Seattle, sold his real-estate
company and all his other Seattle property, and retired to California and obscurity.

Perhaps one reason for Hanson's permanent retirement from
politics was his treatment at the hands of Clarence Darrow, attorney for the defense in the 1920 trial of twenty Communist
Labor party members in Chicago. Hanson, an expert witness on
bolshevism for the prosecution, was expected to tell how the
workers in Seattle attempted to overthrow the government and
establish a Soviet system (an action the prosecution alleged was
part of the Communist Labor party's revolutionary program).[106]

By skillful questioning, Darrow was able to cast doubts on the
sincerity of Hanson's patriotism by bringing to light the financial
rewards of a Red hunter. Hanson was forced to reveal that in
seven months of public speaking he had made $38,000—$500 for
each of his lectures. The tour had netted Ole more than five times
his already adequate yearly salary as mayor. Ole pleaded "poverty,
neuritis and the absolute necessity of earning a living for my
family" as his reason for the lecture tour.[107] Darrow's response
was perhaps Hanson's political epitaph:

> Is Ole Hanson hard to understand? Is he? Doesn't he show, all
> over him, the marks of a cheap poser? Doesn't he show all over him
> evidence of a lightheaded notoriety hunter? Think of it, gentlemen!
> Imagine one of you. Suppose you had been the hero of this bloody

strike. Suppose you had preserved civilization and Americanism because you were such a great and such a brave and such a noble Mayor? Suppose that you had bared your breast to this mob, that opens up milk stations and eating houses and carefully guards the peace of the city. Suppose that you had earned the plaudits of your fellowmen and the encomiums of the press? Suppose that you had done that and suppose that you had been heralded by State's Attorneys as the great savior of the world, what would you have done?

Well, I fancy you would have stuck to your job? I fancy you would have stayed right there and run the job. But not Ole, oh no, not Ole. When he was advertised from one end of America to another for his fool proclamation because he was the jumping jack Mayor of Seattle, when his advertising was worth thousands in lecture courses, he forthwith lays down his job and leaves Seattle to go to the dogs, or to the workingmen, as the case may be.

The captain deserts the army, and the pilot gets off the ship and lets Seattle go to the devil while he rakes in the shekels.

Now, that is Ole; that is Ole Hanson, the cheap vaudeville performer. . . .

Why, he said he needed the money.

That is a fine excuse for a patriot, and pretty near all of the professional patriots need the money; that is the reason they are professional patriots, they need the money.[108]

VIII

Conclusion

INFLAMMATORY statements by the mysterious Russian, Leon Green, and an impassioned, muddled editorial by Miss Anna Louise Strong made national headlines that branded the image of a miniature revolution on Seattle's general strike. Mayor Ole Hanson chose to confirm this impression officially, even though he well knew that Miss Strong's and Green's views were not representative of the sentiments of the official leaders of the strike.

The revolution myth has proved hardy; indeed, it is still alive. Older Seattle residents have passed the story of the desperate days when they faced the revolutionary hordes down to their children and newcomers to their city. Tellers of Northwest tales have put similar accounts into print.[1] Nostalgic old radicals either lament the revolution that failed or recall that heroic men tried their best.[2]

The Seattle general strike was not a revolution. All available evidence points clearly to the fact that revolution was not actively attempted by the strikers. Nor is there any substantial evidence to indicate that the strikers *intended* to overthrow the prevailing political and economic system at one stroke.

First, there was no attempt to sequester private property. Although rumors of the seizure of property abounded during the first days of the shutdown, no private property was touched by the strikers without the consent of the owners. The executive committee borrowed facilities and implements needed for setting up the milk and feeding stations from owners who were willing to lend them. At the end of the strike, the executive committee returned or replaced everything that had been borrowed.

Did the strikers intend or lay plans to appropriate private property which were never put into effect because the strike collapsed so quickly? No doubt there were individuals who were dreaming of this possibility or even scheming to attempt it, but there is no evidence that the executive committee, the General Strike Committee, the Metal Trades Council, or any individual who exerted any influence on these key bodies had such plans.

Second, the strikers neither organized themselves for carrying out a revolution nor gathered together the tools necessary to face active opposition successfully. No shock or assault squads were formed. No attempts were made to seize vital installations. There was no secret stockpile of arms. Even after the United States Army entered the city, labor attempted no violent resistance. The War Labor Guard, wearing armbands, not sidearms, prevented labor men from engaging in violence and did not form a vanguard leading the strikers into violent action.

It is extremely unlikely that Seattle labor had made any secret preparations for revolution, for if such plans had existed, violence would almost certainly have ensued. The fizzling of the Seattle general strike is probably the most anticlimactic moment in any major mass effort by American workingmen. Generally, when troops, goons, or Pinkertons have been brought in to suppress a strike and American workers have had weapons, there has been bloodshed. In Seattle, the "revolutionaries" fired not a single gun. Not one striker was found in possession of a weapon, no laboring man was arrested even for disorderly conduct. If arms had been available and plans made to use them, emotional tension and sheer frustration probably would have compelled their use.

Finally, it is evident that the general strike was not an attempted revolution because the strikers did not try, nor is there evidence that they planned to try in the future, to usurp permanently the functions of the city government. The executive committee was not the "rival government" that Crane Brinton believes necessary for a genuinely revolutionary situation to exist.[3] While the committee did suspend the economic life of the city; control access to vital goods and services, such as food, transportation, sanitation, water, electric power, funerals, and hospital service; and assume police power in controlling its own followers, it conceived its role as temporary. And the committee's attempt to shut down the city and simultaneously to sustain it by providing vital services precluded the executive committee's becoming a "rival government." Only by closing down Seattle completely could labor demonstrate that the populace was entirely in its power; only then would the executive committee have had power or moral authority to take over the normal functions of the city government and private enterprise.

Leon Green's lonely attempt to force the executive committee into sponsoring revolution failed. The committee chose to keep the city from degenerating into chaos and civil upheaval by exempting from the strike all the facilities the city officials needed. City government did not atrophy; its moral and physical power was untouched even though Ole Hanson waited until the last minute to apply it fully. A "rival government" can form only when the legal government either drops its responsibilities or is so powerless that it cannot assume them. Hanson and the organized middle class that rallied to him never lacked the power to keep "the seat of government . . . at the City Hall."

After the General Strike Committee and its executive committee gained control of the strike, their actions made it obvious that they did not intend to create America's first Soviet. Sixteen years later Anna Louise Strong, by then definitely in the camp of the Communists, looked back to remember that "all of us were red in the ranks and yellow as leaders." [4] She preferred to believe that the majority of the strikers intended to stage a revolution but were balked by leaders who had lost their nerve.

But the rank and file had chosen its own leadership and that leadership was not red. The men could be urged on by IWW propaganda from without and by IWW borers and free-wheeling radicals from within, but they would not be led by them. They were not as red as the relatively small group of ardent revolutionaries among them hoped.

If the Seattle general strike was not a revolution, it was, emphatically, a revolt. Seattle workers saw hostile forces or outright enemies in every direction—the United States government and its troops, its agent Charles Piez, Ole Hanson's city-hall regime, obdurate shipyard owners, the threatening Seattle employers and their open-shop movement, the hostile middle class of the community. The overwhelming majority of the strikers wanted a vehicle through which they could "let off steam," vent their fears and frustrations, and lash out against all their enemies at once. The Seattle general strike was a revolt against everything and therefore a revolt against nothing. Labor had so many enemies to punish that it was unable to define specific goals and impose a definite time limit on the strike. Only in the case of a revolutionary general strike could such conduct be useful. But, although failure to impose limits on nonrevolutionary economic general strikes or political mass strikes is dysfunctional, it is also typical. The Seattle general strike is a textbook example of the ineffectiveness of the nonrevolutionary general strike as a labor weapon for attaining any but the narrowest goals. Only if a general strike is limited in duration and the goals are narrowly defined can it be successful.[5] Without narrow goals understood by striker, opponent, and neutral observer, a general strike will be treated as revolution.[6]

No single element caused the Seattle general strike. It occurred only because there was a multiplicity of causes—IWW propaganda which gave Northwest workers name familiarity with the general strike; the class spirit and advanced opinions of Seattle workers; the emotional impact of the Bolshevik Revolution; general world unrest; the obdurate position taken by the shipyard owners; the intervention of Charles Piez and the United States government; fear of employer support for a growing open-shop movement; agitation by revolutionary and nonrevolutionary radicals among local labor; and the distinctive Seattle AFL organization, led by James A. Duncan and his progressives, which insisted that all Seattle workers pull together and which provided a vehicle for such unity. Separately, not even the dominant causes would have provoked the general strike; rather, it was the combination of extraordinary events and the condition of Seattle labor.

Perhaps one element more important than the others, the one condition without which the strike could not have occurred, was the form into which the Duncanites had molded Seattle labor.

This strong organization, which used the Central Labor Council to dominate local unions and enforced the habit of working together, was, if not the powder causing the explosion, at least the fuse without which the powder could not ignite. Essentially, the Seattle general strike is the story of an organization which for a short period escaped from the domination of its progressive leaders; and without Duncan and his cohorts in control, the organization was caught up in momentary passion and temporarily got out of hand.

Paradoxically, the complexity of the strike's causes, while a precondition for its very occurrence, also denied the strike any chance of success. With no stated goals, no specific enemies against whom to direct the strike, and no set time limit so that the middle class would not take fright, each individual striker was a spokesman for the movement as a whole. The inability of the official strike leaders to make policy was compounded by the variety of statements issued by rank-and-file strikers and unofficial spokesmen for various factions. Each was striking for what he thought important. In the absence of stated goals and motivated leadership, the Seattle general strike was all things to all men.

A Note on Sources

THE story of the Seattle general strike has been pieced together from many primary sources.

The Papers on Industrial Espionage, University of Washington Library, proved invaluable for tracing the organization, tactics, and personalities of the Seattle labor movements. They were particularly useful because the Seattle Central Labor Council official records were reportedly lost in a fire many years ago. The Papers on Industrial Espionage (PIE) were originally collected by a large Seattle firm whose workers the Seattle AFL was trying to organize. They contain two sets of labor-spy reports giving a day-by-day account of the Seattle labor movements for most of 1919 and 1920, an incomplete collection of union-meeting minutes, and a fine collection of labor and radical pamphlets, leaflets, flyers, posters, stickers, and magazine and newspaper clippings. The reports of one of the agents, Number 106, who concentrated on AFL affairs, were particularly useful. He made no obvious attempt to inject his own opinions into the reports, and he provided sufficient detail so that it was possible to check his account against other sources. Unfortunately, the same cannot be said of Agent 17, who reported on the IWW. Not only were his reports opinionated, but their accuracy is in doubt; his employer sharply reprimands him for carelessness and mendacity, or both. His reports were used with extreme caution.

The Papers on the Seattle General Strike, University of Washington Library, are all that remains of a study of the strike begun just after World War II by the Bureau of Labor Economics,

University of Washington. It consists of newspaper clippings and transcripts of interviews with major strike participants. The interviews were useful for cross-checking my interviews with the same strike leaders and for divulging the views of those who were dead or unavailable fourteen years later.

Revealing details on the actions and ideology of the antilabor Associated Industries were found in the Papers of Roy John Kinnear, University of Washington Library. In addition, the labor-spy reports in this collection helped prove the value of those in the Papers on Industrial Espionage. The disparity between them is startling. The agents reporting to Associated Industries apparently were concerned only with reinforcing the fixed bias of their employer—facts notwithstanding. In contrast, Agents 106 and 17 were reporting to an employer, under immediate pressure from labor, who could fight back most effectively when supplied with accurate advance information. His efforts to keep his agents under control made even Agent 17's reports seem models of probity and precision compared to the reports submitted to Associated Industries.

Another useful collection in the University of Washington Library was the Papers of James Delmage Ross, superintendent of City Light. Memoranda received and sent out by Ross just before and during the strike were extremely important for placing in perspective Leon Green's attempt to shut down the City Light plant.

While not rich in materials on the conduct of the general strike, the Papers of Robert Bridges, University of Washington Library, were helpful in elucidating the relationship of Seattle labor and its liberal friends, as well as showing the effect of the strike on those allies.

The trial of leaders of the Communist Labor party took place in Chicago in 1920, a year after the general strike. Because the prosecution alleged that the CLP regarded the Seattle strike as a model for revolutionary attempts in the United States, five people directly involved in the strike were put on the witness stand. Over two hundred pages of testimony in the transcript of *People* v. *Lloyd* dealt with the central events of the strike. This transcript, 304 Ill. 23 (136 N.E. 505) (1922), was microfilmed by Remington Rand, Springfield, Illinois, in 1954. It is a treasure of information, particularly about the roles played by two of the witnesses, James A. Duncan and Ole Hanson. The transcript was especially useful because opposing attorneys in cross-examination were able to force testimony on subjects that the witnesses did not discuss voluntarily.

Since one of the interested parties in the situation in Seattle was the United States government, an examination of some of its records deposited in the National Archives in Washington, D.C., was essential. Contemporary Northwest newspapers give a confused, incomplete account of the Seattle shipyard strike of late 1918–early 1919. The records of the United States Shipping Board (Record Group 32) in the National Archives revealed the positions of Charles Piez, the managements of Skinner and Eddy, the smaller yards, and the metal-trades unions. The government was an important participant not only in the genesis of the strike but also in its resolution. Records of the Adjutant General's Office (Record Group 94) and the Western Department of the Army (Record Group 98) provided important details on the timing of bringing troops into the city, their location and function, and the condition of the city while the army was present.

Several important participants in the strike were still alive and living in Seattle and vicinity when this study was begun in 1958-59. I was fortunately able to interview James A. Duncan, Harry E. B. Ault, Frank Turco, Ralph Bean, Professor Theresa Schmid McMahon, Tom Nash, and Ralph Chaplin. Most of their accounts of the strike were remarkably full, considering the passage of time. The general strike was probably the single most important event in which they participated. Their fluency made it evident that they had told their stories of the strike many times. The interviews with James A. Duncan provided the greatest volume of information. Duncan's accounts of the events of 1919—given in Chicago the next year, to the Bureau of Labor Economics interviewer in 1946, and to me forty years after the strike—were remarkably consistent. I was never able to persuade Mr. Duncan to answer direct questions, however; he always returned to his fixed account. Harry Ault, on the other hand, was very cooperative and introspective, although he did not always remember details well. His analysis and critique of the role he and the Seattle *Union Record* played in the strike was most helpful. Frank Turco was, in 1959 as in 1919, pugnacious, argumentative, and self-assertive. His account, characteristically inflating the role of Frank Turco, deviated frequently in detail from other available evidence. Milton Bean, an editor of the business newspaper *Daily Bulletin,* provided valuable information on the attitude of the business community, particularly toward labor, the open-shop movement, and Ole Hanson. The late Theresa Schmid McMahon, Professor Emeritus at the University of Washington, gave information on the condition of Seattle labor; Tom Nash, on the Seattle IWW movement in which he was active in 1919. Ralph Chaplin was not in Seattle during the strike, but as a nationally known leader of the IWW, he was able to give insight into the IWW as an organization.

Two official publications of the Seattle labor movement concerning the general strike were *The Seattle General Strike* by Anna Louise Strong (Seattle, n.d.), and *History of Activities of the Seattle Labor Movement* . . . by William Short (Seattle, 1919). These were used with caution. The sins of these sources were those of omission rather than commission. What the authors revealed checked well with other materials, but they left out anything that might prove embarrassing or damaging to labor's image.

Notes

CHAPTER I

1. Ole Hanson, *Americanism versus Bolshevism* (Garden City, N.Y.: Doubleday, Page, 1920), p. 65; Ralph Potts, *Seattle Heritage* (Seattle, Wash.: Superior Publishing Co., 1955), p. 69; John S. Gambs, *The Decline of the I.W.W.* (New York: Columbia University Press, 1932), pp. 133-34; Robert L. Tyler, "Rebels of the Woods," *Oregon Historical Quarterly,* LV (1954), 35; Robert K. Murray, *Red Scare: A Study in National Hysteria, 1919-20* (Minneapolis: University of Minnesota Press, 1955), pp. 59-60; William E. Leuchtenburg, *The Perils of Prosperity, 1914-32* (Chicago: University of Chicago Press, 1958), p. 71; Rowland H. Hill, *Samuel Gompers: Champion of the Toiling Masses* (Stanford, Calif.: Stanford University Press, 1935), p. 306.

2. Henry F. May, *The End of American Innocence* (New York: Knopf, 1959), p. xi.

3. Richard Hofstadter, *The Age of Reform: From Bryan to F.D.R.* (New York: Knopf, 1955), p. 273.

4. See George Kennan, *Russia Leaves the War* (Princeton, N.J.: Princeton University Press, 1956), pp. 12-14, for a full discussion of the reaction in the United States to the downfall of czarist autocracy.

5. The state of Washington went dry by initiative in 1914. Charles Merz, *Dry Decade* (New York: Doubleday, Doran, 1931), p. 42.

6. See, for example, "Partial List of Prisoners," *One Big Union,* II (March, 1920), 6-21; "Partial List of IWW Prisoners in the Northwest," *One Big Union,* II (April, 1920), 12-14; and "Partial List of IWW Deportees," *One Big Union,* II (June, 1920), 39. These are consolidated lists of IWW prisoners rounded up during the wartime, immediate postwar, and Palmer raids who, at the time of writing, still remained in custody.

7. Philip Taft, "The Federal Trials of the IWW," *Labor History,* III (Winter, 1962), 57-91; and H. C. Peterson and Gilbert Fite, *Opponents of War* (Madison: University of Wisconsin Press, 1957), pp. 242-46.

8. Seattle *Post-Intelligencer,* Jan. 15, 1919, p. 1; "The Sabotage Law," *The Town Crier,* XIV (Jan. 18, 1919), 4.

9. As Eldridge Foster Dowell points out in *A History of Criminal Syndicalist Legislation in the United States* (Baltimore, Md.: Johns Hopkins Press, 1939), p. 42, note 75: "The Seattle strike is important because at the time of its occurrence criminal syndicalism bills were before the legislatures of eleven states and were to appear later in the same year in four additional states and Alaska and Hawaii."

10. Papers on Industrial Espionage (MSS in University of Washington Library, Seattle), report of Agent 106, July 17, 1919. Hereafter this collection will be cited as PIE.

11. Peterson and Fite, *Opponents of War,* pp. 235-36, and PIE, report of Agent 17, June 29, 1919.

12. PIE, report of Agent 17, July 4, 1919.

13. PIE, report of Agent 106, June 27, 1919.

14. Peterson and Fite, *Opponents of War,* p. 169.

15. "The Case of Louise Olivereau," *One Big Union,* I (October, 1919), 11.

16. *Ibid.*

17. Peterson and Fite, *Opponents of War,* p. 162. For other interesting details of the case, see: Anna Louise Strong, *I Change Worlds* (New York: Holt, 1935), p. 62; Murray Morgan, *Skid Road* (New York: Viking, 1951), pp. 208-9; Harvey O'Connor, *Revolution in Seattle* (New York: Monthly Review Press, 1964), pp. 248-61.

18. PIE, report of Agent 17, April 12, 1920.

19. Peterson and Fite, *Opponents of War,* pp. 22-23.

20. PIE, reports of Agent 106, June 3, Aug. 29, 31, Sept. 3, 6, 7, 9, 12, 13, 14, 17, 28, 1919; report of Agent 17, Sept. 4, 1919.

21. For a discussion of the extensive use of labor spies by American industrial management, see John A. Fitch, *The Causes of Industrial Unrest* (New York: Harper, 1924), pp. 171-85.

22. PIE, report of Agent 106, July 17, 1919.

23. As did Agent 172: "Three delegates to district council, I being one of them. Will now be in shape to give more first hand information and am in a position to give better work." Papers of Roy John Kinnear 1881-1959 (MSS in University of Washington Library, Seattle), report of Agent 172, March 31, 1920.

24. *Ibid.,* and PIE.

25. See reports of Special Agent J. H. in file 18252-1, General Records of the Industrial Relations Division, United States Shipping Board, National Archives, Record Group 32.

26. W. H. Crook, *The General Strike* (Chapel Hill: University of North Carolina Press, 1931), p. 532.

27. Seattle *Post-Intelligencer,* Jan. 14, 1919, p. 2.

28. *War Directory* (Seattle, Wash.: Seattle *Post-Intelligencer,* 1918), p. 31.

29. Transcript of *People* v. *Lloyd* [304 Ill. 23 (136 N.E. 505) (1922), microfilmed by Remington-Rand, Springfield, Ill., 1945]. The testimony of a Seattle Minuteman, Harry S. Wilson, reveals much on the methods and sense of responsibility of the organization. Also see the comments of H. Austin Simons in Max Eastman's Marxist journal, *Liberator,* III (August, 1920), 12.

30. Theodore Draper, *The Roots of American Communism* (New York: Viking, 1957), p. 139.

31. Seattle *Post-Intelligencer,* Jan. 4, 1919, p. 2.

32. On IWW and AFL cooperation, see transcript of *People* v. *Lloyd,* p. 478.

33. "Mayor Declares Charges False," Seattle *Post-Intelligencer,* Jan. 23, 1919, p. 2. For some of the propaganda which caused this apprehension when it was distributed on Seattle streets, see a leaflet titled "Mustered Out" (State's Exhibit 41), transcript of *People* v. *Lloyd,* p. 471.

34. On the extent of Minuteman infiltration, see transcript of *People* v. *Lloyd,* pp. 449-535.

35. PIE, report of Agent 106, July 16, 1919.

36. *Ibid.,* May 6, 1919.

37. PIE, report of Agent 17, July 16, 1919; reports of Agent 106, May 11, 24, June 25, 1919.

38. *Ibid.,* Nov. 26, 1919.

39. Kinnear Papers, report of Agent 317, March 12, 1920.

40. Seattle *Union Record,* Jan. 3, 1919, p. 1; Seattle *Post-Intelligencer,* Jan. 4, 1919, p. 2; and transcript of *People* v. *Lloyd,* pp. 523-25.

41. *Daily Bulletin,* Jan. 15, 1919, p. 7.

42. Seattle *Times,* Jan. 22, 1919, p. 1; and Seattle *Post-Intelligencer,* Jan. 5, 1919, p. 13.

43. See chapter 3, "The Shipyard Strike," and chapter 7, "Aftermath," for more extended discussions of the open-shop movement.

44. David A. Shannon, *The Socialist Party of America* (New York: Macmillan, 1955), pp. 122-23.

45. Seattle *Post-Intelligencer,* Jan. 1, 1919, p. 2.

46. PIE, report of Agent 106, Nov. 28, 1919.

47. Seattle *Post-Intelligencer,* Dec. 16, 1918, p. 1.

48. *Ibid.,* Jan. 1, 1919, p. 22.

49. *Daily Bulletin,* Jan. 15, 1919, p. 7.

50. PIE, report of Agent 106, Aug. 22, 1919. A representative of the state Grange and a friend of labor is said to have made the following statement at a meeting of Boilermakers' Local 104: "Yes, the other side has started on a slandering campaign. . . . A speech was made in Raymond to the business men in which it was stated that the Triple Alliance should be destroyed if not they will get control of the government of the State of Washington then confiscate all property and nationalize the women. Can you beat that? You don't believe it? Well,

it is true, we have stenographic reports of that speech and of many others like it. Yes, I have something right here with me, an article printed to [*sic*] our friend Edwin Selvin. He says right here that we are the propagators of Bolshevism. That our ultimate aim is the nationalization of women. It is printed right here so you must believe it. Now this article and many others are being sent to the unsuspecting farmers. We must guard them against such propaganda and I am sending letters to the same farmers exposing the lies."

51. For example, Samuel Gompers took an anti-Soviet position based on an accurate perception of the realities of the unfolding events in Europe. In a March, 1919, memorandum to the American Peace Commission, he pointed out that the Bolsheviks came to power with the aid of the German government, that the Weimar government was established only by agreement between the Socialist Premier Ebert and a representative of the army, General Groner, and that the new Soviet government was dictatorial in structure. Philip Taft, *The A. F. of L. in the Time of Gompers* (New York: Harper, 1957), pp. 446-51.

52. PIE, report of Agent 106, Sept. 18, 1919.

53. Seattle *Union Record*, Dec. 12, 1918, p. 1; *ibid.*, Jan. 9, 1919, p. 1.

54. There were no negative votes on a resolution approved by the Central Labor Council pledging aid to the Seattle branch of the International Longshoremen's Association in its efforts to halt arms shipments to Kolchak. PIE, report of Agent 106, Sept. 18, 1919.

55. Strong, *I Change Worlds*, p. 67.

56. *Ibid.*, p. 69.

57. Seattle *Union Record*, Dec. 12, 1918, p. 4. Anna Louise Strong was named chairman. Other members were: Leon Green, J. C. Mundy, Fred Nelson, F. Lighter, Andy Mulligan, Blanche Johnson, Hulet Wells, and James Walsh.

58. Papers of Robert Bridges 1861-1921 (MSS in University of Washington Library, Seattle), A. J. Rhodes to Robert Bridges, June 20, July 20, Aug. 17, 1917.

59. William Short, *History of Activities of Seattle Labor Movement and Conspiracy of Employers to Destroy It and Attempted Suppression of Labor's Daily Newspaper, the Seattle Union Record* (Seattle, Wash.: Union Record Publishing Co., 1919), p. 17; also, PIE, reports of Agent 106, Sept. 17, 18, 20, Oct. 15, 16, 20, 1919, and reports of Agent 17, Oct. 11, 13, 15, 16, 1919.

60. Seattle *Post-Intelligencer*, Jan. 13, 1919, p. 1.

61. *Ibid.*, Jan. 14, 1919, p. 2. The meeting was sponsored by the Central Labor Council, the Hope Lodge of Machinists, and the Socialist party and was endorsed by the Metal Trades Council. According to the Seattle *Star* (Jan. 16, 1919, p. 1), Anna Louise Strong—without authority, as President Robert Proctor later informed her—lent the name of the Central Labor Council as sponsor.

62. Seattle *Post-Intelligencer,* Jan. 14, 1919, p. 6.
63. Seattle *Star,* Jan. 3, 1919, p. 1.
64. *Daily Bulletin,* Jan. 14, 1919, p. 7. Also see *ibid.,* Jan. 18, 1919, p. 7.
65. Seattle *Post-Intelligencer,* Jan. 17, 1919, p. 3.
66. *Ibid.;* also see Hanson's contradictory testimony where he confuses the two riots, transcript of *People* v. *Lloyd,* pp. 542-49, 580-81.
67. Quoted in John Graham Brooks, *Labor's Challenge to Social Order* (New York: Macmillan, 1920), pp. 364-65.
68. *Ibid.*
69. Morgan, *Skid Road,* p. 203.
70. Quoted in *ibid.,* p. 204.
71. Transcript of *People* v. *Lloyd,* p. 583.
72. *Ibid.,* pp. 538-41. According to Morgan, *Skid Road,* p. 203, the Rooseveltian belief in "ruggedness" was emulated by Hanson with great success, which confirmed his faith in his mentor. Hanson injured his back in Butte, Montana, in 1900. By walking the seven hundred miles to Seattle in an elaborate harness attached to the rear of a covered wagon driven by his wife, he restored his own health.
73. Transcript of *People* v. *Lloyd,* p. 537.
74. *Business Chronicle,* VI (Jan. 11, 1919), 75.

CHAPTER II

1. Dorothy O. Johansen and Charles M. Gates, *Empire of the Columbia* (New York: Harper & Bros., 1957), p. 382.
2. Murray Morgan, *Skid Road* (New York: Viking, 1951), p. 159.
3. Dun and Bradstreet, Inc., *Seattle* (n.d.), p. 13.
4. Frederick Jackson Turner, "The West and American Ideals," reprinted in *Frontier and Section,* ed. by Ray Allen Billington (Englewood Cliffs, N.J.: Prentice-Hall, Inc., 1961), p. 106.
5. As one Tacoma businessman complained in 1957. Quoted by Robert C. Nesbit, *"He Built Seattle": A Biography of Judge Thomas Burke* (Seattle: University of Washington Press, 1961), p. 402.
6. Dun and Bradstreet, *Seattle,* p. 24.
7. Oscar O. Winther, *The Great Northwest: A History* (New York: Knopf, 1947), p. 336.
8. William Short, *History of Activities of Seattle Labor Movement and Conspiracy of Employers to Destroy It and Attempted Suppression of Labor's Daily Newspaper, the Seattle Union Record* (Seattle, Wash.: Union Record Publishing Co., 1919), pp. 1-2.
9. Bridges Papers, letter of James A. Duncan to Robert Bridges, April 21, 1919.
10. Transcript of *People* v. *Lloyd,* p. 631.
11. *Ibid.,* pp. 460, 556, 620-25.
12. *Ibid.,* p. 621.

13. *Ibid.,* p. 460.

14. The position of Gompers on the immediate postwar labor situation is ably summarized by Lewis L. Lorwin, *Labor and Internationalism* (New York: Macmillan for the Institute of Economics of the Brookings Institution, 1929), p. 258.

15. *The Rebel Worker* (March 1, 1919), p. 1.

16. Transcript of *People* v. *Lloyd,* p. 657; interview with James A. Duncan, Dec. 30, 1958; Anna Louise Strong, *I Change Worlds* (New York: Holt, 1935), p. 73.

17. See the statement of Ed Levi in the Seattle *Union Record,* Feb. 4, 1919, quoted in transcript of *People* v. *Lloyd,* p. 571.

18. PIE, report of Agent 106, Aug. 4, 1919.

19. Papers on the Seattle General Strike (MSS in University of Washington Library, Seattle), interview of Charles Doyle by Margaret Aller, Jan. 7, 1947.

20. PIE, report of Agent 106, June 11, 1919.

21. *Ibid.,* June 24, 25, 27, 30, July 13, 14, Oct. 8, 1919.

22. *Ibid.,* July 13, Sept. 30, Dec. 25, 1919.

23. *West Coast Metal Trades Worker,* I (Feb. 21, 1920), 1.

24. PIE, report of Agent 106, March 7, 1920.

25. Nicolai Lenin, *The Soviets at Work,* with foreword and paragraph headings by Anna Louise Strong (Seattle, Wash.: Seattle Union Record Publishing Co., n.d.).

26. Strong, *I Change Worlds,* p. 67.

27. PIE, report of Agent 106, Aug. 18, 1919.

28. *Ibid.,* May 18, 1919.

29. Kinnear Papers, report of Agent 317.

30. For an excellent account of industrial-union agitation within the AFL, see James O. Morris, *Conflict Within the AFL: A Study of Craft Versus Industrial Unionism, 1901-1938* (Ithaca, N.Y.: Cornell University, 1958), pp. 16-17.

31. PIE, report of Agent 17, Aug. 14, 1919.

32. Philip Taft, *The A.F. of L. in the Time of Gompers* (New York: Harper & Bros., 1957), pp. 452-53.

33. PIE, reports of Agent 106, Aug. 20, 21, 1919. See *The Rebel Worker* (May 7, 1919), p. 7, for the IWW view of the industrial-union referendum at the Bellingham convention.

34. PIE, reports of Agent 106, July 19, Aug. 16, 1919.

35. *Ibid.,* May 9, 14-16, 21, 27, Aug. 15, 1919.

36. *Ibid.,* and attached semiannual report of Boilermakers' Local 104, Aug. 1, 1919.

37. *Ibid.,* May 6, 31, 1919.

38. *Ibid.,* Jan. 30, 1920. Bridges was, of course, a middle-class supporter of organized labor. See the tributes of organized labor on his retirement from the Seattle Port Commission: Bridges Papers, letter from J. A. Madison, secretary-treasurer, Pacific Coast District of the

ILA, April 25, 1917; letter from C. Lancaster, secretary, Local 38-12, ILA, April 28, 1917; letter from J. M. Wilson, secretary, United Dockworkers, April 30, 1917.

39. Arthur Gleason, *Workers' Education* (rev. ed.; New York: Bureau of Industrial Research, 1921), p. 37.

40. PIE, reports of Agent 106, Jan. 14, Feb. 11, 1920.

41. *Ibid.*, March 7, 1920.

42. *Ibid.*, Aug. 1, 1919. For details on the British Triple Alliance, see: G. D. H. Cole, *A Short History of the British Working Class Movement 1789-1947* (London: George Allen and Unwin, 1948), p. 350.

43. PIE, reports of Agent 106, Feb. 15, 17, March 20, 21, 1920.

44. *Ibid.*, July 26, 1919.

45. *Ibid.*, Nov. 27, Dec. 5, 25, 1919, Jan. 8, 1920.

46. *Ibid.*, July 22, 1919.

47. *Ibid.*, June 10, 1919. This is another indication of how little the men of the Seattle labor movement knew of Russia and the Bolshevik Revolution. The absence of legal facilities for the consumption of liquor was, however, a factor in the growth of Seattle labor's militancy, as this report indicates: "12. The abolishing of the saloon in this locality has entered into the strike situation. The saloon by many persons has been regarded as the poor man's club. With many saloons in existence, the workmen who did not care to remain at home scattered of an evening and distributed themselves among the many saloons, and because they were scattered it was harder to agitate. Now of an evening they drift in large numbers to the Labor Temple where it is easy for a few soap box orators to collect and harangue a mob." (W. G. Wiley, Commandant's Office, 13th Naval District, Jan. 22, 1919, file 18252-2, General Records of the Industrial Relations Division, United States Shipping Board, National Archives, Record Group 32.) Those in the local labor movement concerned with prohibition simply read into a distant event about which they knew little, factors from their own situation.

48. PIE, report of Agent 106, April 30, 1920.

49. *Ibid.*, Dec. 9, 1919.

50. *Ibid.*, May 20, 1919.

51. *Ibid.*, May 5, 1919; report of Agent 17, July 27, 1919.

52. Jacob Margolis, "The Orthodox Wobbly and the Borer from Within," *One Big Union*, I (October, 1919), 27.

53. PIE, report of Agent 106, July 17, 1919. Also see his reports for July 5, Oct. 26, Nov. 6, 1919.

54. *Ibid.*, Aug. 22, 1919.

55. PIE, report of Agent 17, July 27, 1919.

56. For widely varying labor-spy reports (some of which have minutes of IWW meetings attached), see *ibid.*, June 1, 20, 28, 29, July 15, Aug. 16, 23, 28, 29, Oct. 22, 24, 1919.

57. PIE, report of Agent 106, June 1, 1919; reports of Agent 17, Jan. 29, June 10, 1920.

58. PIE, reports of Agent 106, May 31, Aug. 24, 1919, Jan. 9, Feb. 19, 1920.

59. *Ibid.*, March 31, 1920.

60. Taft, *The A. F. of L. in the Time of Gompers,* pp. 452-53.

61. PIE, report of Agent 17, July 7, 1919.

62. PIE, reports of Agent 106, May 16, 21, 1919.

63. *Ibid.*, May 30, June 19, 25, 1919.

64. *Ibid.*, June 19, 1919.

65. Robert Michels, *Political Parties: A Sociological Study of the Oligarchical Tendencies of Modern Democracy* (New York: Collier Books, 1962), p. 6.

66. PIE, reports of Agent 17, Jan. 15, 30, Feb. 6, 11, 1920.

67. PIE, reports of Agent 106, May 29, 1919, Jan. 28, 1920; interview with Frank Turco, Aug. 5, 1959.

68. PIE, report of Agent 106, May 17, 1919.

69. *Ibid.*, May 29, 1919.

70. See articles treating Turco as a beloved local character: Seattle *Post-Intelligencer,* June 18, 1961, Pictorial Review, p. 5, and Seattle *Times,* Feb. 5, 1959, p. 29.

71. Transcript of *People* v. *Lloyd,* pp. 663, 691.

72. James Stevens, "Liberals in Seattle," *Plain Talk,* I (1930), 605.

73. Seattle *Star,* Feb. 13, 1919, p. 1.

74. Daniel Bell, "The Capitalism of the Proletariat: A Theory of American Trade-Unionism," *The End of Ideology* (rev. ed.; New York: Collier Books, 1961), pp. 211-18.

75. Stevens, "Liberals in Seattle," pp. 604-5. James A. Duncan emphasized this point in an interview with the author, Dec. 30, 1958.

76. PIE, report of Agent 106, Dec. 10, 1919.

77. Letter from Harry E. B. Ault to the author, Oct. 9, 1959.

78. Taft, *The A. F. of L. in the Time of Gompers,* pp. 455-57.

79. Transcript of *People* v. *Lloyd,* p. 619.

80. Interview with James A. Duncan, June 7, 1960, and transcript of *People* v. *Lloyd,* pp. 619-20.

81. PIE, report of Agent 106, Feb. 21, 1920.

82. Transcript of *People* v. *Lloyd,* pp. 620, 656-57.

83. *Ibid.*, pp. 656-57.

84. *Ibid.*, pp. 535-36, 659-60.

85. Letter from Harry E. B. Ault to the author, Oct. 9, 1959.

86. Kinnear Papers, undated and untitled address (probably 1920-21).

87. Seattle *Post-Intelligencer,* obituary for Harry E. B. Ault, Jan. 6, 1961, p. 34.

88. PIE, report of Agent 106, March 7, 1920.

89. Strong, *I Change Worlds,* pp. 25, 27, 32, 36-37, 39, 45, 48-49, 51, 54-55, 59, 62; and Morgan, *Skid Road,* pp. 208-9.

90. Interview with James A. Duncan, Dec. 30, 1958.

CHAPTER III

1. Seattle *Union Record,* Jan. 10, 1919, p. 1.

2. Paul M. Zeis, *American Shipping Policy* (Princeton, N.J.: Princeton University Press, 1938), pp. 81-83.

3. Alexander M. Bing, *Wartime Strikes and Their Adjustment* (New York: E. P. Dutton, 1921), p. 20.

4. Zeis, *American Shipping Policy,* p. 12.

5. *Report of Director General Charles Piez to the Board of Trustees of the United States Shipping Board Emergency Fleet Corporation— (Philadelphia) April 30, 1919* (Washington, D.C.: Government Printing Office, 1919), p. 8.

6. Zeis, *American Shipping Policy,* pp. 95-114. Zeis's account is a scathing attack on the inefficiency of the Board. He views the shipbuilding program as a gigantic raid on the Treasury by rapacious private interests.

7. For Piez's account of the struggles, see *Report of Director General . . . 1919,* p. 7.

8. United States Shipping Board, Emergency Fleet Corporation, *Report of the President . . . to the Board of Trustees* (Washington, D.C.: Government Printing Office, 1919), p. 7.

9. *Report of Director General . . . 1919,* p. 6.

10. See Zeis's *American Shipping Policy,* pp. 87-94, for the controversy over government ownership versus private ownership.

11. Willard E. Hotchkiss and Henry R. Seager, *History of the Shipbuilding Labor Adjustment Board 1917-1919* (Bulletin of the United States Bureau of Labor Statistics No. 283 [Washington, D.C.: Government Printing Office, 1921]), p. 15.

12. Seattle *Times,* Jan. 21, 1919, p. 1; *Business Chronicle,* I (Jan. 4, 1919), 69. The following were the shipyards in Seattle at the end of the war: metal yards—Skinner and Eddy, Ames Shipbuilding and Dry Dock Company, J. F. Duthrie and Company, Seattle Construction and Dry Dock Company, Seattle North Pacific Shipbuilding Company; wood yards—Patterson-MacDonald Shipbuilding Company, Meacham-Babcock Shipbuilding Company, Puget Sound Bridge and Dredging Company, Nilson & Keley Shipbuilding Company, Elliott Bay Shipbuilding Company, Allen Shipbuilding Company, Anderson Shipbuilding Company, Price Shipbuilding Company, Madison Shipbuilding Company, Alaska Pacific Construction Company, Ballard Shipbuilding Company, McAtee Shipbuilding Corporation.

13. *Report of Director General . . . 1919,* Exhibit 4, Part 3.

14. Seattle *Post-Intelligencer*, Jan. 1, 1919, p. 13.
15. *Report of Director General . . . 1919*, Exhibit 4, Part 4.
16. Anna Louise Strong, *The Seattle General Strike* (Seattle, Wash.: Union Record Publishing Co., n.d.), p. 80.
17. *Business Chronicle*, VI (Jan. 4, 1919), 69.
18. Transcript of *People* v. *Lloyd*, p. 621.
19. *Ibid.*, and Strong, *The Seattle General Strike*, p. 1.
20. *West Coast Metal Trades Worker*, I (Feb. 21, 1920), 1.
21. W. H. Crook, *The General Strike* (Chapel Hill: University of North Carolina Press, 1931), p. 529.
22. F. T. Underwood to J. S. Holl, March 6, 1919, file 18252-1, General Records of the Industrial Relations Division, United States Shipping Board, National Archives, Record Group 32. Hereafter records in the National Archives are indicated by the symbol NA, followed by the record group (RG) number.
23. As the strikers' official history claimed; see Strong, *The Seattle General Strike*, p. 8. Prior to the Shipbuilding Labor Adjustment Board's assumption of jurisdiction over questions of wage, hours, and working conditions, Seattle labor and management did sign a closed-shop agreement. Hotchkiss and Seager, *History of the Shipbuilding Labor Adjustment Board*, p. 17.
24. Interview with James A. Duncan, Dec. 30, 1958.
25. Transcript of *People* v. *Lloyd*, pp. 459, 537.
26. Dorothy O. Johansen and Charles M. Gates, *Empire of the Columbia* (New York: Harper and Bros., 1957), p. 548.
27. William Short, *History of Activities of Seattle Labor Movement and Conspiracy of Employers to Destroy It and Attempted Suppression of Labor's Daily Newspaper, the Seattle Union Record* (Seattle, Wash.: Union Record Publishing Co., 1919), pp. 1-2. After the Centralia incident, the Seattle *Union Record* was suppressed. Short, in arguing against shutdown of the newspaper, used the Wobblies in the shipyard as an argument indicating the difficult position of the Seattle AFL—pressed on one side by the IWW and conspired against on the other side by local employers.
28. Anna Louise Strong, *I Change Worlds* (New York: Holt, 1935), p. 65.
29. *Report of the Director General . . . 1919*, p. 17.
30. Hotchkiss and Seager, *History of the Shipbuilding Labor Adjustment Board*, p. 16.
31. *Ibid.*, p. 19.
32. George Soule, *Prosperity Decade* (New York: Rinehart, 1947), p. 31. For details on the Hog Island yards—reputed to be the largest in the world at that time—see *Hearings on United States Shipping Board Emergency Fleet Corporation*, U.S. Senate Committee on Commerce, 65th Cong., 3d sess. (Washington, D.C.), part 8.
33. Seattle *Union Record*, Feb. 4, 1919, p. 6.

34. Franklin Delano Roosevelt, Assistant Secretary of the Navy and at that time Acting Secretary of the Navy, signed the agreement for his department.

35. But only informally, after a meeting of Gompers and Macy with Joseph Tumulty, representing President Wilson. Formal recognition had to wait until a new agreement was signed Dec. 8, 1917.

36. Quoted in Hotchkiss and Seager, *History of the Shipbuilding Labor Adjustment Board,* p. 21.

37. Strong, *The Seattle General Strike,* p. 11.

38. Bing, *Wartime Strikes and Their Adjustment,* p. 27.

39. Seattle *Post-Intelligencer,* Jan. 3, 1919, p. 7.

40. Conference between Charles A. Piez, Charles M. Schwab, and shipyard employees, held at New Washington Hotel, Seattle, Washington, July 18, 1919, transcripts of hearings, October, 1917, March and December, 1918, Records of the Shipbuilding Labor Adjustment Board, United States Shipping Board, NA, RG 32.

41. C. N. Piez to E. N. Hurley, Feb. 26, 1919, file 18252-1, General Records of the Industrial Relations Division, United States Shipping Board, NA, RG 32.

42. Undecipherable signature (Division of Steel Ship Construction, United States Shipping Board, Emergency Fleet Corporation, Seattle, Washington) to J. F. Blain, Jan. 30, 1919, file 18252-2, General Records of the Industrial Relations Division, United States Shipping Board, NA, RG 32. According to the Seattle official of USSB: "At the time the Northwest Shipbuilders Association prepared a joint wire to Mr. Piez advising him officially of the strike and the compromise offered the strikers, it was my impression that they were not in a position to make a compromise offer which they had done. This resulted in their request that I wire through you requesting Piez to withdraw that letter which, in my opinion, was the lever used by the labor unions against the builders for more money."

43. Piez to Hurley, Feb. 26, 1919, file 18252-1, NA, RG 32.

44. Strong, *The Seattle General Strike,* p. 9.

45. *Ibid.*

46. Seattle *Star,* Jan. 20, 1919, p. 1.

47. Seattle *Union Record,* Dec. 11, 1918, p. 3.

48. Strong, *The Seattle General Strike,* p. 10. This account released after the strike was over indicated that of seventeen unions affiliated with the Metal Trades Council at that time, ten gained majorities required by their constitutions and six gained majorities but not sufficient to satisfy constitutional requirements. Only one local voted no.

49. PIE, report of Agent 106, June 3, 1919.

50. Strong, *The Seattle General Strike,* p. 3.

51. Seattle *Post-Intelligencer,* Jan. 4, 1919, p. 2.

52. Seattle *Union Record,* Jan. 16, 1919, p. 3.

53. Seattle *Times,* Jan. 21, 1919, p. 1.

54. *Ibid.,* Jan. 22, 1919, p. 1.
55. Seattle *Post-Intelligencer,* Jan. 17, 1919, p. 1.
56. *Ibid.*
57. *Ibid.*
58. Seattle *Star,* Jan. 22, 1919, p. 1.
59. Bing, *Wartime Strikes and Their Adjustment,* p. 26.
60. Strong, *I Change Worlds,* pp. 74-75. EFC officials in Seattle later became acutely conscious of their lack of telegraphic security. One official in a telegram to Piez commented: "Third that you remember that telegrams sent to Seattle pass through the Labor Temple there before delivery." (Marshall to Piez, Feb. 22, 1919, file 18252-2, General Records of the Industrial Relations Division, United States Shipping Board, NA, RG 32.) Management and government had competition in the spying business!
61. Interview with Harry E. B. Ault, Jan. 10, 1959. Ault believed his view to be correct because of his association with David E. Skinner. According to Ault, Skinner had advanced the *Union Record,* a newspaper owned by organized labor, sizeable sums to keep it in operation. Ault believed that if Skinner, the capitalist, could keep a union newspaper going for his own reasons, he could have manipulated the union movement to strike at the time he wished, again for his own reasons. His mistake was to assume that Skinner had the support of the other shipyard management for this maneuver. If the opinion of the other yard owners of Skinner's labor tactics is accurate, it is possible that Skinner deliberately cultivated the impression that the other shipbuilders supported his efforts. According to Henry Marshall, Skinner had already misrepresented their positions on the compromise offer to the skilled men of 86½ cents per hour. See note 65, below.
62. *Report of Director General . . . 1919,* pp. 39-42, 121.
63. Short, *History of Activities of Seattle Labor Movement . . . ,* p. 4.
64. Strong, *The Seattle General Strike,* pp. 4-6.
65. Marshall to Piez, Feb. 22, 1919, file 18252-2, NA, RG 32.
66. *Ibid.*
67. C. W. Wiley to W. H. Todd, Feb. 11, 1919, file 18252-2, General Records of the Industrial Relations Division, United States Shipping Board, NA, RG 32.
68. Piez to Hurley, Feb. 26, 1919, file 18252-1, NA, RG 32.
69. Report of Special Agent J. H., Feb. 5, 1919, file 18252-1, General Records of the Industrial Relations Division, United States Shipping Board, NA, RG 32.
70. Interview with James A. Duncan, Dec. 30, 1958. He based his views on two points: (1) management's strenuous efforts to discredit the strike after its termination, and (2) Skinner's telegram to Piez of January 26 stating that the workers were forced to strike.
71. *Business Chronicle,* VI (Jan. 4, 1919), 2.

72. Seattle *Times,* Jan. 28, 1919, p. 1.
73. The IWW took the same position after the general strike when an open-shop drive by an employers' organization, Associated Industries, did take place. PIE, reports of Agent 106, Oct. 26, Nov. 6, 1919.
74. Seattle *Post-Intelligencer,* Jan. 18, 1919, p. 1.
75. *Ibid.*
76. *Ibid.*
77. See, for example, *Argus,* XXVI (Jan. 25, 1919), 1.
78. Seattle *Star,* Jan. 20, 1919, p. 1. Signed by A. E. Miller, G. F. Soultzer, J. Duschak, J. Von Carnop, E. Rowan, and J. N. Bellinger.
79. Seattle *Times,* Jan. 20, 1919, p. 1.
80. Seattle *Star,* Jan. 20, 1919, p. 1.
81. Seattle *Union Record,* Jan. 21, 1919, p. 1.
82. Seattle *Times,* Jan. 21, 1919, p. 1.
83. Bing, *Wartime Strikes and Their Adjustment,* p. 24.
84. Seattle *Post-Intelligencer,* Jan. 22, 1919, p. 1.
85. Seattle *Union Record,* Jan. 21, 1919, p. 1.
86. Seattle *Post-Intelligencer,* Jan. 22, 1919, p. 1.
87. *Ibid.*
88. Seattle *Times,* Jan. 22, 1919, p. 1.
89. Seattle *Post-Intelligencer,* Jan. 22, 1919, p. 1.
90. Seattle *Times,* Jan. 23, 1919, p. 1.
91. Transcript of *People* v. *Lloyd,* pp. 552-54.
92. Seattle *Post-Intelligencer,* Jan. 23, 1919, p. 7.
93. *Daily Bulletin,* Jan. 23, 1919, p. 7.
94. Seattle *Post-Intelligencer,* Jan. 24, 1919, p. 3.
95. Seattle *Times,* Jan. 24, 1919, p. 1.
96. *Ibid.*
97. Seattle *Union Record,* Jan. 25, 1919, p. 1.
98. Crook, *The General Strike,* p. 531.
99. Strong, *I Change Worlds,* p. 72.
100. Most of these letters were too well written to be acccpted un-critically as authentic communications from strikers. Many of them could have been written only by educated men. For example, here are some excerpts from a letter labeled "Striker speaks his mind" in the Seattle *Post-Intelligencer,* Jan. 30, 1919, p. 5:
"45,000 men ordered out on a strike in the dead of winter against their wills by a few Bolshevik and IWW Junkers bespeaks a specific instance of actual autocracy in America. . . . The minority who favored the strike almost invariably did so by reason of being in friendly sympathy with the Bolshevists and the IWW . . . the order for a strike was actuated by a hope of plunging this country into a revolution."
101. Seattle *Star,* Jan. 27, 1919, p. 1.
102. Seattle *Union Record,* Jan. 27, 1919, p. 1.
103. Seattle *Post-Intelligencer,* Jan. 26, 1919, p. 1.
104. Seattle *Union Record,* Jan. 27, 1919, p. 1.

105. Seattle *Post-Intelligencer,* Jan. 27, 1919, p. 1.
106. *Ibid.*
107. See, for example, Ole Hanson, *Americanism versus Bolshevism* (Garden City, N.Y.: Doubleday, Page, 1920), p. 39.

The Seattle metal trades' effort to gain support from unions working in other shipyards was no secret to Atlantic and Gulf Port shipyard managements or the Emergency Fleet Corporation. The Pinkertons had procured a copy of the telegrams the Seattle Metal Trades Council had sent. A copy is in EFC files in S. L. Stiles, Superintendent, Pinkerton National Detective Agency, to P. O. Knight, Vice President, American International Shipbuilding, Jan. 30, 1919, file 18252-2, General Records of the Industrial Relations Division, United States Shipping Board, NA, RG 32.

108. Seattle *Times,* Jan. 28, 1919, p. 1.
109. Seattle *Star,* Jan. 22, 1919, p. 1.
110. Seattle *Post-Intelligencer,* Jan. 23, 1919, p. 1.

CHAPTER IV

1. Mooney remained in prison until 1939 when he was pardoned by Governor Cuthbert Olson. Robert Burke, *Olson's New Deal for California* (Berkeley and Los Angeles: University of California Press, 1953), pp. 48-58.

2. Lewis Lorwin, *American Federation of Labor: History, Policies and Prospects* (Washington, D.C.: Brookings, 1933), p. 191.

3. The other two were Oakland and Chicago.

4. Seattle *Post-Intelligencer,* Jan. 1, 1919, p. 22. The remaining twenty were: C. E. Kingery, auto drivers; A. W. Dolan, blacksmiths; James Lansbury, boilermakers; Phil Greenfield, butchers; Lee A. Vaughan, Carpenters' District Council; J. F. Cotton, Carpenters' Local 1184; John Potts, Carpenters' Local 1335; Frank McCarthey, Carpenters' Local 1271; W. F. DeLaney, Electrical Workers' Local 46; William Goldthorpe, laundry workers; Paul C. Bickel, machinists; B. F. Gellerman, iron moulders; James King, painters; John Young, pipe fitters; Andy Raynor, ship laborers; J. C. Sandal, street railway employees; A. G. Dentler, structural iron workers; Forrest L. Hudson, structural iron shopmen; George O. Johnson, foundry workers; J. C. Bower, municipal employees.

5. Interview with Harry E. B. Ault, Jan. 10, 1959.

6. Seattle *Star,* Jan. 15, 1919, p. 1. Turco attempted to place other issues on the conference agenda which were not germane to the task of freeing Mooney. He was agitating for conference endorsement of Soldiers', Sailors' and Workingmen's Councils, the unrestricted issue of passports, and a popular referendum on the treaty drawn up at the Paris Peace Conference.

7. Seattle *Star,* Jan. 23, 1919, p. 1. According to the late Dr. Theresa Schmid McMahon, Professor Emeritus of Economics at the University of Washington who frequently observed the Wednesday night meetings, it was not unusual to have Wobblies in the galleries of the AFL hall during meetings. A large percentage of the Wobblies in the city were homeless. One of the few buildings which was open to them and heated was the Labor Temple. Interview with Dr. McMahon, Aug. 5, 1959.

8. Seattle *Times,* Jan. 23, 1919, p. 1.

9. Seattle *Star,* Jan. 23, 1919, p. 1.

10. Transcript of *People* v. *Lloyd,* p. 625.

11. Seattle *Union Record,* Jan. 24, 1919, p. 1.

12. Seattle *Times,* Jan. 28, 1919, p. 1.

13. *Daily Bulletin,* Jan. 25, 1919, p. 1.

14. Or as the international lawyer would put it, *rebus sic stantibus.*

15. Seattle *Times,* Jan. 27, 1919, p. 1; *ibid.,* Jan. 28, 1919, p. 1.

16. Transcript of *People* v. *Lloyd,* p. 626.

17. Seattle *Union Record,* Jan. 28, 1919, p. 1. The members of the *ad hoc* committee appointed by the Central Labor Council were: Leon Green, electricians; Phil Pearl, barbers; O. F. Dozier, millmen; Alice Lord, waitresses; and Lee G. Holson, longshoremen.

18. *Ibid.*

19. The following statement appears on the masthead of the *Business Chronicle*:

The Fearless Editorial Policy
of an Untrammeled Journal
Edited by its Owner, is pledged to maintenance of the existing order of society and preservation of "open shop" in industry. Our editorial policy personifies Conservatism as opposed to Radicalism that would pull down and destroy—whether under the stolen name of Democracy, hides behind the skirts of State Socialism, or appears in the guise of a highly Centralized as opposed to a Representative form of Federal Government.

20. Note from Harry E. B. Ault to the author, Oct. 6, 1959.

21. The original can be found in *Business Chronicle,* VI (Jan. 25, 1919), 1. See also the same scheme proposed in an earlier editorial, *Business Chronicle,* VI (Jan. 4, 1919), 2.

22. This was not the only time that Selvin's attempt to address the people of Seattle via the daily newspapers brought him into direct conflict with the union movement. He bought space in the *Post-Intelligencer* in November, 1919, but so vicious was his message that the issue containing it was banned from the mails by the Post Office Department. For labor's reaction to the ad, see PIE, reports of Agent 106, Nov. 23, Dec. 4, 1919.

23. Seattle *Post-Intelligencer,* Jan. 29, 1919, p. 1. The exact voting figures are as follows:

Union	For	Against
Electrical Workers' Local 77	74	64
Millmen Local 338	128	91
Leather Workers' Local 40	21	11
Hotel Maids' Local 528	25	5
Jewelry Workers	94	17

24. Figures taken from the Seattle *Times,* Jan. 29, 1919, p. 1.
25. *Ibid.*
26. Only 89 of the 110 locals affiliated with the Central Labor Council were eligible. The 21 locals affiliated with the Metal Trades Council at this time (four more since the Metal Trades shipyard-strike vote was taken) did not vote in the general-strike referendum.
27. Seattle *Post-Intelligencer,* Jan. 30, 1919, p. 1. As reported there, the twenty-four unions voting to strike were: auto painters, barbers, blacksmiths, boilermakers, building laborers, carpenters, cigarmakers, cooks and assistants, foundry workers, garment workers, hotel maids, hod carriers, housebuilders, housepainters, jewelry workers, laundry workers, longshoremen, milk-wagon drivers, newsboys, plumbers, riggers, structural-iron workers, tailors, and teamsters and auto truck drivers.
28. *Ibid.*
29. *Ibid.*
30. For an example of the IWW's writings on the general strike, see the leaflet distributed during the shipyard strike by Shipbuilders' Industrial Union No. 325, quoted in *Hearings on Investigation of Brewing and Liquor Interests and German and Bolshevik Propaganda,* U.S. Senate Subcommittee of the Judiciary, 66th Cong., 1st sess., S. Doc. 62, Vol. III, p. 1049.

It would be a major mistake to attribute to working-class anarcho-syndicalist movements the conception of the general strike held by Georges Sorel and other so-called theorists of anarcho-syndicalism. While the French anarcho-syndicalist movement was aware of Sorel's writings, it was not guided by them. To real working-class anarcho-syndicalists, Sorel was a middle-class intellectual, and even friendly such specimens were not to be trusted. The IWW was even less influenced by the middle-class rationalizers of anarcho-syndicalism, as any reader of Wobbly journals could attest.
31. Seattle *Times,* Jan. 30, 1919.
32. *Ibid.*
33. *Argus,* XXVI (Feb. 1, 1919), 2.
34. Seattle *Post-Intelligencer,* Jan. 30, 1919, p. 1.
35. *Ibid.,* p. 2.
36. Piez to O. S. Larson, Jan. 31, 1919, file 18252-2, General Records of the Industrial Relations Division, United States Shipping Board, NA, RG 32.
37. Seattle *Times,* Jan. 30, 1919, p. 1.
38. Seattle *Union Record,* Jan. 31, 1919, p. 3.

39. Seattle *Times*, Jan. 31, 1919, p. 1.
40. Seattle *Post-Intelligencer*, Feb. 2, 1919, p. 1.
41. *Ibid.*
42. Seattle *Star*, Feb. 3, 1919, p. 9; Seattle *Post-Intelligencer*, Feb. 3, 1919, p. 16; Tacoma *News Tribune*, Feb. 3, 1919, p. 4.
43. It is likely that Piez was influenced by Edwin Selvin's view of the nature of the struggle in Seattle. A copy of Selvin's editorial, "Spectacle of a City Committing Suicide," is in the EFC files, the only Seattle newspaper material in the file. The content of Piez's second ad and Selvin's editorial are similar. See file 18252-2, General Records of the Industrial Relations Division, United States Shipping Board, NA, RG 32.
44. Seattle *Star*, Feb. 4, 1919, p. 9; Seattle *Post-Intelligencer*, Feb. 4, 1919, p. 7.
45. Seattle *Star*, Feb. 4, 1919, p. 6.

CHAPTER V

1. Seattle *Times*, Jan. 30, 1919, p. 1.
2. Murray Morgan, *Skid Road* (New York: Viking, 1951), p. 5.
3. Seattle *Post-Intelligencer*, Feb. 1, 1919, p. 7. Selvin's advertisement was published the same day as an editorial in his *Business Chronicle*, VI (Feb. 1, 1919), 111.
4. Seattle *Times*, Feb. 2, 1919, p. 4. In the fall of 1917 the Macy Board set $5.50 per day as the wage scale for skilled men in the shipyards of the Puget Sound District. See chapter 3, "The Shipyard Strike."
5. Seattle *Union Record*, Feb. 3, 1919, reprinted as Defendants' Exhibit 5, transcript of *People* v. *Lloyd*, pp. 636-37.
6. Seattle *Post-Intelligencer*, Feb. 1, 1919, p. 1.
7. Morgan, *Skid Road*, pp. 169-98.
8. Transcript of *People* v. *Lloyd*, p. 654.
9. Vernon H. Jensen, *Lumber and Labor* (New York: Farrar & Rinehart, 1945), p. 128.
10. Transcript of *People* v. *Lloyd*, pp. 653-54.
11. Seattle *Post-Intelligencer*, Feb. 1, 1919, p. 1.
12. *Ibid.*, Feb. 3, 1919, p. 1; Anna Louise Strong, *The Seattle General Strike* (Seattle, Wash.: Union Record Publishing Co., n.d.), p. 13.
13. Seattle *Post-Intelligencer*, Feb. 1, 1919, p. 1.
14. Strong, *The Seattle General Strike*, pp. 13-14.
15. *Ibid.*, p. 16. Before the general strike commenced, nine more locals were seated on the General Strike Committee.
16. Interview with Frank Turco, Aug. 5, 1919. Turco stated that he presided over most of the sessions of the General Strike Committee.
17. Analogous events in Tacoma have been omitted from the text for two reasons: (1) Seattle labor clearly led in the demand for a general strike in the Puget Sound area, and (2) the general strike was not com-

plete in Tacoma. In fact, it fared badly. A referendum vote of unionists not already involved in the shipyard strike was taken to determine whether Tacoma unions should join Seattle in calling a general strike. It resulted in 4,160 unionists voting for, and 1,605 unionists voting against holding a general strike in Tacoma. However, the Tacoma *News Tribune* claimed that more than half of the men voting were members of the remaining unions affiliated with the Metal Trades Council which were not directly involved in the shipyard strike but who came out strongly in support of their striking brothers. As a result of the referendum and the decision of the metal-trades unions already on strike in the shipyards, only sixteen unions committed themselves in favor of a general strike. Of the remaining thirty-four unions affiliated with the Central Labor Council (of a total of fifty), twenty-one were opposed to a general strike, four refused to put the question to a vote of their membership, and the remaining nine took no action at all. Nevertheless, under the leadership of A. L. Dickson, its secretary-treasurer, the Central Labor Council by a vote of sixty-five to twenty-seven decided, on February 5, to authorize a general strike.

The response was poor. Only the meat cutters, timber workers, barbers, 5 per cent of the retail clerks, the streetcar men (contrary to expectations), and the unions affiliated with the Metal Trades Council struck. The brewery workers, movie operators, tailors, gas workers, allied printing trades workers, teamsters and chauffeurs, cereal and flour mill workers, boot and shoe workers, longshoremen, smelter workers, and carpenters remained on the job in defiance of the Central Labor Council order. The city of Tacoma was able to function quite normally during the course of the strike. The unions that did strike broke more quickly than their counterparts in Seattle. By February 7, when federal troops were brought into Tacoma, it was reported that the most radical of the labor leaders had fled the city. A full-scale revolt began in labor ranks against Dickson's leadership on February 10. For further details see the Tacoma *News Tribune*, Feb. 3 to Feb. 15, 1919.

18. Strong, *The Seattle General Strike*, p. 17.

19. Seattle *Post-Intelligencer*, Feb. 3, 1919, p. 1.

20. Strong, *The Seattle General Strike*, p. 17. Miss Strong states that "in practice, repeal [of a decision of the Executive Committee of 15] was not found necessary." While this is technically correct, it must be pointed out that the General Strike Committee did vote down the executive committee's *recommendation* to end the strike on Saturday, February 8.

21. Seattle *Post-Intelligencer*, Feb. 4, 1919, p. 1. Members were: B. F. Nauman, T. Egan, W. L. Hingsley, E. Cram, L. Berndal, D. Thompson, D. S. Turner, Miss May Montgomery, Miss Gladys Small, J. A. Stevenson, A. G. Heller, W. Coffey, E. B. Tryon, L. Glaser, and B. F. Dwyer. Coffey and Heller were the radicals.

22. Strong, *The Seattle General Strike*, p. 18.

23. Seattle *Post-Intelligencer*, Feb. 4, 1919, p. 1.

24. Seattle *Union Record*, Feb. 3, 1919, p. 1; Seattle *Post-Intelligencer*, Feb. 3, 1919, p. 1.

25. Seattle *Union Record*, Feb. 3, 1919, p. 1.

26. *Ibid.*, Feb. 3, 1919, reproduced as Defendants' Exhibit 4, Transcript of *People* v. *Lloyd*, p. 636.

27. For examples of this literature see "Extract From Leaflet Headed 'Strikers' (Seattle Washington, January 20, 1919)," and George Harrison, "The Red Dawn, and Strike Bulletin of Shipbuilders' Industrial Union (IWW), No. 325, January 25, 1919," quoted in *Hearings on Brewing and Liquor Interests and German and Bolshevik Propaganda*, U.S. Senate Subcommittee of the Judiciary, 66th Cong., 1st sess., S. Doc. 62, Vol. III, pp. 1044, 1049, 1074.

28. For a photocopy of the original, see State's Exhibit 40, transcript of *People* v. *Lloyd*, p. 467. Paraphrased and inaccurate versions can be found in *Business Chronicle*, VI (Feb. 8, 1919), 121, and Edgar Lloyd Hampton " 'They Made Us Strike': The Story of the Attempted Revolution in Seattle," *Saturday Evening Post* (April 4, 1919), p. 144. Harvey O'Connor claims authorship of "Russia Did It," in *Revolution in Seattle* (New York: Monthly Review Press, 1964), p. 143.

29. Seattle *Star*, Feb. 3, 1919, p. 1.

30. Strong, *The Seattle General Strike*, p. 28.

31. Seattle *Star*, Feb. 3, 1919, p. 1.

32. Strong, *The Seattle General Strike*, p. 18, and Seattle *Post-Intelligencer*, Feb. 4, 1919, p. 1.

33. Transcript of *People* v. *Lloyd*, p. 501.

34. Seattle *Star*, Feb. 4, 1919, p. 2; Seattle *Post-Intelligencer*, Feb. 4, 1919, p. 1.

35. *Ibid.*; Strong, *The Seattle General Strike*, pp. 19-20.

36. *Ibid.*, p. 19.

37. *Ibid.*

38. Transcript of *People* v. *Lloyd*, pp. 672, 694-95.

39. Strong, *The Seattle General Strike*, pp. 21-22.

40. Bridges Papers, Tom Egan to Robert Bridges, Feb. 7, 1919.

41. Seattle *Post-Intelligencer*, Feb. 4, 1919, p. 1.

42. Transcript of *People* v. *Lloyd*, p. 487.

43. *Ibid.*, pp. 496-500. Harry J. Wilson, the Minuteman *agent provocateur*, claims that he saw baskets filled with revolvers brought to the headquarters of the War Veterans' Guard. There is no other evidence to corroborate this story. No member of the Guard was reported or arrested for carrying arms.

44. Seattle *Star*, Feb. 4, 1919, p. 1; Seattle *Post-Intelligencer*, Feb. 4, 1919, p. 1.

45. The Seattle *Times* was the only downtown paper which neither attempted to publish during the first days of the strike (February 6-9)

nor condemned the strike as a revolution. It shut down quietly after the issue of February 5, requesting its readers not to inundate the newspaper's telephone switchboard with calls.

46. Seattle *Post-Intelligencer,* Feb. 1, 1919, p. 1.

47. For Duncan's testimony see transcript of *People* v. *Lloyd,* pp. 652-53. In an interview by the author, Dec. 30, 1958, Mr. Duncan discussed in great detail the effort of the four men to establish a time limit for the general strike. In addition, it is mentioned in Strong, *The Seattle General Strike,* p. 22.

48. General Strike Papers, interview of James A. Duncan by Margaret Aller and Ralph Thayer, Dec. 12, 1946.

49. *Ibid.*

50. *Ibid.*

51. Transcript of *People* v. *Lloyd,* p. 706.

52. General Strike Papers, interview of James A. Duncan by Margaret Aller and Ralph Thayer, Dec. 12, 1946.

53. Interview of Frank Turco by the author, Aug. 5, 1959. Forty years after the event, Turco stated that he did not accuse Swain of "selling out." His objections, he said, were not to a limit on the strike, but rather to Swain's "poor leadership" and "mistakes" in strike tactics. As he recalled, he also objected to Swain's service on a wartime draft board when he was not an American citizen.

54. Seattle *Post-Intelligencer,* Feb. 5, 1919, p. 9.

55. Seattle *Star,* Feb. 4, 1919, p. 1. The italicized portions were in bold-face type in the original. The editorial was also republished the next day. An editorial similar in content played a leading role in the British General Strike of 1926. When union printers refused to print an editorial by Thomas Marlowe, editor of the *Daily Mail,* the Baldwin cabinet broke off all relations with the General Council of the Trades Union Congress. See Julian Symons, *The General Strike* (London: Cresset Press, 1957), p. 49.

56. Represented were: The National League for Women's Service, The Seattle Federation of Women's Clubs, The Seattle Chapter of the American Red Cross, the Ministerial Federation, the Seattle Clearing House Association, the Seattle Bar Association, the Auto Club, the College Club, the Elks' Lodge, the Building Owners' and Managers' Association, the Seattle Chamber of Commerce and Commercial Club, the Fire Insurance Exchange, the Grand Army of the Republic, the Service and Ex-service Men's Association, the YMCA, the War Camp Community Service, the Washington Chapter of the American Institute of Architects, the University Commercial Club, the Importer and Exporters Association, the Sales Managers' Association, the Young Men's Business Club, the Transportation Club, the Rotary Club, the 100% Club, the Knights of Columbus, the Manufacturers' Association, the Real Estate Association, the Kiwanis Club, the King County Medical Association, the Retail Meat Dealers' Association, the Seattle Press

Club, the Puget Sound Underwriters' Association, the Brotherhood of the University Baptist Church, the Engineers' Club, and the Alliance Francaise. Seattle *Post-Intelligencer*, Feb. 5, 1919, p. 1.

57. Seattle *Star*, Feb. 10, 1919, p. 2.

58. Reprinted in full in Strong, *The Seattle General Strike*, pp. 4-6, and reprinted in part in Anna Louise Strong, *I Change Worlds* (New York: Henry Holt, 1935), p. 79.

59. Although Ault conceded that the Seattle labor movement was more radical than the parent AFL, he personally was convinced that it had no revolutionary intentions. Interview with Harry Ault, Jan. 10, 1959.

60. Miss Strong, however, claimed that the content of the editorial was approved by the conference committee of the Metal Trades Council. *The Seattle General Strike*, p. 6.

61. Seattle *Post-Intelligencer*, Feb. 5, 1919, p. 2.

62. *Ibid.*, Feb. 4, 1919, p. 11. For additional details, see transcript of *People* v. *Lloyd*, pp. 480-89.

63. Seattle *Post-Intelligencer*, Feb. 5, 1919, p. 2.

64. General Strike Papers, interview of Frank L. Curtis by Margaret Aller, Jan. 13, 1947. Also see Robert K. Murray, *Red Scare: A Study in National Hysteria 1919-1920* (Minneapolis: University of Minnesota Press, 1955), p. 60.

65. Seattle *Times*, Feb. 9, 1919, p. 5.

66. Strong, *The Seattle General Strike*, p. 3; Strong, *I Change Worlds*, p. 72.

67. The italicized portions were in large italicized type in the original.

68. Strong, *The Seattle General Strike*, p. 23.

69. *Ibid.*

70. *Argus,* XXVI (Feb. 15, 1919), 2-3.

71. Seattle *Union Record*, Feb. 5, 1919, reproduced as State's Exhibit 48, transcript of *People* v. *Lloyd*, p. 572.

72. Seattle *Post-Intelligencer*, Feb. 5, 1919, p. 1.

73. Quoted in Seattle *Times*, Jan. 31, 1919, p. 1.

74. Seattle *Star*, Feb. 5, 1919, p. 1. A slightly different version can be found in Ole Hanson, *Americanism versus Bolshevism* (Garden City, N.Y.: Doubleday, Page, 1920), p. 85.

75. PIE, report of Agent 106, May 12, 1919.

76. Strong, *The Seattle General Strike*, pp. 26-27.

77. Seattle *Star*, Feb. 1, 1919, p. 1.

78. *Ibid.*, Feb. 4, 1919, p. 2; Seattle *Union Record*, Feb. 5, 1919, p. 1.

79. "Our men may vote against it but even then conditions may be beyond us. . . ." Papers of James Delmage Ross, 1871-1939 (MSS in University of Washington Library, Seattle), memorandum from J. D. Ross to John L. McCartney, Jan. 31, 1919.

80. For Duncan's analysis of the reasons for Hanson's sense of insecurity over City Light, see transcript of *People* v. *Lloyd*, p. 675.

81. *Town Crier*, XIV (Feb. 15, 1919), 1; and *Business Chronicle*, VI (Jan. 11, 1919), 75.

82. Transcript of *People* v. *Lloyd*, p. 638. Also see pp. 674-75. The substance of the exchange between Duncan and Hanson is also reported in H. Austin Simons, "Guilty: The General Strike," *Liberator*, III (August, 1920), 13; and Strong, *The Seattle General Strike*, p. 32. For Doyle's recollection of the meeting, see General Strike Papers, interview with Charles Doyle by Margaret Aller, Jan. 7, 1947.

83. Transcript of *People* v. *Lloyd*, p. 639.

84. *Ibid.*

85. Strong, *I Change Worlds*, p. 81.

86. Ross Papers, memorandum from Ross to Mooers, Feb. 13, 1919. Also see Seattle *Star*, Feb. 5, 1919, p. 1.

87. For union support of City Light's Skagit Valley hydroelectric project, see PIE, reports of Agent 106, Aug. 31, Sept. 17, 23, 1919.

88. Transcript of *People* v. *Lloyd*, p. 558.

89. Strong, *The Seattle General Strike*, p. 25.

90. Transcript of *People* v. *Lloyd*, p. 559.

91. Strong, *The Seattle General Strike*, p. 26.

92. Hanson's telephone call requesting the dispatch of troops to Seattle was made at 11:00 P.M., February 5. Telegram, Ernest Lister to Department Commander, Western Department, 11:59 P.M., Feb. 5, 1919, Records of U.S. Army Commands, NA, RG 98.

93. Papers of Henry Suzzallo, 1875-1933 (MSS in University of Washington Library, Seattle), "Seattle 1919 Revolutionary Strike," by Vaughn Tanner, as told to Edith M. Suzzallo, Nov. 15, 1940.

In addition to the governor's office, federal officials in Seattle representing the Food Administration Grain Corporation and the Emergency Fleet Corporation requested federal troops to protect government property. The EFC's request was made as early as January 22. Telegram, M. H. Houser to Commander, Western Department, Feb. 6, 1919; telegram, Wooley to Commanding Officer, Western Department, Jan. 22, 1919, Records of U.S. Army Commands, NA, RG 98.

94. Telegram, Lister to Department Commander, Western Department, 4:48 P.M. Feb. 5, 1919, Records of U.S. Army Commands, NA, RG 98.

95. Telegram, Harris to Morrison, Feb. 6, 1919, Records of U.S. Army Commands, NA, RG 98.

96. Telegram, Morrison to Adjutant General, Washington, D.C., Feb. 7, 1919, Records of U.S. Army Commands, NA, RG 98.

97. Telegram, Morrison to Lister, Feb. 6, 1919, Records of U.S. Army Commands, NA, RG 98.

CHAPTER VI

1. Ole Hanson, *Americanism versus Bolshevism* (Garden City, N.Y.: Doubleday, Page, 1920), p. 84.
2. "The Iron Heel," in Philip S. Foner (ed.), *Jack London, American Rebel: A Collection of His Social Writings* (New York: Citadel Press, 1947), p. 163. London also wrote a short story on the theme of the general strike: "Dream of Debs," *International Socialist Review* (January-February, 1909).
3. General Strike Papers, interview by Margaret Aller with Bert Swain, Jan. 7, 1947.
4. Anna Louise Strong, *The Seattle General Strike* (Seattle, Wash.: Union Record Publishing Co., n.d.), p. 55.
5. On rumors, see: *ibid.*, p. 49; Portland *Oregonian*, Feb. 7, 1919, p. 1; Edgar Lloyd Hampton, " 'They Made Us Strike': The Story of the Attempted Revolution in Seattle," *Saturday Evening Post* (April 4, 1919), p. 144; Murray Morgan, *Skid Road* (New York: Viking, 1951), p. 212.
6. New York *Times,* Feb. 8, 1919, p. 1.
7. Strong, *The Seattle General Strike,* p. 28.
8. *Ibid.* The estimate of thirty-five hundred is based on John S. Gambs, *The Decline of the IWW* (New York: Columbia University Press, 1932), pp. 133-35.
9. Transcript of *People* v. *Lloyd,* p. 631.
10. Ross Papers, memorandum, Ross to Ragge, Feb. 7, 1919.
11. Seattle *Post-Intelligencer,* Feb. 6, 1919, p. 1; Seattle *Times,* Feb. 9, 1919, p. 1.
12. Strong, *The Seattle General Strike,* p. 46, and W. H. Crook, *The General Strike* (Chapel Hill: University of North Carolina Press, 1931), p. 535.
13. Report, C. G., 13th Division to Adjutant General of the Army, March 3, 1919, Records of the Adjutant General's Office, NA, RG 94.
14. Strong, *The Seattle General Strike,* p. 50.
15. "Strike That Oiled Its Own Troubled Waters: Seattle Strike," *Literary Digest,* LXI (April 12, 1919), 90.
16. Interview of Frank Turco by the author, Aug. 5, 1959.
17. Strong, *The Seattle General Strike,* pp. 48-49.
18. State's Exhibit 45, transcript of *People* v. *Lloyd,* pp. 564, 630.
19. Strong, *The Seattle General Strike,* pp. 41-42.
20. State's Exhibit 46, transcript of *People* v. *Lloyd,* p. 566.
21. State's Exhibit 47, *ibid.,* p. 568.
22. Report, Commanding Officer, U.S. Military Forces, Seattle, to Major General J. D. Leitch, Feb. 20, 1919; Special Order No. 1, H.Q., U.S. Forces, Seattle, Feb. 6, 1919; General Order No. 1, H.Q., U.S. Forces, Seattle, Feb. 6, 1919, Records of the Adjutant General's Office, NA, RG 94.

23. See, for example, Bridges Papers, letter of Robert Bridges to the Central Labor Council, Feb. 14, 1919; and a speech Bridges delivered before the National Popular Government League, Washington, D.C., reported in Seattle *Union Record*, March 14, 1919, p. 1.

24. Seattle *Star*, Feb. 7, 1919, p. 1.

25. General Strike Papers, interview of Frank L. Curtis by Margaret Aller, Jan. 13, 1947.

26. Strong, *The Seattle General Strike*, pp. 29-30.

27. Seattle *Star*, Feb. 7, 1919, p. 1. The front page also featured a large American flag with the caption "Under This Flag the Star Will Continue to Publish an American Newspaper." The proclamation was also reprinted in the *Star* the next day, as well as in the New York *Times*, Feb. 8, 1919.

28. See the Seattle *Star*, Feb. 8, 1919, p. 1, for photographs of the distribution of the previous issue under police protection.

29. Clarence Darrow pointed this out in his summation to the jury in the case of *People* v. *Lloyd*. He said: "Now, gentlemen, pray tell me why, on the 7th day of February, after this strike had been brewing for a week, after repeated conferences by the Mayor with the strike committee; after this sleuth [Harry J. Wilson, the Minuteman *agent provocateur*] had been going in and out and making his reports; after every effort had been made to stir up violence by these agents; after all this time, pray tell me why Ole Hanson issued his proclamation and never in any way referred to any effort of these strikers to take control of the city; to interfere with property, to usurp the functions of the State; or do any single unlawful thing?" Reprinted in *Argument of Clarence Darrow in the Case of the Communist Labor Party in the Criminal Court, Chicago* (Chicago: Charles H. Kerr, 1920), p. 86.

30. New York *Times*, Feb. 9, 1919, p. 1.

31. Transcript of *People* v. *Lloyd*, p. 640.

32. Strong, *The Seattle General Strike*, p. 33. A similar version of the exchange as remembered by Duncan can be found in transcript of *People* v. *Lloyd*, p. 642.

33. Hanson, *Americanism versus Bolshevism*, p. 89. Hanson's version is also consistent with his remarks on the stand in the trial of *People* v. *Lloyd*, p. 578.

34. See: Seattle *Star*, Feb. 6, 1919, p. 1; Seattle *Post-Intelligencer*, Feb. 6, 1919, p. 1; *Daily Bulletin*, Feb. 6, 1919, p. 11.

35. Transcript of *People* v. *Lloyd*, p. 646. Except for where otherwise noted, the account of the three meetings is drawn from the trial record. Duncan's version is contained in pp. 640-47, 689; Hanson's, 577-79.

36. Seattle *Star*, Feb. 10, 1919, p. 2.

37. Reprinted in *Daily Bulletin*, Feb. 8, 1919, p. 1; New York *Times*, Feb. 8, 1919, p. 1. Also see, for the circumstances surrounding the issuing of the notice, transcript of *People* v. *Lloyd*, p. 577.

38. Interview with Milton Bean, Dec. 29, 1958. Also see, for business opinion of Hanson, General Strike Papers, interview with Frank L. Curtis by Margaret Aller, Jan. 13, 1947.

39. Hanson, *Americanism versus Bolshevism,* p. 89.

40. Seattle *Star,* Feb. 7, 1919, p. 1.

41. *Daily Bulletin,* Feb. 8, 1919, p. 1.

42. General Strike Papers, interview with Charles Doyle by Margaret Aller, Jan. 7, 1947. This was also Duncan's opinion. See transcript of *People* v. *Lloyd,* p. 648.

43. Hanson, *Americanism versus Bolshevism,* pp. 92-93, states incorrectly that the strike ended on Saturday.

44. Portland *Oregonian,* Feb. 8, 1919, p. 7.

45. *Daily Bulletin,* Feb. 10, 1919, p. 3.

46. Seattle *Star,* Feb. 8, 1919, p. 1.

47. *Ibid.*

48. *Argus,* XXVI (Feb. 8, 1919), 7.

49. *Daily Bulletin,* Feb. 8, 1919, pp. 1, 3.

50. Seattle *Post-Intelligencer,* Feb. 5, 1919, p. 2.

51. Strong, *The Seattle General Strike,* pp. 37-38.

52. Lewis Lorwin, *The American Federation of Labor: History, Policies, and Prospects* (Washington, D.C.: Brookings Institution, 1933), p. 190.

53. Strong, *The Seattle General Strike,* pp. 35-36.

54. General Strike Papers, interview of James A. Duncan by Margaret Aller and Ralph Thayer, Dec. 12, 1946; interview of Charles Doyle by Margaret Aller, Jan. 7, 1947.

55. Interview with Harry Ault, Jan. 10, 1959.

56. Transcript of *People* v. *Lloyd,* p. 649.

57. Seattle *Post-Intelligencer,* Feb. 9, 1919, p. 1.

58. Seattle *Union Record,* Feb. 10, 1919, p. 1.

59. Seattle *Post-Intelligencer,* Feb. 10, 1919, p. 1.

60. Seattle *Union Record,* Feb. 10, 1919, p. 1.

61. Strong, *The Seattle General Strike,* p. 37.

62. Interview with James A. Duncan by author, Dec. 30, 1958; General Strike Papers, interview with James A. Duncan by Margaret Aller and Ralph Thayer, Dec. 12, 1946; transcript of *People* v. *Lloyd,* pp. 650, 670-71.

63. Strong, *The Seattle General Strike,* p. 39. See also transcript of *People* v. *Lloyd,* p. 651.

64. Seattle *Star,* Feb. 11, 1919, p. 1.

65. *Ibid.*

CHAPTER VII

1. Seattle *Star,* Feb. 11, 1919, p. 1.

2. *Town Crier,* Vol. 14, No. 7 (Feb. 15, 1919), p. 1. Also see page 4

for the editor's apology for his previously stated opinion of Hanson.

3. *Argus*, XXVI (Feb. 15, 1919), 1.

4. New York *Times*, Feb. 8, 1919, p. 1.

5. Most of the journalistic literature written during and immediately after the strike heavily reinforced Hanson's version. See: "Mayor Ole Hanson, Who Sat Tight at Seattle," *Literary Digest*, LX (March 8, 1919), 47-50; Edgar Lloyd Hampton, " 'They Made us Strike': The Story of the Attempted Revolution in Seattle," *Saturday Evening Post* (April 4, 1919); Paul C. Henrick, "The IWW and Mayor Hanson," *Unpartisan Review*, XII (July, 1919), 35-45; W. V. Woehlke, "Revolution in America: Seattle Crushes the First Soviet Uprising," *Sunset*, XLII (April, 1919), 13-16; "Bolshevism Cowed in Seattle," *Modern City*, IV (February, 1919), 25.

6. Bridges Papers, Hallinan to Robert Bridges, May 23, 1919.

7. *Ibid.*, George Hampton to Robert Bridges, April 24, 1919.

8. Seattle *Union Record*, March 14, 1919.

9. New York *Times*, Feb. 11, 1919, p. 1.

10. Feb. 11, 1919, p. 7.

11. *Argus*, XXVI (Feb. 15, 1919), 1.

12. Note to the author from Harry E. B. Ault, Oct. 9, 1959. In fact, Boilermakers' Local 104 had $54,700 invested in Liberty Bonds as of June 30, 1919. See PIE, Semi-Annual Report—Boilermakers' Local 104, attached to report of Agent 106, June 30, 1919.

13. They were Robert L. Proctor and Frank Gates of the Central Labor Council; R. M. McCullough of the Typographical Union. C. H. Hanford, *Seattle and Environs 1852-1924*, I (Chicago, Ill. and Seattle, Wash.: Pioneer Historical Publishing Co., 1924), 351.

14. Anna Louise Strong, *I Change Worlds* (New York: Holt, 1935), pp. 84-85.

15. New York *Times*, Feb. 15, 1949, p. 1; Feb. 16, 1949, p. 20; Feb. 18, 1949, p. 1; Feb. 20, 1949, p. 13; Feb. 22, 1949, p. 1; Feb. 24, 1949, p. 1.

16. Seattle *Times*, Dec. 2, 1959, p. 7.

17. *Ibid.*, Feb. 13, 1919, p. 1; Seattle *Star*, Feb. 14, 1919, p. 1.

18. Transcript of *People* v. *Lloyd*, p. 663; Ole Hanson, *Americanism versus Bolshevism* (Garden City, N.Y.: Doubleday, Page, 1920), pp. 92-93.

19. General Strike Papers, interview with Adell Parker by Margaret Aller, Nov. 25, 1946.

20. Note from Harry E. B. Ault to the author, Oct. 9, 1959.

21. Seattle *Star*, Feb. 15, 1919, p. 1.

22. Anna Louise Strong, *The Seattle General Strike* (Seattle, Wash.: Union Record Publishing Co., n.d.), p. 57.

23. Seattle *Star*, Feb. 14, 1919, p. 1; *One Big Union*, I (July, 1919), 9; *The Industrial Worker*, II (May 4, 1919), 1.

24. *One Big Union*, I (July, 1919), 9.

25. See *The Industrial Worker*, I (June 11, 1919), 1, for an extensive discussion of the trial from the IWW point of view.

The arrests of the Wobblies and Miss Strong, and the attempted arrest of Leon Green, occurred not long after a trainload of deportees called the "Red Special" was sent from Seattle to Ellis Island. The fifty-four prisoners it contained were said to be mostly Russians and former enemy nationals, most of whom were affiliated with the IWW. They were not involved in the general strike and had been picked up for deportation before it began. As the *Star* put it (Feb. 10, 1919, p. 2), "deportation at this time came only as a coincidence." They were, however, confused with the participants in the general strike. (See New York *Times*, Feb. 8, 1919, p. 1, quotation from Washington State representative to Congress, Royal Johnson.) Most of the men arriving at Ellis Island recanted and were not deported. For more details, see Robert K. Murray, *Red Scare* (Minneapolis: University of Minnesota Press, 1955), pp. 194-95.

26. PIE, report of Agent 106, June 5, 1919.

27. *The Industrial Worker*, I (June 18, 1919), 1; and VIII (June 25, 1919), 1. On the police campaign to keep the IWW hall closed, see Ole Hanson's statement quoted in John Graham Brooks, *Labor's Challenge to Social Order* (New York: Macmillan, 1920), pp. 364-65.

28. Ross Papers, memorandum, Ross to Williams, May 26, 1919. Also see: Ross Papers, memorandum, G. N. Sheldon to J. D. Ross, May 22, 1919; memorandum, J. D. Ross to B. C. Mooers, February 1, 1919; memorandum, J. D. Ross to Mooers, G. Smith, W. J. and F. McKeen, Hendricks, Lamb, Ferguson, G. Meagher, Riddoch, Rose, Kenney, Swyney, Gilmur, Ragge, and Sheldon, May 20, 1919.

29. "More Lessons Than One in Seattle Strike," *American Federationist*, XXVI (March, 1919), 243.

30. For Gompers' attitude on industrial unionism, see Louis S. Reed, *The Labor Philosophy of Samuel Gompers* (New York: Columbia University Press, 1930), pp. 131-47. For his attitude on sympathetic strikes, see Florence C. Thorne, *Samuel Gompers—American Statesman* (New York: Philosophical Library, 1957).

31. Interview with James A. Duncan, Dec. 30, 1958.

32. "More Lessons Than One in Seattle Strike," *American Federationist*, p. 243.

33. Seattle *Union Record*, Feb. 14, 1919, p. 1.

34. General Strike Papers, interview with Bert Swain by Margaret Aller, Jan. 7, 1947; similar opinions were expressed by Ed Weston and Frank L. Curtis in interviews with Miss Aller, Jan. 16, 1946, and Jan. 13, 1947.

35. PIE, report of Agent 106, Nov. 3, 1919.

36. *Ibid.*, Oct. 28, 1919.

37. Kinnear Papers, report of Agent 181, April 2, 1920.

38. PIE, report of Agent 106, March 25, 1920.

39. *Ibid.,* Oct. 16, 1919.

40. *Ibid.,* Nov. 19, 1919.

41. *Ibid.,* Oct. 29, 1919.

42. See *ibid.,* March 25, 1920, for information on the Committee of 15 designed to eliminate radical interference. This is not to be confused with the executive committee of the General Strike Committee, also frequently referred to as the "Committee of 15."

43. *Ibid.,* June 15, 1919.

44. *Ibid.,* Aug. 20, 1919; report of Agent 17, Aug. 21, 1919.

45. PIE, report of Agent 106, Nov. 26, 1919.

46. *Ibid.,* Nov. 17, 1919.

47. *Ibid.,* May 15, 20, Aug. 3, 1919.

48. PIE, report of Agent 17, Aug. 29, 1919; report of Agent 106, May 16, 1919.

49. *Ibid.,* May 3, 5, 1919.

50. *Ibid.,* July 5, Oct. 27, 1919; reports of Agent 17, July 15, Aug. 23, 1919.

51. PIE, reports of Agent 106, May 3, 5, 1919.

52. Kinnear Papers, address by Roy John Kinnear before the annual meeting of the Associated Industries of Seattle, June 6, 1924.

53. Quoted in William Short, *History of Activities of Seattle Labor Movement and Conspiracy of Employers to Destroy It and Attempted Suppression of Labor's Daily Paper, the Seattle Union Record* (Seattle, Wash.: Union Record Publishing Co., 1919), p. 19.

54. See Kinnear Papers, reports of Agents 317 and 172, and Operator C.

55. Committee on Labor Relations of Seattle Chamber of Commerce and Commercial Club, *Profitism, Slackism, and YOU* (1920), p. 5.

56. Interestingly, some forty years later the International Ladies Garment Workers Union struck a California dress firm because it hired Mrs. Edwin Selvin as a labor consultant. Seattle *Times,* March 23, 1960, p. 10.

57. William Short, *History of Activities . . .* , p. 15.

58. PIE, reports of Agent 106, Oct. 18, 20, 22, 23, 25, Nov. 8, 25, Dec. 23, 1919, March 20, 1920; report of Agent 17, March 30, 1920.

59. *Daily Bulletin,* Feb. 10, 1919, p. 3.

60. PIE, reports of Agent 106, Sept. 13, 18, 20, 23, Oct. 11, 18, 20, 25, Dec. 15, 18, 1919; Jan. 5, 31, 1920.

61. W. H. Crook, *The General Strike* (Chapel Hill: University of North Carolina Press, 1931), pp. 540-41.

62. Kinnear Papers, report of Agent 172, April 2, 1920.

63. PIE, report of Agent 106, Nov. 8, 1919.

64. *Ibid.,* July 18, 1919; reports of Agent 17, July 27, Oct. 6, 1919.

65. PIE, report of Agent 106, April 24, 1920.

66. Dun and Bradstreet, Inc., *Seattle* (n.d.), pp. 11-12, 24.

67. Leo Wolman, *The Growth of American Trade Unions 1880-1923* (New York: National Bureau of Economic Research, 1924), pp. 22, 41.

68. Commanding Officer, U.S. Forces, Seattle, to Major General J. D. Leitch, Commanding Officer, Camp Lewis, Washington, Feb. 20, 1919, Records of the Adjutant General's Office, NA, RG 94; C. J. Erickson to Piez, Feb. 3, 1919, McBride to Blain, Feb. 26, 1919, Piez to Blain, March 15, 1919, file 18252-2, General Records of the Industrial Relations Division, United States Shipping Board, NA, RG 32.

69. PIE, reports of Agent 106, Aug. 5, Nov. 4, Dec. 1, 1919, Jan. 3, 1920.

70. *Ibid.,* March 22, April 27, 1920.

71. *Ibid.,* Dec. 18, 1919.

72. *Ibid.,* Aug. 10, 1919, March 18, 1920; report of Agent 17, May 15, 1920.

73. *Ibid.,* May 13 (and *Union Record* clipping, May 12, 1920, attached), May 14, 1920 (and *Union Record* clipping, May 13, 1920, attached).

74. See *United States* v. *Skinner and Eddy,* 28 F (2d), 373.

75. Seattle *Times,* March 5, 1919. The returns were as follows:

Labor candidate		*Conservative candidate*	
R. L. Proctor	21,210	C. B. Fitzgerald	29,022
E. T. Levi	19,683	W. H. Moore	28,298
C. H. Gallant	19,767	R. H. Thomson	27,302

76. Ole Hanson, *Americanism versus Bolshevism,* p. 96. Also see "Labor Rebuked," *Argus,* XXVI (March 8, 1919), 1, for press attempts to link the general strike with the labor candidates for the City Council.

77. For details on the Triple Alliance, see chapter 2, "The AFL in Seattle."

78. PIE, report of Agent 17, Nov. 30, 1919; reports of Agent 106, Dec. 2, 5, 19, 1919.

79. *Ibid.,* Jan. 17, 1920.

80. Interview with James A. Duncan, Dec. 30, 1958.

81. *Argus,* XXVII (Feb. 7, 1920), 1; PIE, report of Agent 106, Feb. 21, 1920.

82. *Argus,* XXVII (Jan. 31, 1920), 7.

83. PIE, report of Agent 106, Feb. 12, 1920. Also see his reports for Jan. 22, 23, 29, 30, 1920.

84. *Ibid.,* Feb. 27, 1920. Also see his reports for Feb. 28 and March 1, 1920.

85. C. H. Hanford, *Seattle and Environs 1852-1924,* I, 370. The exact returns were: Caldwell—50,875; Duncan—33,777.

86. PIE, report of Agent 106, March 2, 1920.

87. Interview with James A. Duncan, Dec. 30, 1958.

88. This was not Duncan's last venture into the political arena. In 1922 Duncan ran for the Senate on the Farmer-Labor ticket (an outgrowth of the Triple Alliance). Although his candidacy was supported by the Seattle labor movement—he was endorsed by the Central Labor Council—it was repudiated by Samuel Gompers. Gompers endorsed the victorious Democratic candidate, Clarence C. Dill. Duncan ran third in a field of five, even in his home county (King County).

89. For accounts of the bombings, see Robert Murray, *Red Scare*, pp. 60-72, and William E. Leuchtenburg, *The Perils of Prosperity, 1914-32* (Chicago: University of Chicago Press, 1958), pp. 71-72.

90. Murray, *Red Scare*, p. 61.

91. Edward T. Devine, "Winnipeg and Seattle," *Survey*, XLIII (Oct. 4, 1919), 5-8; W. H. Crook, *The General Strike*, p. 528; Lewis Lorwin, *American Federation of Labor* (Washington, D.C.: Brookings Institution, 1931), p. 191. For the IWW view of the Winnipeg general strike, see *One Big Union*, I (September, 1919), 13.

92. Murray, *Red Scare*, p. 113.

93. Interview with James A. Duncan, Dec. 30, 1958.

94. Murray, *Red Scare*, pp. 122-65.

95. For details of the Centralia incident, see *The Centralia Case*, A Joint Report on the Armistice Day Tragedy at Centralia, Washington, November 11, 1919, issued by the Federal Council of Churches, National Catholic Welfare Conference, Central Conference of American Rabbis (October, 1930). For a literary treatment, see John Dos Passos, *Nineteen Nineteen* (New York: Modern Library, 1937), pp. 456-61.

96. Short, *History of Activities . . .* , p. 9. The *Union Record* was restored to its owners on Nov. 21, 1919.

97. See Murray, *Red Scare;* Leuchtenburg, *The Perils of Prosperity,* pp. 77-81.

98. Ole Hanson, "Bolshevism," *The American Legion Weekly,* I (July 11, 1919), 13.

99. Quoted in Murray, *Red Scare,* p. 70. Later he denied having said this.

100. PIE, report of Agent 106, May 21, 1919.

101. Quoted in R. H. Harvey, *Samuel Gompers: Champion of the Toiling Masses* (Stanford, Calif.: Stanford University Press, 1935), p. 307.

102. Hanson, *Americanism versus Bolshevism,* preface.

103. "The I.W.W. and Mayor Hanson," *Unpartisan Review,* XII (July, 1919), 35.

104. *One Big Union,* II (January, 1920), 16.

105. Quoted in Leuchtenburg, *The Perils of Prosperity,* p. 81.

106. See the prosecutor's opening statement to the jury, transcript of *People* v. *Lloyd,* pp. 48-49.

107. *Ibid.,* p. 583.

108. A complete reprint of Darrow's speech can be found in *Argument of Clarence Darrow in the Case of the Communist Labor Party in the Criminal Court, Chicago* (Chicago: Charles H. Kerr & Co., 1920), pp. 90-92. For a shortened version see Arthur Weinberg (ed.), *Attorney for the Damned* (New York:Simon & Schuster, 1957), p. 160.

CHAPTER VIII

1. See the reprint of Nard Jones's radio comment on "Revolution in Seattle," *Northwest Narratives* (Seattle, Wash.: Peoples National Bank, 1959), p. 80; Howard Brier, *Sawdust Empire* (New York: Knopf, 1958), p. 158; and Ralph Potts, *Seattle Heritage* (Seattle, Wash.: Superior Publishing Co., 1955), pp. 69-71.

2. Harvey O'Connor, *Revolution in Seattle: A Memoir* (New York: Monthly Review Press, 1964), p. 145.

3. Crane Brinton, *Anatomy of Revolution* (New York: Vintage, 1957), pp. 134-44.

4. Anna Louise Strong, *I Change Worlds* (New York: Holt, 1935), p. 82.

5. For a good discussion of the subject, see W. H. Crook, *The General Strike* (Chapel Hill: University of North Carolina Press, 1931), pp. viii, 223.

6. Bert Swain ruefully admitted almost thirty years later: ". . . any general strike is doomed to failure before it begins unless there is a virtual dictatorship of control . . . complete control of all strikers and all unions must be vested in the hands of the few people who have the power to limit the duration of the strike, to call out any one group of workers at a particular time, and to make all decisions without having to resort to a rank-and-file vote. When a general strike is run by the rank and file, it must end only in chaos." General Strike Papers, interview with Bert Swain by Margaret Aller, Jan. 7, 1947.

Index